BLOOD AND INK

BLOOD AND INK

THE BARBARY ARCHIVE IN EARLY AMERICAN LITERARY HISTORY

JACOB CRANE

University of Massachusetts Press
AMHERST AND BOSTON

Copyright © 2023 by University of Massachusetts Press
The electronic version has been made freely available under a Creative Commons
(CC BY-NC-ND 4.0) license, which permits noncommercial use, distribution,
and reproduction provided the author and University of Massachusetts Press are
fully cited and no modifications or adaptations are made. Details of the license
can be viewed at https://creativecommons.org/licenses/by-nc-nd/4.0/.

This book will be made open access within three years of publication thanks
to Path to Open, a program developed in partnership between JSTOR, the
American Council of Learned Societies (ACLS), University of Michigan Press,
and The University of North Carolina Press to bring about equitable access
and impact for the entire scholarly community, including authors, researchers,
libraries, and university presses around the world. Learn more at https://about
.jstor.org/path-to-open/

All rights reserved
Printed in the United States of America

ISBN 978-1-62534-741-1 (paper); 742-8 (hardcover)

Designed by Sally Nichols
Set in Minion Pro
Printed and bound by Books International, Inc.

Cover design by adam b. bohannon
Cover art by unknown artist, *Portrait of Sengbe Pieh*, from *A True History of
the African Chief Jingua and His Comrades* (New York: The Booksellers, 1839),
9.—Courtesy Beinecke Rare Book and Manuscript Library, Yale University, New
Haven, CT

Library of Congress Cataloging-in-Publication Data
A catalog record for this book is available from the Library of Congress.

British Library Cataloguing-in-Publication Data
A catalog record for this book is available from the British Library.

Chapter 2 is, in part, reprinted from *Early American Literature* 50, no. 2 (2015):
331–358, originally titled "Barbary(an) Invasions: The North African Figure in
Early American Print Culture." An earlier version of chapter 6 appeared as "Peter
Parley in Tripoli: Barbary Slavery and Imaginary Citizenship," *ESQ: A Journal
of Nineteenth-Century Literature and Culture* 65, no. 3 (2019): 512–50.
Copyright © 2022 by the Board of Regents of Washington State University.

For Mom,
Barbara Ann Crane

CONTENTS

List of Illustrations   ix

Acknowledgments   xi

INTRODUCTION
Appealing to the Nation   1

PART ONE:
OF PIRATES AND PRINT

CHAPTER ONE
The Patriot and the Sable Bard   31
CHAPTER TWO
Barbary(an) Invasions   57

PART TWO:
THE BARBARY AND THE
JEWISH ATLANTIC

CHAPTER THREE
"A Vague Resemblance to Something Seen Elsewhere"   87
CHAPTER FOUR
Performing Diaspora in Noah's *Travels*   121

PART THREE:
THE LONG SHADOW OF THE BARBARY

CHAPTER FIVE
"The Advantage of a Whip-Lecture"   147
CHAPTER SIX
Peter Parley in Tripoli   179
CODA
Selim's Archive Fever   203

Notes   209

Index   251

ILLUSTRATIONS

FIGURES

FIGURE 1. Valentine Verax, *The Allied Despots; or, The Friendship of Britain for America* (1794) 18

FIGURE 2. Frontispiece Portrait of Phillis Wheatley from *Poems on Various Subjects* (1773) 45

FIGURE 3. Frontispiece and title page of Mordecai Noah's *Travels in England, France, Spain, and the Barbary States* (1819) 132

FIGURE 4. "Merchant, Slave and Arab" from Noah's *Travels* 133

FIGURE 5. Playbill for *Yusef Caramalli; or, The Siege of Tripoli* (1822) 141

FIGURE 6. Sengbe Pieh from *A True History of the African Chief Jingua and His Comrades* (1839) 159

FIGURE 7. "Riley and His Men Seized by Arabs" from Samuel Griswold Goodrich's *Tales about Africa* (1830) 194

FIGURE 8. "Wreck of the Brig Commerce on the Coast of Africa" from James Riley's *Authentic Narrative* (1817) 199

FIGURE 9. "Riley Attempting to Escape" from Samuel Griswold Goodrich's *The Story of Captain Riley* (1834) 199

TABLE

TABLE 1. Listing of ransom prices for the crew of the *Dauphin* 11

ACKNOWLEDGMENTS

There are so many people I have to thank for making this work possible. My journey started as an undergraduate in the English Department of Boston University, where I had the pleasure of taking phenomenal courses that still influence my research today from Laura Korobkin and Christopher Lukasik. The senior thesis I completed there, with the support of my advisor Kevin Van Anglen, gave me my first opportunity to exercise my scholarly ambitions.

Of course, so much of this project was shaped by the graduate courses I took at Tufts University from Christina Sharpe, Elizabeth Ammons, Joseph Litvak, Lee Edelman, Kevin Dunn, Sonia Hofkosh, and Lecia Rosenthal. At Tufts I was very fortunate to work closely with Virginia Jackson. It was for her extraordinary seminar that I wrote the first version of my analysis of Peter Markoe's *The Algerine Spy*, which would later become the article that helped me get my position at Bentley University and is now a chapter in this book. Her feedback and support over the years has been vital in helping me direct my scholarship. Radiclani Clytus, who oversaw my dissertation, introduced me to the kind of scholarship I wanted to pursue and taught me to take ownership of my work. I have his advice and encouragement to thank for many of the accomplishments that brought me to this point. I also want to thank the other members of my dissertation committee: Douglas A. Jones Jr., who provided me with brilliant and much-needed feedback on how I worked with theatrical sources, and Lisa Lowe, whose questions during my defense helped me develop a much stronger and more meaningful argument for this book. Finally, at Tufts, I want to thank Heather Nathans, with whom I have had the great pleasure of discussing the work of Mordecai Manuel Noah.

The research for this book would not have been possible without the generous support of several archival fellowships. I would like to thank in particular James Green and Connie King, who worked with me at the Library Company of Philadelphia when this project was still in its infancy;

Paul Erickson and Laura E. Wasowicz of the American Antiquarian Society; and the Touro National Heritage Trust and the late Bernard Bell for supporting my work at the John Carter Brown Library. Each fellowship came at a critical time in the development of this book, and I am grateful for having had the opportunity to explore these great collections. Outside the archives, this project benefited immensely from the NEH summer seminar "City of Print," directed by Mark Noonan, who greatly encouraged me with his enthusiasm and commitment to this community of scholars. I would also like to thank the Futures of American Studies Institute and Duncan Faherty in particular for helping me in the final stages of my work. I am extremely grateful for Duncan's generosity with his time and his insightful feedback. Among the journal editors I have worked with over the years, I want to thank Sandra Gustafson for her help in getting my second chapter to publication in *Early American Literature* and Johanna Heloise Abtathi for shepherding my sixth chapter to publication in *ESQ*. I am incredibly fortunate to have worked with some of the smartest, kindest, and most generous people in the field.

Over the long process of putting together this book, I benefited greatly from the support and encouragement of my colleagues in the English and Media Studies Department at Bentley University: Ben Aslinger, Tzarina Prater, Claudia Stumpf, Samir Dayal, Luke Mueller, Anna Siomopoulos, Erica Arkin, Ken Stuckey, Liz LeDoux, Casey Hayward, Val Wang, Barbara Paul-Emile, Traci Abbott, Wiley Davi, Jennifer Gillan, and Greg Farbor-Mazor. In some cases, they read my materials, in many cases they patiently listened to me talk about my research, and in all cases they supported me with my day-to-day work so that I could carve out space to move my scholarship forward.

But really, none of this would have been possible without the help of the venerable Medford School: Leif Eckstrom, Erin Kappeler, Jacqueline O'Dell, James Mulder, Maik Stanitzke, Bryn Gravitt, and Caroline Gelmi. In addition to providing the moral support to help me through graduate school, the job market, and finally five complicated years on the tenure track, they have provided generous feedback on every one of these chapters. I could not have even imagined taking on such a big project without their support and encouragement.

Finally, thank you to Barbara Crane, for teaching me to love reading. Thank you to Charles Crane and Casey Crane for helping me through tumultuous times and always letting me know that they are proud of me. Most of all, I am so, so grateful for my partner, Jessica Crane, and my children, Amy and Max. It goes without saying that I would never have made it here without Jessica's love and support over many years. She inspires me every day to work harder and to care about what I am doing. Thank you, so much.

BLOOD
AND
INK

INTRODUCTION

APPEALING TO THE NATION

The mystic spell of Africa is and ever was over all America.

—W. E. B. Du Bois, *John Brown* (1909)

In September 1786, Philadelphia's *Columbian Magazine* printed a short piece by Mathew Carey, inspired by the French novel *Memoirs of the Year Two Thousand Five Hundred* (1771), which begins with the narrator awaking from a deep sleep to find himself "transported to so distant a period, as the year 1850." He walks into a nearby coffeehouse and encounters a local newspaper, the contents of which evoke "surprise and pleasure."[1] These reports from the future highlight the rapidly expanding borders of American territorial and commercial influence. One story, for example, announces the completion of a canal across the isthmus of Panama, while another reports on the admission of the thirtieth state to the union.[2] The very first story at the top of the column, however, concerns the United States' conflicts with Algerian pirates:

> *Philadelphia, May 5, 1850.* A letter received from Cadiz, dated the 10th of March, says "We have authentic accounts that the American admiral, Beaunale, with 10 sail of the line, has lately had a desperate engagement with a grand fleet of the Algerines, of 11 sail of the line, 6 frigates, and 4 gallies. Both fought with the utmost bravery—but two of Algerine first rate vessels being blown up, and a great havock being made among the crews of the rest, three struck, and the remainder fled. . . . The brave admiral immediately sailed to Algiers, which he bombarded with such vigor, that in a short time all the fortifications were levelled, and the city almost entirely reduced to ashes."[3]

The author imagines U.S. naval power emerging victorious and ending forever Algerian piracy in the Mediterranean. That this is the very first prediction presented in the piece suggests that North African piracy loomed large

2 **INTRODUCTION**

in Carey's mind.[4] At the time he was writing, the crews of two American merchant vessels, captured the year before, were being held as slaves in Algiers, with no end to their captivity in sight. As with the piece's other predictions, this story includes both hits and misses. The United States would eventually defeat North African pirates at sea in a series of conflicts from 1801 to 1815 now called the Barbary Wars. It was, however, Great Britain that devastated Algiers with a punitive bombardment in 1816, and France that put an ultimate end to Algerian piracy with its invasion in 1830. With hindsight, we can see how Carey's prediction marginalizes Europe, imagining a future in which the United States stands at the center of the Atlantic world, facilitating trans-Atlantic prosperity and policing its margins.[5]

While the report of the final defeat of Algiers reflected the late-eighteenth-century American public's belief in the inevitability of full-scale war with North Africa, another important historical conflict is notably absent. The real year 1850 was marked by a political compromise, brokered by Henry Clay, that aimed to avoid the start of a civil war while strengthening provisions such as the Fugitive Slave Act, effectively nationalizing the institution of slavery and heightening sectional tensions.[6] However, the only mention of slavery in this newspaper of the future suggests that the crisis had long passed: "*Charleston, April 15.* No less than 10,000 blacks have been transported from this state and Virginia, during the last two years to Africa, where they have formed a settlement near the mouth of the river Goree. Very few blacks remain in this country now; and we sincerely hope that in a few years every vestige of the infamous traffic, carried on by our ancestors in the human species, will be done away."[7] In this alternate future, a successful colonization movement in West Africa solves any tensions between North and South, averting a civil war and allowing a united country to focus on its real enemy: the Barbary Coast.[8]

I emphasize these two predictions concerning Algerian pirates and African colonization because they demonstrate how Carey in 1786 saw the future of the country playing out in relation to *both* North and West Africa. Writing in the early years of what we now call the Algerine Crisis (1785–1797), he assumed that conflicts with the Barbary Coast would play a formative role in defining America's future, on the same level as the problem of domestic slavery. In his study of early American temporalities, Lloyd Pratt notes that these imaginative forays into the future were common in this period, as writers "staged dialogues with the future undertaken less for reasons of vanity than out of a desire to influence how their descendants would understand their relationship to the past and in turn come to know themselves." Carey's predictions convey both anxiety and ambition—a concern for the long-term threat of Barbary piracy combined with the expectation that America *will* overcome that challenge. More than traditional rivals Britain and France, Algiers serves in Carey's mind as the chief adversary of American growth and prosperity, and its defeat would signal a crucial turning point in the nation's identity and role in the larger Atlantic world. If, as Pratt argues, authors like Carey "occupied the future—our present—by captioning their own and earlier periods as the origin of an inevitable national fate," the story overall envisions the predestined transition from weak republic to powerful empire.[9] Carey presents as a key part of that process the consolidation of the nation's white identity through imperial engagements with both West African colonization and the subjugation of North Africa.

The prominence of Algiers in Carey's thinking about America's present and future might surprise readers today, but he was by no means the only early American writer who assigned critical importance to the country's conflicts with North Africa. As I briefly mentioned above, Carey composed his semi-prophetic article during the Algerine Crisis, which began when two American merchant ships, the *Maria* of Boston and the *Dauphin* of Philadelphia, were captured by Algerian pirates in 1785.[10] Their crews were carried to Algiers and enslaved; the survivors would remain in the city awaiting ransom for the next decade. This first Barbary crisis came to an end in 1797 once peace treaties were finalized with the dey of Algiers, the bey of Tunis, and the bashaw of Tripoli that included annual tribute payments to ensure the safety of American shipping. Peace lasted until 1801, when the recently elected President Thomas Jefferson refused to pay tribute and the bashaw of Tripoli declared war in response. The Tripolitan War saw the U.S. military actively engage with the Barbary corsairs and eventually invade Tripoli to unseat the bashaw and install his more pro-American brother. After this conflict, a second brief war erupted between the United States and Algiers in 1815, during which a squadron under the command of Stephen Decatur defeated the Algerian flagship *Meshouda*, forcing an end to the conflict. After 1815, the Barbary States ceased to be a significant threat to

American shipping, but the stories of white slavery emerging from the crises and later captivity narratives from castaways such as James Riley continued to circulate in the decades leading up to the Civil War, often in the context of intensifying debates over American slavery.

Covering roughly the first thirty years of the United States' independence, the Barbary crises engendered a vast array of responses from American writers that reflected the diverse practices and genres of early republican print, from captivity narratives, novels, plays, and poems to broadsides, newspaper articles, histories, travel narratives, and visual ephemera. These works constitute a unique, multi-generic, and multifaceted archive that I call the Barbary archive. *Blood and Ink: The Barbary Archive in Early American Literary History* seeks to recover and reconstruct the largely forgotten role of the Barbary as a site for literary experimentation with notions of publicity, fictionality, and racial and national identity from independence to the Civil War. Across this book I posit that the threat of Barbary pirates, spies, and slavedrivers, along with the appeals of their enslaved American victims, were more present in the minds of early American writers and circulated much longer in the public imagination than literary historians have yet recognized. Through my readings of works explicitly about the crises, such as Carey's short fiction above or Susanna Rowson's 1794 play *Slaves in Algiers*, and of those in which Barbary tropes and figures reside just below the surface, including Charles Brockden Brown's *Arthur Mervyn* (1801) and even Frederick Douglass's *The Heroic Slave* (1852), I explore how anxieties around the Barbary crises shaped representations of trans-Atlantic African and Jewish bodies and identities in print well into the antebellum era, contributing to a wide variety of emergent cultural formations, from early journalism, literary nationalism, and abolitionism to the discourses surrounding foreign interventionism, Jewish rights, and juvenile citizenship. Tracing Barbary texts and figures across time, I argue, allows us to begin to fill in longstanding critical gaps in American literary history and to index the major cultural shifts leading into the mid-nineteenth century that would come to characterize American modernity.[11]

While Algerian pirates were apparently a major concern for prominent early republicans like Carey, literary and journalistic works surrounding the Barbary crises were for much of the twentieth century largely overlooked by critics. Since the publication in 1999 of Paul Baepler's landmark anthology of Barbary narratives, *White Slaves, African Masters*, attention to these texts has been steadily building, fueled by both a renewed interest in early American engagements with the Muslim world and the critical shift toward transnational and oceanic paradigms for literary study.[12] Despite this rising interest, exploration into the broader cultural impact of these crises has been limited. To date critics have primarily focused on popular captivity narratives written by American sailors such as John Foss, James Leander Cathcart, and James Riley. As Gordon Sayre has noted, the rise in scholarship on Barbary captivity narratives within the well-established field of captivity studies under the auspices of the much-discussed "transnational turn" has done important work in challenging the critical associations of that genre—traditionally centered on Native American captivity narratives—with notions of American exceptionalism and stale conceptions of national character.[13]

Although these narratives indeed offer opportunities for innovative multilateral and transnational readings, I would suggest that they constitute only a small portion of the cultural response to the North African threat and therefore only a narrow understanding of how Algerians, Tunisians, Tripolitans, and their enslaved victims were depicted in early American print.[14] Comparatively few studies have engaged at length with the many fictional works circulating during and after the crises, with two notable exceptions: Royall Tyler's fictional captivity narrative *The Algerine Captive* (1797) has long been a fixture in critical discussions of the early American novel, just as Susanna Rowson's *Slaves in Algiers* (1794) has been important in studies of early American drama and women's literature. However, until recently it has been rare to see these works placed in relation to each other or to the many other Barbary materials that circulated in the period. What do we glean from the fact that the liberation plots in both works rest in the hands of duplicitous Barbary Jews? How does Tyler's enslaved protagonist, Updike Underhill, compare to the figure of the Patriot in the long poem *The American in Algiers*, published the same year, and how do these representations of white suffering evoke (and limit) the writers' antislavery messages?

Blood and Ink makes the case for what we can gain from reading representations of white slaves and North Africans, predominantly Muslims and Jews, across multiple texts and genres. First and foremost, I argue that these works can tell us quite a bit about how early Americans grappled with the complexities of racial identity beyond the Black-white binary that frequently structures our discussions of race in this period. Too often, readings of

Tyler and Rowson have focused on what Algerians (or any of the many diverse peoples of North Africa) could have "stood in" for. In Jared Gardner's reading of *The Algerine Captive*, for example, he argues that the novel "imagines [in Algiers] racial 'landscapes' upon which its hero comes to discover his 'American' identity." It "adds a fourth term to the question of his country's racial destiny: not black, not Indian, not European—but American." Notably absent in Gardner's rehearsal of the racial presences evident or implied in the novel are any of the actual races or peoples Underhill encounters in Algiers: Moors, Arabs, Turks, Jews, and others. Gardner reads the Algerian as "the composite of all the racial and national destinies [Tyler] does not want for his country."[15] My point is not necessarily to contest Gardner's reading; rather, I would assert that Algerian, Tripolitan, and Tunisian figures were not mere composites of more consequential races but rather complex identities that *did*, in fact, have their own role to play in how writers articulated the "country's racial destiny." As I have suggested in my reading of Carey's piece above, the distinction between North Africa and West Africa was central to those discussions. Attending to moments in which this geographic/racial distinction is maintained—as in my discussion of the dueling white and Black slave laments in chapter 1—and where that distinction is collapsed—as in the examination in chapter 6 of depictions of the leader of the *Amistad* uprising Sengbe Pieh as an Algerine pirate—can tell us a lot about both national anxieties and the contours of evolving racial ideology.

As a number of scholars in recent decades have posited, the late eighteenth and early nineteenth centuries marked a significant shift in the way that Americans understood race.[16] Katy Chiles observes that up to the end of the eighteenth century, race was most often depicted as "an exterior bodily trait, incrementally produced by environmental factors . . . and continuously subject to change."[17] To articulate the movement toward modern, essentialist understandings of race, she points to Tyler's protagonist in *The Algerine Captive*. In one poignant scene, after Underhill aids an enslaved West African, the latter wonders how God would have put a "good *black* soul" in the doctor's "*white* body."[18] As Chiles explores, this depiction of the protagonist's "racialized interior" coincides with contemporaneous developments in racial science.[19] It is not particularly surprising that *The Algerine Captive* provides critical documentation for how shifting ideas about race manifested in literature; across

Blood and Ink's six chapters, we will see how Barbary works frequently offered a testing ground for the latest developments in racial thought.

Consequently, the Barbary archive allows us not only to pinpoint specific developments around the turn of the century but also to track the evolving relationships between race, slavery, and print well into the antebellum period as racial categories were being consolidated. More than a decade ago Paul Baepler noted the "loose but intriguing connection" between white slavery texts and the most prominent nineteenth-century African American slave narratives, inviting scholars "to ask what role the Barbary narratives play in American abolition debates."[20] Surprisingly few critics have taken up this invitation, and these relationships remain elusive. This book seeks to develop these connections through two distinct approaches. The first involves understanding how American audiences were conditioned to understand and to *read* slavery in the early nineteenth century as the institution itself became increasingly racialized. Specifically, this involves thinking about how writers thought through the role of the speaking slave in print; how could that voice be understood, and how could it be situated within the dominant ideology of publicity?

The second approach involves thinking about what Barbary slavery meant for abolitionist and minority writers in the antebellum period. For many twenty-first-century scholars, Barbary captivity warrants investigation precisely because it challenges our normative assumptions of slavery and racial hierarchy in early America—the title of Baepler's anthology, *White Slaves, African Masters*, points directly to the appeal of this "inversion." Yet, in broader historical terms, this was not an inversion at all; abolitionist and African American writers could look back on examples of white slavery in recent memory that were part of a centuries-long history of conflicts between Africa and the West that predated the trans-Atlantic slave trade. As I explore in the later chapters of this book, the historical reality of Barbary slavery was invoked by abolitionist writers such as William Lloyd Garrison, John Greenleaf Whittier, Frederick Douglass, and James McCune Smith to decouple the institution of slavery from the present day and from its association with Blackness. Building on Martha Schoolman's work on abolitionist spatial practice, I explore in chapter 5 how, in the decades leading up to the Civil War, the cultural memory of the Barbary crises gave abolitionists access to alternative spatial and temporal frames through which they could deconstruct and

8 **INTRODUCTION**

interrogate the conditions of the "peculiar institution" within a global context that included Muslim slaveholders and white slaves.

THE ALGERINE HISTORY OF THE NOVEL

Through my primary interest in fictions of Barbary piracy and captivity, rather than in the popular captivity narratives themselves, I hope to contribute to the growing body of scholarship exploring early American concepts of fictionality. Since the publication in 2006 of Catherine Gallagher's foundational essay "The Rise of Fictionality," studies of fictionality have become central to our understanding of the rise of the novel.[21] Yet, Gallagher largely dismisses early American fiction, declaring that "fictionality seems to have been but faintly understood in the infant United States at the end of the eighteenth century." Of *The Power of Sympathy* (1789), recognized by Gallagher as the most common candidate for the status of first American novel, she notes its roots in "the earlier *chronique scandeleuse* form" rather than in the important precursor works of fictionality like *Robinson Crusoe* (1719).[22] Matthew Pethers and Thomas Koenigs remark in a recent special issue of *Early American Literature* that Americanists have been slow to contest Gallagher's claim, in part because critics often take it for granted that skeptical early republicans viewed fiction as a dangerous, corrupting influence. Pethers and Koenigs call for "alternative accounts of fictionality's emergence" within the field of early American literature.[23] This book aspires to take up that challenge. Beginning chronologically with works like Carey's article above and Peter Markoe's *The Algerine Spy in Pennsylvania* (1787), a very different contender for the status of first American novel, I argue that Barbary works offer a particularly productive approach to diverse forms of fictionality through the way they imagine readers' individual and collective engagement with national crises.

In efforts to recover the multiple genealogies of early American fictionality, once again critics have turned to Royall Tyler's *The Algerine Captive*—a fictionalized captivity narrative that, in fact, preceded the major true-life accounts of the period.[24] The novel's preface nods to the kind of antifiction critique so common to early republican novels that critics often suggest slowed the development of fictionality in America. In it, Updike Underhill, having returned from seven years' captivity in Algiers, comments on both the expansion of print networks and the changing tastes of American readers. He remarks that when he left New England, "books of biography, travels, novels, and modern romances, were confined to our sea ports," while inland, "farmer's libraries consisted largely of sermons and funeral orations." In his absence, "social libraries" were established throughout the country, "composed of books designed to amuse rather than to instruct; and country booksellers, fostering the new born taste of the people, had filled the whole land with modern travels, and novels almost as incredible." Underhill understands his enslavement abroad, from 1788 to 1795, as a transition period at home during which fanciful novels have captivated the public. Underhill sees the problem as twofold: the books being circulated are "not of our own manufacture," and the fancy and levity of these foreign popular novels have led to corruption and vice.[25] Tyler's novel, therefore, positions itself as both a critique of and intervention into the rise of fictionality.[26] Lindsay DiCuirci remarks on how the novel "blurs the lines between real and imaginary documentary evidence" as it constructs a colonial history for its fictional protagonist in the work's picaresque first half.[27] The novel's complex mix of fiction and fact underlies too Thomas Koenigs's reading of how the two very different halves of the novel stage "fiction's transformation from a vehicle for private amusement to a tool for grappling with the political concerns of its moment." He argues that the Barbary captivity narrative of the novel's second half offers a "specific mode of fictionality" through which the reader must recognize, in Underhill's ethnographic observations of Algiers and remarks on the evils of slavery, the potential for fiction to provide reliable information that can form the foundation for political action.[28]

Building on these highly generative readings, I want to draw attention to a specific moment in Tyler's novel that marks the complex confluence of fiction and fact typical of the Barbary works I take up in this book. While Underhill's enslavement coincides with the Algerine Crisis, the novel makes scant reference to other Americans held in the city at the time, with the notable exception of the twenty-ninth chapter of the work's second half. The chapter begins with the captive Underhill, who had formerly roamed the city of Algiers freely, suddenly confined to a cell. Puzzled by the abrupt turn in his fortunes, he learns that new American captives had just arrived in the city, and the Algerian authorities feared that Underhill would aid their escape. The jailors release Underhill from confinement only after he swears never to speak to his "miserable countrymen." Nevertheless, the captive muses on his almost overwhelming desire to make contact:

> If a man is desirous to know how he loves his country, let him go far from home; if to know how he loves his countrymen, let him be with them in misery

10 **INTRODUCTION**

> in a strange land. I wish not to make a vain display of my patriotism, but I will say, that my own misfortunes, upon this intelligence, were so absorbed in those of my unfortunate fellow citizens, . . . that, I thought, I could again have willingly endured the lashes of the slave driver, and sink myself beneath the burthens of slavery, to have saved them from an Algerine captivity.

In the final sentence of the chapter, Underhill adds, "Often, when I have drawn near the places of their confinement and labours, I have regretted my submitting to this oath, and once was almost tempted to break it, at seeing Captain O'Brien at some distance."[29] Tyler here references Richard O'Brien, captain of the *Dauphin*, the capture of which, as previously mentioned, precipitated the Algerine Crisis. The real-life O'Brien would remain in captivity in Algiers for about ten years, until he was freed by treaty in 1795.

Many critics, including Jared Gardner and Gesa Mackenthun, have noted the extensive intertextuality woven throughout *The Algerine Captive*. In this case, Tyler's specific reference to O'Brien may have evoked for readers their own encounters with the captain and his fellow captives, albeit in the pages of their local newspaper.[30] In his survey of communications from Algiers during the crisis, Lawrence A. Peskin counts as many as twenty different letters from captives in North Africa that circulated in American newspapers in the short period from 1785 to 1787, most from O'Brien himself. In fact, the dey of Algiers had a strong incentive to allow his captives to write home, as their appeals might stoke public support for heavy ransom payments.[31] These letters ranged from petitions for aid and descriptions of Algerian barbarity to more mundane reports on the progress of diplomacy. One of the most well-known letters, published only months after the *Dauphin*'s capture and signed by O'Brien and two other captives, begins, "We, the subscribers, subjects of the United States of America, have had the misfortune to be captured by the Algerines—brought into this port, and made slaves. We were stript of all our wearing apparel, and brought to a state of bondage and misery,—the severities which we endure are beyond your imagination."[32] Notably, their call for national sympathy anticipates the opening line of the Constitution, written two years later. This would be the first of many petitions sent from North Africa that aimed to appeal directly to the American people, often including complaints about the slow pace of negotiations. One such letter, addressed to clergy across the country, called for a petition to be read "in every house of worship" on a specific Sunday to increase public pressure on the government.[33]

O'Brien would continue to write home over the course of his decade of captivity, with several noteworthy letters coming in the years leading up to the publication of *The Algerine Captive*. In a letter first published in December 1793 and circulated throughout the early months of 1794, the captain, having now been a captive for eight years, asks that a new petition be published on his behalf so that "the Citizens of the United States will know the melancholy situation of the American Captives; and we hope we shall know what our fate is to be, and be put out of this intolerable state of suspence."[34] O'Brien would use the term "suspence" again a year later to refer not to the captives but to their loved ones back home. In that letter, he announced the death of fourteen American captives over the last year, to be published so as to "relieve from a tormenting state of suspence the surviving friends of the deceased."[35] Both uses of the term carry with them the potential for a variety of meanings. On a basic level, they point to the anguish and anxiety that attended the delays of trans-Atlantic travel and the captives' physical and temporal distance from their fellow citizens. The former letter also calls forth a now obsolete meaning, of a deferred payment, reinforced by a list that appeared at the end of the petition including the name of each captive and their ransom price.[36] Certainly some readers must have noted the similarities with the Atlantic slave trade, particularly when these "terms of redemption" appeared in some publications only columns away from escaped slave advertisements and notices of upcoming auctions.

TABLE 1. THE UNDERWRITTEN CREW OF THE *DAUPHIN,* OF PHILADELPHIA, BELONGING TO THE MESSRS. MATTHEW AND THOMAS IRVING

	SPANISH DOLLARS
Richard O'Brien, Master, at	4,000
Andrew Montgomery, Mate, at	3,000
Philip Sloan, at	1,400
Peleg Loring, at	1,400
James Hull, at	1,400
Jacobus Tiffanier, at	4,000
William Patterson, at	3,000
	18,200

Source: *Newhampshire Journal* (Walpole), January 10, 1794.

Taken together O'Brien's letters over the decade are an affecting mix of pathos, fortitude, and urgency. They, along with the later captivity narratives published after the end of the Algerine Crisis, inspired many works like *The Algerine Captive* that offered similar appeals to American cultural unity and national action, emerging from what Lennard J. Davis has called the "novel/news" matrix of the eighteenth century. In his classic study of the rise of the English novel, *Factual Fictions* (1983), Davis focuses on the development of print technologies in the seventeenth and eighteenth centuries that "permitted, but did not guarantee, a text of recentness," giving rise to both journalism (fact) and the novel (fiction). The latter Davis defines as "framed works . . . whose attitude toward fact and fiction is constitutively ambivalent[,] . . . a factual fiction which is both factual and factitious."[37] The fictional Underhill's brief nonencounter with the real O'Brien offers a fleeting glimpse of how that novel/news matrix functioned in the American context. Algiers becomes the newspaper page, and Underhill's enforced separation from his countrymen and concern for their welfare reproduces the "suspence" of early American readers, including Tyler himself, awaiting news of their suffering compatriots in North Africa. To the extent that the novel, as Koenigs argues, "centers on Updike's education as a reader," the protagonist models the ways in which the encounter with the appeals of fellow Americans should prompt political action, in this case seen in his willingness to subject himself to the lash for his countrymen.[38] However, unlike other notables such as Benjamin Franklin, whom Underhill meets in the first part of the novel, O'Brien and the other captives never truly enter the narrative, and so they mark the boundary of fiction's operation in the novel while drawing attention to the protagonist's fictionality. Their narratives parallel but never intersect Underhill's, never really threatening the distinction between fact and fiction.

Koenigs and DiCuirci read *The Algerine Captive*'s engagement with fictionality primarily within the context of the rise of the novel, reflecting certainly the genre's centrality in studies of fiction more broadly. However, it is also important to examine how the work that Tyler's novel performs in sorting fiction from fact would have seemed especially vital in the historical moment of the Algerine Crisis. Alongside letters from O'Brien and other captives, newspapers of the 1780s and 1790s printed a variety of suspect reports and outright hoaxes. Peskin observes that the capture of the *Dauphin* and the *Maria* in 1785 provoked as many as fourteen other *false* reports of captures in the two years that followed.[39] During this period the London newspapers were still the chief source of information on North Africa, and this residual colonial dependence led to the spread of one of the most notorious examples of fake news in the early republic: the alleged capture and enslavement of Benjamin Franklin by Algerian pirates.[40] While historians of the Barbary crises almost invariably mention the brief but widespread circulation of this erroneous report, it is worth exploring a bit more at length the questions this episode raises for republican print media.

The report in question originated from London's *Daily Universal Register* in September 1785 in the form of a letter from Thomas Truxton, captain of the *London Packet*, to the ship's English owners. Written from Algiers, the letter claims that the *Packet* had been captured by corsairs, and now Truxton and all his crew and passengers, including Benjamin Franklin himself, who was returning to Philadelphia from France, were now slaves on the Barbary Coast. Of the sudden enslavement of one of America's most famous statesmen, Truxton writes only, "Poor Doctor Franklin bears this reverse of fortune with more magnanimity than I could have imagined." While we know that some publications and readers assumed the letter was authentic, a closer reading suggests a subtle if clumsy satire of post-revolutionary American identity in the Atlantic. It begins with Truxton complaining that flying the American flag at sea, rather than the British flag, made him a target for pirates, a grievance notably out of character for the New York native and former Revolutionary War privateer. Truxton expresses regret over American independence because it meant sacrificing British protections. This dynamic manifests too in the closing comment attached by the paper's editor, declaring that, "by the capture of the ship *London Packet* by the Algerines, the celebrated Dr. Franklin, after all his struggles for *liberty*, will most probably end his days in *slavery*."[41] The not-so-subtle implication of this parting shot is that Americans, with all their rhetoric of liberty, have only exchanged the relatively benign dominion of their colonial master for "true" slavery at the hands of the African menace.

Like many fake news articles today, the report played on specific national anxieties as it circulated in the United States. In this case, the letter stoked the fear that no one was safe from the Algerine menace, and that after the Revolution, Americans might not be able to maintain their freedom and independence. The Truxton letter was soon discovered to be a hoax, but this seemingly did not prevent some American editors from circulating the letter *as a fiction*. Hoax, as Koenigs argues, provided a powerful tool for training skeptical readers, as seen in the way the letter was received and framed by American editors and writers.[42] For example, Isaiah Thomas's

Massachusetts Spy included a short preface in brackets, announcing that "the following letter was fabricated in London, and published in the London papers in September last, no doubt with the design to raise the premium of insurance on American vessels, and is, perhaps, as barefaced a falsehood as ever was imposed on the publick."[43] Other papers carried a quotation originating from John Adams that observed the hoax as fueled by trans-Atlantic celebrity culture: "The editors of news-papers find, that nothing contributes more to the sale of their merchandize in this city, than paragraphs respecting Dr. Franklin. . . . They send him a captive to Algiers [or] wreck him on the coast of the island of Madeira; such anecdotes answer their purpose as well as if they were true."[44] Still others focused on America's postcolonial dependence on British papers and the possibility of meddling from a foreign power. One Charleston paper published a series of "Lies Collected from British News-Papers," with Truxton's letter topping the list.[45] As one editor noted regarding the Truxton letter: "The story . . . of Dr, Franklin being sent to Algiers, is a very good one, but like many good stories, it requires confirmation."[46]

I treat this particular case study of early American virality at length because of the questions it raises about both print networks and republican readers. In the majority of cases in which the letter circulated without commentary from newspaper editors, did readers recognize it as a hoax? Did they understand it as satire? How many knew that, at the time of the letter's circulation, Franklin was already at home in Philadelphia?[47] It may be impossible to know in any precise detail how audiences across the United States received the Truxton letter, but we can infer from various reprintings that it was sometimes taken seriously and sometimes dismissed; it was read by different audiences as a harmless hoax and as an insidious slander aiming to undermine the republic.[48] For editors that reprinted the letter even as they condemned it as false, this particular instance of fake news served as a convenient pseudo-crisis that allowed American papers to articulate a break with the British newspapers from which they received so much of their information. They could offer the Truxton letter as evidence that this state of affairs was fundamentally dangerous, and that a stronger national print network capable of overcoming what Daniel Walker Howe terms the "tyranny of distance" was essential not just for convenience but also for national security.[49]

The circulation of the Truxton letter sheds light on the complex landscape of the novel-news matrix and of fictionality in early America. As a somewhat over-the-top fabrication imitating accounts of captives like O'Brien and anticipating (or even perhaps inspiring) the many fictional Barbary slave tales to follow, the Truxton letter inhabits a liminal space from which several American works of the period emerged. Furthermore, exposing the letter as fiction provided American newspaper editors the opportunity to decouple an American print public from a British one, a process akin to what Kariann Akemi Yokota describes not as a positive "becoming" American but rather as "unbecoming British," facilitated by the intervention of silent but menacing Algerians into the Anglo-American Atlantic.[50] The letter itself does little to describe these pirates other than to call them "piratical barbarians." They are presented almost as a force of nature that exposes the challenge and perhaps the folly of American independence. Most importantly, they represent an unambiguous distinction between liberty and slavery. In this sense, they crystallize and clarify the rhetorical force of the concept of liberty to a degree that many writers struggled to achieve in the revolutionary era.

The O'Brien and Truxton letters and their connections to *The Algerine Captive* point to two defining features of the Barbary archive as I formulate it in this book. First is the importance of timeliness. The circulation (or imagined circulation) of the letters across the Atlantic, the "presentness" of the captives' suffering, and the urgency of relief efforts point to the way print connected American citizens across vast distances. In this early period Barbary works were effectively ripped from the headlines, while later in the mid-nineteenth century, writers would attempt to recapture this sense of national synchronicity by invoking that collective past. Second is the mutability and porousness of genre across fiction and nonfiction within the archive, as letters and reports circulated like captivity narratives in miniature, and novels, novellas, poems, and plays adapted the news to new purposes. Reading across this archive, therefore, gives us an opportunity to partially decenter the novel form in favor of tracing the myriad of ways in which early American writers leveraged "different modalities of fiction for community building and social reform."[51] While I explore the more particular aspects of each genre, such as Barbary dramas' connections to benefit performances that sought to raise funds for the ransom of Algerian captives, I argue throughout that more innovative readings are available to us as we track tropes and characters like

16 **INTRODUCTION**

Richard O'Brien across page and stage, fiction and fact. Along these same lines, we can learn much about evolving national and racial discourses by comparing earlier representations of Barbary pirates with the Algerines that resurface beyond the works explicitly about the crisis, in abolitionist meeting proceedings, court documents, and even eulogies for antislavery crusader John Brown.

HAZARDOUS CROSSINGS

Focusing on the circulating works of the Barbary crises like O'Brien's letters and the Truxton hoax allows us to recenter the textual history of American national identity on the trans-Atlantic. Representations of Barbary slavery leveraged anxieties surrounding the North African threat to intervene in the space between the local and the national, populating it with bodies that signaled national belonging through the scars of their enslavement. By focusing on the trans-Atlantic movements of bodies and texts—of blood and ink—this book stages a constructive intervention into the expanding critical field of Atlanticist/oceanic studies, a field with its roots in Paul Gilroy's seminal book *The Black Atlantic: Modernity and Double-Consciousness* (1993). Gilroy's work imagined the "Black Atlantic world" as an alternative to nation-state–centered modernity; the Black Atlantic includes "structures of feeling, producing, communicating and remembering" engendering "stereophonic, bilingual, or bifocal cultural forms" beyond "discrete national dynamics."[52] In the context of literary studies, Gilroy's Black Atlantic allowed for critical models that move beyond traditional nationally or territorially constituted canons.

In the last two decades, Black Atlantic studies have strongly influenced what has been called the "New Atlanticism." William Q. Boelhower describes this new oceanic order as "fundamentally a space of dispersion, conjunction, distribution, contingency, heterogeneity, and of intersecting and stratified lines and images." The ocean "leaves no traces, and has no place names, towns or dwelling places; it cannot be possessed."[53] Through an emphasis on points of contact (usually ports) rather than territories, an oceanic model for literary studies has the potential to bring to the fore previously ignored literary works—in a sense, to reconfigure the dominant criteria of literary value and, more importantly, to "overhaul our understanding of archives." In Boelhower's reading of Frederick Douglass's novel of the revolt on the slave-ship *Creole, The Heroic Slave* (1852), which he labels "an important Atlantic-world *exemplum*," Boelhower emphasizes the novel as "a hybrid act of the historical imagination." Central to his analysis is what he calls the "*Creole* archive," an expansive collection of texts that transcends genre, nation, and the fiction/nonfiction divide.[54] As I suggest in my analysis of O'Brien's letters and the Truxton hoax above, this book too is invested in a project of archival construction that crosses disciplinary boundaries as well as geopolitical territories; similar to Boelhower's reading of *The Heroic Slave*, we can see how *The Algerine Captive* and works like it compile the disparate materials of the Barbary archive and function themselves as "hybrid act[s] of the historical imagination," even as they ultimately seek to consolidate modes of national belonging by speaking to the young country's most pressing political and social concerns.[55]

Most of the Barbary texts that I explore are set primarily in North Africa, but each text includes or rests on the Atlantic crossing between America and Africa as a movement into and back out of enslavement that reverses the polarity of the trans-Atlantic slave trade's middle passage. In her influential book *Freedom's Empire: Race and the Rise of the Novel in Atlantic Modernity, 1640–1940* (2008), Laura Doyle focuses on the "swoon moment" that accompanies the trope of the Atlantic crossing in many British and American works of the eighteenth and nineteenth centuries. *Blood and Ink* owes a debt to her formulation of the crossing as a trope implicated in the "race plot" of Anglo-Saxon Atlantic print culture. Doyle argues, "The Anglo-Saxon race's entry into a 'state' of liberty is from the beginning associated with an Atlantic crossing and trauma of exile. . . . The pattern constitutes a central chronotope in English-language texts—in other words, a vehicle for the cultural reorganization of space, time, and subjectivity."[56] For Doyle's study, this reorganization of space made possible the rise of white liberal thought, but the terms just as easily describe the processes by which cultures of print circulation reorganized space around an understanding of a postcolonial national public.

How, then, might we read Doyle's articulation of trans-Atlantic liberty in the context of Barbary materials such as Valentine Verax's print *The Allied Despots* (1794?)? As the commentary below the image reads, King George instructs his "Cousin Mustapha" on how to best oppress the upstart Americans. On the left, as Timothy Marr notes, images of Native Americans slaughtering settlers reference Britain's continued presence on the northwestern

FIGURE 1. An engraving of King George III and the dey of Algiers observing Americans attacked by Native Americans and Barbary pirates in Valentine Verax, *The Allied Despots; or, The Friendship of Britain for America* (Philadelphia, 1794). The text at the bottom of the image reads, "The Imperial George instructeth his good Ally and Cousin Mustapha in the mysteries of regal policy—sheweth him as a proof of their efficacy, how Billy manageth John Bull—Relateth with Delight the depredations which his allies the Savages by his instigation make on the sons of Liberty—Exorteth him to annoy them by Sea. As implacably, as the Savages do by land—Which Mustapha performeth—Then sheweth his Royal preceptor how prompt a pupil he is." —Museum purchase, courtesy of Winterthur Museum, Garden & Library.

frontier, while the man shackled on the bottom left is an American merchant whose goods are being illegally seized in the West Indies.[57] The representations on the right side are somewhat more straightforward, as white bodies are being stripped of clothes and whipped by turbaned figures, a pirate flag flying in the background. The overt political message demands that Americans stand up to indignities both at home and abroad, yet more subtle is the use of space, the connection of North America and Africa in a seamless landmass. The Atlantic is represented simply as an uninhabited field, littered by the commodities stolen from their rightful American owners. The image effectively globalizes oppression; with no geographical referent but perhaps the pine tree on the far left of the image, Americans can only be identified as beaten and enslaved bodies. The Atlantic crossing as the boundary marking the critical borders of the race plot disappears, and America itself becomes Africa.

There are still other aspects of the racial narrative of the Barbary archive that we might glean from this image. If Americans fought a globalized revolution against oppression, the print depicts Native American and North African aggressors as agents of the British Empire rather than independent actors. In this sense, the hierarchy of power presented might have been subtly comforting to its American audience since it reframed the conflicts in terms they could understand. In practice, writers in the period often struggled to make sense of an Africa that could assert itself, could threaten the West, and could seek revenge. This is the confusion and anxiety that I examine throughout this book. Important studies like Paul Giles's *Transatlantic Insurrections* (2001) have shown how we might read the comparative development of British and American literatures in the nineteenth century as a dialectic, as "intertwined with a play of opposites, a series of reciprocal attractions and repulsions between opposing national situations."[58] Attention to the Barbary offers us the opportunity to look beyond the British-American binary and to the multilateral relationships at play in the period in ways that recover Africa as an important site for representation. While my focus on American literary history cannot claim to transcend the longstanding critical fixation on European-American Atlanticism, I emphasize how the Barbary crises exposed ruptures within Whiggish histories of the West that, like Hegel, treated Africa as "beyond the day of self-conscious history, . . . enveloped in the dark mantle of night," and how they imagined what it would mean to recognize other histories, other presents, and other futures.[59]

At the same time, I must acknowledge that the expansiveness of my archive is more imagined than real. For several reasons related to the focus of my argument, I limit the works I examine mainly to those published, performed, and circulated in public, most often in the major American cities of New York, Boston, Philadelphia, and Charleston. Because I am primarily interested in fiction rather than in the popular captivity narratives of the period, few of the writers I examine ever set foot in North Africa and few would have had any significant contact with Islamic society. This project does not engage with what must be a rich archive of Arabic- and Turkish-language sources from the period nor does it pretend to offer any insights into Islamic practices. Rather, the guiding principle in my reading across these texts is to assume that commentaries on Islam and North African society as a whole have little to tell us about the actual conditions in those communities but much to tell us about how early Americans mapped their own intractable political and social conflicts onto Africa as a way to process their Atlantic anxieties.

A final note regarding *The Allied Despots*: although my focus in this book is not on firsthand Barbary accounts, I would suggest that the image offers a convenient visualization of how Native American and Barbary narratives in this period constituted parallel but distinct genres that call for different critical approaches. The first and most obvious point is that the Muslim world offered a very different setting and cast of antagonists than we see in narratives of Native American contact. Early Americans were fascinated by the racial and cultural diversity North Africa, making it, as I have already suggested, the ideal proving ground for new forms of racial thinking. Second, since the Barbary crises themselves were a direct result of American independence, many of the victims spent significant time pondering the meaning of liberty along with larger political issues such as the structure of the state, government power, and even the effectiveness of legislation and diplomacy. Far more so than Native American captivity narratives, Barbary accounts offered a direct commentary on the Revolution, the instability that followed, and the internal contradictions left unresolved.[60] Unsurprisingly, these issues became central to much of the early fiction produced during the crises, such as in Washington Irving's Mustapha letters (1807–1808), which I read in chapter 2. Third, while they are often described as captives, the victims of the dey of Algiers on the right side of the image would have been considered, and would have seen themselves, as *slaves* held by an organized, slaveholding society that assigned them a monetary value, making connections with American slavery almost inevitable. These accounts are then particularly useful as a bridge between the genres of captivity narrative and slave narrative. Lastly, the Barbary crises prompted the public to imagine a different kind of empire in response to the pirate threat—not the settler colonialism and "civilizing" mission of western expansion but rather a projection of military power that sought intervention, pacification, and ultimately regime change (in the case of the Tripolitan War), a program that is rather familiar to us today.[61] These divergences between Native American and Barbary narratives, I argue, offer the potential to explore alternate understandings of how Americans conceived of their identity in a global context beyond the traditional models for reading colonial dominance of the western landscape.

FROM HERE TO THERE (AND THEN)

The fictional Underhill's brush with the real O'Brien in Algiers and Verax's *The Allied Despots* offer contrasting visions for the collapse of Atlantic space prompted by the first Barbary crisis. I opened this introduction, however, with a very different gap: the broad temporal gap imagined by Carey as he constructed a fictional 1850 from his position in 1786. By way of articulating the broader, meta-critical contributions of the Barbary archive to American literary history, I want to turn briefly to those vital coordinates in national space-time. After all, it is a remarkable coincidence that, writing a year before the drafting of the Constitution, Carey sent his narrator forward to the year identified by F. O. Matthiessen as the start of the half-decade period he labeled the "American Renaissance."[62] Carey's piece implies that in the intervening sixty-four years, the United States was steadily accomplishing the dual ambitions of national consolidation and imperial expansion. For twenty-first-century literary critics looking back, it is far less clear how we might characterize the first half of the nineteenth century. When do the early postcolonial periods—whether defined as "republican" or "early national"—end, and when does the romantic period and the antebellum era begin? While the profession has seen a growing skepticism regarding the efficacy of periodization in both research and pedagogy, the gap between early American and antebellum literary aesthetics, studied by "early Americanists" and "U.S.-Americanists" respectively, seems too significant to dismiss. The failure to reconcile these critical projects has led to what Sandra M. Gustafson has called a "critical aporia," as the increasingly transnational framework of early Americanists seems to drift further and further away from the national focus of antebellum-era scholarship.[63]

To understand the ways in which the Barbary archive might productively intervene on these debates, I want to approach this critical aporia by focusing on the various temporal coordinates that have marked where early republican literature ends. Writing more recently on the question of the temporality of early American literature, Gustafson offers four key dates for consideration. The first, 1789, is marked by the publication of William Hill Brown's *The Power of Sympathy* and with the ratification of the Constitution. The second, 1800, marks both the "high point" of Charles Brockden Brown's career as a novelist and the election of Thomas Jefferson, which served as a "decisive break from a quasi-aristocratic political culture based on hierarchy and deference," ushering in a new and different political future. Gustafson then leaps twenty years into the future to note in the 1820s the rise of American romanticism with the major works of Washington Irving, James Fenimore Cooper, William Cullen Bryant, Lydia Maria Child, and Catherine Maria Sedgwick. Finally, by 1830, "the trajectory of American literature was set" as two of the major writers of the American Renaissance, Nathaniel Hawthorne and Edgar Allen Poe, emerged and the country entered the period known as "Jacksonian Democracy." Gustafson argues that the selection of any of these dates as a critical turning point in the evolution of American literature denotes a distinct set of narrative priorities, privileging the cultural shift from coloniality to emergent nationalism (1789), the rise of the novel (1800), the turn to westward expansion (1820), or the period leading up to the American Renaissance.[64]

The wide range of dates Gustafson presents emphasizes the lack of a critical consensus about exactly what in American literature constitutes "early" when dealing with such a diverse set of genres, reading practices, political landmarks, and social changes. The result is that our choices in periodization are more affected by retrospection than usual; independence looms over late colonial literature, the rise of romanticism and the Civil War are projected back on early national works, and all of it is tinted by our understanding of how American nationalist sentiment evolved in the late nineteenth century when, as Trish Loughran argues, advances in technology and infrastructure finally made possible the understanding of the United States as a singular, coherent political entity.[65]

If major political landmarks provide a rather slippery handhold on this evolving narrative, something of a scholarly consensus does exists concerning a major cultural shift between 1800 and the mid- to late 1820s—the largest gap between dates Gustafson offers—that dramatically altered the social and aesthetic parameters of American literature to form what we recognize as American modernity. Michael Warner, for example, describes somewhere in between Charles Brockden Brown and James Fenimore Cooper a shift from the ideology of republican print to that of liberal readership. Loughran, in her opposition to such totalizing theories, suggests a different turning point, characterizing the early United States as a "long-forgotten Rip Van Winkle" that finally wakes after 1830 to grapple with the internal contradictions of half a century of unionist rhetoric.[66] Similarly, for theorists of temporality like Lloyd Pratt, literature after 1830 is fundamentally marked by technological advances such as steam power that allowed for the imagining of multiple temporalities within the same territorial space. This multiplicity of temporalities characteristic of American modernity complicated rather than facilitated the processes of national/racial consolidation just as the epistemology of race became increasingly the domain of the sciences rather than the realm of religion and culture.

To summarize the problem, no single date or even decade seems to mark with enough precision the end of republican postcoloniality and the advent of American modernity, but if we must refer to two temporal coordinates that might come dozens of years apart, what lies in between? Enter the Barbary. The narrative of the Barbary crises starts with notions of the public in the post-revolutionary United States, but it expands to encompass multiple overlapping trends that would shape American modernity in print: the consolidation of racial taxonomies through emergent scientific discourse, the ascendance of sentiment and sentimental literature in organized abolition, the rise of distinct minority—in this case African American and Jewish American—print cultures and literary traditions, and the development of children's literature and new pedagogical practices focused on notions of liberal citizenship and racial literacy. Barbary figures are ideally suited to function as an index for the political and cultural shifts of the early nineteenth century precisely because these menacing pirates, spies, and slave masters functioned as harbingers for the destabilizing forces of modernity: linguistic incoherence, temporal plurality, growing technological power, and shrinking distances. They are, in some senses, metonyms for larger processes of social change, and their defeat, dramatized again and again across the Barbary archive, posited new forms of empirical/imperial discipline necessary to national citizenship in the post-republican era.

By focusing on the Barbary, we can map onto the dates outlined by Gustafson a new set of temporal coordinates: 1785, 1797, 1805, and 1815. In 1785, as I have already discussed, the first American ships were captured by Algerian pirates, sparking the Algerine Crisis. Because no captives had yet returned from North Africa to tell their story, short newspaper accounts and longer fictionalized narratives of captivity pervaded the public sphere in the decade to follow. The year 1797 saw the end of that crisis and the return of American captives. Their accounts circulated widely while the United States enjoyed several years of peace with the Barbary States at the cost of massive tribute payments. Captivity narratives written in the period, including

John Foss's influential account, focused on regaining national pride after the humiliation of enslavement. Continuing on, 1805 was a turning point in the archive, when General William Eaton led his expedition against Tripoli, the United States' first invasion of a foreign country, and emerged victorious from the first Barbary War. From that war we also have the exploits of Stephen Decatur, who led a raid to burn the American frigate *Philadelphia*, which had fallen into Tripolitan hands after running aground. The literary works produced in the period celebrated the country's transition from vulnerable republic and tributary to the despotic Barbary States to a rising imperial power in the Atlantic. Finally, 1815 brought the close of the Barbary Wars and the effective end of the threat of North African corsairs. As Christopher Apap argues, 1816 represented a pivotal year in the "Jacksonian geographical imagination," when, "as migration explodes and new states are hewed out of existing territories," American authors turned decisively to the task of national consolidation.[67] That project was both facilitated and complicated by the history of the Barbary conflicts. With the effective end of the threat of North African piracy, accounts published after 1815 were less concerned with the immediacy of white captivity than in exploring the racial complexities of North Africa and what they meant for the articulation of American identity. At the same time, anachronistic "Algerine" figures continued to circulate and threaten the margins of this national project.

Throughout this book I explore how these temporal coordinates can complement our traditional understanding of early American periodization. While the narrative in each chapter crosses one or more of these dates, the book overall divides into three parts. The first section, "Of Pirates and Print," is primarily situated in the early republic, exploring responses to the late-eighteenth-century Algerine Crisis through to the Tripolitan War and the aftermath of William Eaton's 1805 invasion of Tripoli. The first chapter, "The Patriot and the Sable Bard," examines how minor fictions of Barbary captivity in the late eighteenth century developed the parallels between Algerian and American slavery. At the center of the chapter, I read an early Barbary poem, *The American in Algiers; or, The Patriot of Seventy-Six in Captivity* (1797), and explore how the work counterposes the narratives of an American captive in North Africa and an African captive in the American South. The first half of the two-canto poem is told from the perspective of a Revolutionary War veteran who is, after the war, captured and enslaved by Algerian corsairs and deprived of the liberty for which he had fought.

In a dramatic turn, the perspective of the second canto shifts to that of an enslaved African in the American South who tells his story of being kidnapped from his family in Africa and brought to America by the middle passage. My reading examines the concepts of trans-Atlantic mobility and translation that operate within the poem—and in between the cantos—to frame the African slave's lament within a larger discourse of natural rights and liberation established by the voice of the enslaved patriot. I then use this framework to read two other very different slave narratives: the novella *Humanity in Algiers* (1801) and the "Story of Prince Moro" (1825), the former a relation of the life of a virtuous Algerian slave, Azem, allegedly written by an American captive in Algiers, and the latter the account of the life of the literate African Muslim slave Omar ibn Said in North Carolina. Taken together, these texts route understandings of authorship and access to the public sphere through tropes developed in the republic's engagements with North Africa.

My second chapter, "Barbary(an) Invasions," focuses on the satirical oriental observer/spy genre in early America. I examine three specific works. First, I analyze Benjamin Franklin's 1790 "On the Slave Trade," an article attacking proslavery arguments in Congress. While comparatively well known, this work is rarely discussed in the context of other Barbary texts and the genre of the oriental observer, despite what I argue to be clear lines of influence. The second, Peter Markoe's 1787 *The Algerine Spy in Pennsylvania*, is an epistolary novel that follows a spy sent by the dey of Algiers to observe American society and government in Philadelphia during the Constitutional Convention. My reading of this long-neglected work focuses on its articulation and transgression of the boundaries of the American public sphere through concepts of espionage and assimilation. The third text is the Mustapha letters from *Salmagundi* (1807–1808), a periodical published by Washington Irving in collaboration with his brother William Irving Jr. and James Paulding. The Mustapha letters provide a fictional, firsthand account of a real event—the feting in New York of a group of Tripolitan prisoners of war—from the perspective of the corsair captain Mustapha Rub-a-Dub Kelli Khan. Through these serialized letters, Mustapha criticizes the ephemerality and incoherence of a republic built entirely of words and print: what he dubs a "logocracy." Taken together, these works offer three distinct examples of how Barbary figures in print circulated within and intervened on social and political debates, ultimately critiquing the ideological assumptions of the early American public sphere and playing on anxieties surrounding print and the rhetorical construction of the republic within a wider Atlantic network. Furthermore, the adoption of the North African observer position in these works allowed writers to test the limits of the public to assimilate the voices of minority races and cultures.

The chapters of the second section of this book, "The Barbary and the Jewish Atlantic," offer a narrative bridge in two parts, beginning in the early republic but extending into the post-Barbary crises period following the common thread of racialized and orientalized Jewish characters in Barbary works. In the first chapter, "A Vague Resemblance to Something Seen Elsewhere," I assert that the Barbary archive played a major but almost entirely unacknowledged role in representing contemporary diasporic Jews and Jewishness to early American audiences. I read Jewish characters in Markoe's *The Algerine Spy*, Tyler's *The Algerine Captive*, and Rowson's *Slaves in Algiers* to analyze the problems the racially ambiguous figure of the Jew posed for notions of citizenship and naturalization still only vaguely defined in the period. I then use these readings as a lens through which to understand the problematic and enigmatic figure of Achsa Fielding in Charles Brockden Brown's *Arthur Mervyn* (1800). The significance of Fielding's Jewish identity, revealed late in the second half of the novel, has long eluded critics who have often focused on the race plot of the novel in terms of Mervyn's relationship with its Black and Afro-Caribbean characters. Fielding's appearance is, in part, explained by the Barbary referents that surround her, and her role in the novel resembles that of other North African Jewish characters that challenged and disrupted racial epistemologies, raising again the question of whether trans-Atlantic Jewish figures could ever effectively be nationalized.

Taking up the second half of this narrative in the 1810s, the next chapter, "Performing Diaspora in Noah's *Travels*," examines how one prominent Jewish writer of the period, Mordecai Manuel Noah, participated in the republic's increasingly imperialistic ambitions in the Atlantic world while writing back against orientalized depictions of Jews in North Africa and the United States. A relatively obscure figure today, Noah was the most prominent Jewish public figure in early nineteenth-century America. His book *Travels in England, France, Spain and the Barbary States* (1819) relates his controversial tenure as the U.S. consul to Tunis from 1813 to 1815. I posit in this chapter that *Travels* offers a unique series of performances through which

Noah attempts to reconcile his American and diasporic Jewish identities, effectively founding a tradition of American minority discourse that comes much later to be known as multicultural or multiethnic literature. Noah, I argue, functions as a transitional figure from the ideology of republican print to the racialized texts and performances of the antebellum era. Specifically, his work offers insight into how minority writers negotiated and performed their embodied authorial identities while contributing to emerging forms of mainstream American literary nationalism.

Part 3 projects the Barbary archive forward into the antebellum period to study the continued circulation of Barbary materials within two very different midcentury discourses: abolitionist print culture and popular children's literature. Across these final chapters, I demonstrate how after 1830 abolitionist works continued to circulate the increasingly anachronistic figure of the "Algerine" as distinct from the colonial subjects of French Algiers. The first chapter of the section, "The Advantage of a Whip-Lecture," explores the constellation of references to the Barbary conflicts that pervaded American abolitionism in the decades approaching the Civil War. Specifically, I look at how references to North Africa sought to redefine the circum-Atlantic geography of slavery and freedom in the period for both white and Black writers. These references surround and permeate not only the pages of influential antislavery newspapers such as the *Anti-Slavery Standard* and *The Liberator* but also the works of Frederick Douglass, including his autobiographies and his first and only foray into long fiction, *The Heroic Slave* (1852). Additionally, both Black and white abolitionists used the history of North African captivity to deracialize slavery and challenge the universality of white supremacy, suggesting that narratives of enslavement and the emergence from it, far from marking the enslaved body as inferior, could be seen as integral to American identity from the country's very beginnings.

My final chapter, "Peter Parley in Tripoli," asks how Barbary texts might contribute to our understanding of children's literature and, in particular, children's abolitionism. Barbary pirates abound in nineteenth-century juvenile literature, from textbooks and national histories to adventure tales and dime novels. Recently, studies of nineteenth-century children's literature have shifted from a primary focus on the definition of childhood to an examination of social and racial taxonomies and how they functioned to define citizenship for young readers. These studies have primarily explored abolitionist messages in children's textbooks, geographies, and short stories, yet none has explored in depth the prevalence of Barbary types in children's works, particularly in North African captivity narratives adapted for young readers. This chapter looks specifically at Samuel Griswold Goodrich's use of Barbary pirates and captivity narratives to teach children about race and citizenship. White slavery narratives offered the ideal manifestation of "imaginary" or deferred citizenship—the state in which children, born into the rights of citizenship, must wait to take full advantage of them. My closing chapter proposes ways in which an engagement with the Barbary archive can expand and deepen our understanding of the racial and nationalistic discourses underlying nineteenth-century children's pedagogy.

What takes shape across these six chapters is a network of texts and allusions that have a remarkably long reach in this critical period and that can be traced back to the anxieties and ambitions expressed in the Algerine Crisis–era speculations with which I opened this introduction. Mathew Carey may have missed the mark when describing the scale of future conflicts with the Barbary Coast, but Algerine pirates sail on in American print culture to reappear at surprising times and in unexpected places. My hope is that this book establishes a foundation for future studies of Barbary texts that can strengthen our understanding of the complex relationships between race and print and between republic and empire in American literary history.

PART ONE

OF PIRATES AND PRINT

CHAPTER ONE

THE PATRIOT AND THE SABLE BARD

To be oneself in pain is to be more acutely aware of having a body, as so also to see from the outside the wound in another person is to become more intensely aware of human embodiedness.

—Elaine Scarry, *The Body in Pain: The Making and Unmaking of the World* (1987)

The Spaniards say, that he's a filthy dunce,
Whose house is glass, yet 'gins at throwing stones;
So he who lords it o'er his fellow man,
Should ne'er of wrongs or tyranny complain.

—Anonymous, *The American in Algiers* (1797)

In the preface to his 1798 account of his enslavement in Algiers, Newburyport, Massachusetts, native John Foss attests to offering a "simple statement of facts" concerning the "hellish tortures" he experienced. Foss had been a common sailor on the *Polly*, captured during the surge of piratical activity at the height of the Algerine Crisis in the last months of 1793. Foss's account describes in detail the dehumanizing brutality of Barbary slavery for a public eager for firsthand accounts of conditions in North Africa. In the final line of the preface, Foss commends his narrative to the public sphere with the desire that it might serve as a warning that will save his fellow citizens from the "miseries of Algerine slavery."[1] As one of the first and most popular accounts published in the post-crisis period, *A Journal, of the Captivity and Sufferings of John Foss* set the standard for the new wave of American Barbary captivity narratives. Its mix of ethnographic observations and harrowing anecdotes of brutality proved immensely popular with republican-era audiences.

32   CHAPTER ONE

Throughout his narrative, Foss frames his experiences using the language of the Revolution. Observing the halting progress of diplomatic efforts in Algiers, he "despaired of ever tasting the sweets of Liberty again," yet notes proudly that with the aid provided to the American captives by public efforts back home, "the Republican government of the United States have set an example of humanity to all the governments of the world." Foss presents American public virtue as triumphant over tyranny, with his own final liberation realized by the publication of his account for the benefit of his compatriots. The work's title and preface emphasize how Foss drew the details of his account directly from a journal he kept during his enslavement; he describes writing nightly in his jail cell to "amuse and relieve" his mind, without any expectation that the account would be read or published in the future.[2] Writing, Foss suggests, is a tool for surviving and transcending the mental effects of enslavement. Timothy Marr argues that by narrativizing their captivity, former Barbary slaves "purged themselves of the shame of their prior powerlessness and became agents of national survival." The liberation of Foss's body and the publication of his text for his "fellow citizens" together provided "symbolic proof of the viability of American Independence."[3]

The image of Foss composing his journal in his cell speaks to the power that he, a common white sailor, retained even in captivity. In his influential reading of Barbary captivity narratives as early ethnographies, Paul Baepler observes that while white slavery inverted the racial power dynamic, the genre demonstrates how the "ability to 'decode and encode' the situation remains with the white narrator."[4] Foss's narrative mastery over his enslavement often manifests in the *Journal* in an objective, disembodied tone with which he is able to distance himself from the dehumanizing effects of slavery. While cataloguing the "particular occurrences" of brutality he witnessed in Algiers in the work's first edition, he only vaguely describes the violence he personally experienced. Writing is, in fact, one of the few forms of labor he depicts himself performing in Algiers.[5] He does, however, remark on the story of one specific fellow American captive: Scipio Jackson, a crew member of the *Minerva* described in a brief parenthetical as "(a black man)."[6] Jackson falls ill with cholera but is forced to return to heavy labor by his cruel Algerian taskmaster. He only works for a half an hour before collapsing and soon after expiring. This anecdote stands out as one of the few instances in which Foss names one of his fellow captives, begging the question of why he chose to illustrate his account with this short episode of an enslaved African American worked to death. Would Foss's audience have made the connection between the fate of Scipio Jackson in Algiers and that of nearly a million enslaved Africans in the American South?

Foss's singling out of Jackson's story seems to invite readers to consider the parallels between Algerian and American slavery, yet the writer actively undercut just such an interpretation when he revised this passage in the *Journal*'s second edition later in 1798. Leading into the anecdote in this edition, Foss comments on how Algerians treated the death of a Christian like the death of a common "domestic animal," setting up the introduction of Jackson: "A particular instance of this nature happened on the 30th of January, 1796. The unhappy sufferer being an American. I have thought it worthy remark." Foss then provides an expanded relation of the death of Jackson, now described as "(a blackman belonging to New-York)." He follows the anecdote by commenting that the episode "is sufficient to ascertain the depth of the wretchedness of Christians . . . thrown into the hands of those detestable piratical barbarians."[7] The revised story provides a more vivid relation of the events leading to Jackson's death, but Foss no longer leaves it to the audience to interpret the meaning of the incident. While Jackson's status remains ambiguous in the fact that he "belongs" to New York, his death derives meaning from his identity as an "American" and a "Christian," not his race.[8] By attempting to avoid it, the *Journal*'s second edition places in sharp relief the problem of readerly sympathy provoked by Jackson's story and Foss's own attempts to transcend his former enslavement. Foss expresses the hope in his preface that his account would provoke the kind of collective sentiment that will further bind the young nation together—"the tears of sympathy will flow from the humane and feeling, at the tale of hardships and sufferings of their unfortunate fellow countrymen"—yet the success of this sympathetic union depends on his ability to offer Jackson as a proxy for his own largely absent body while controlling his audience's reading across racial lines.[9]

Foss's revision of Jackson's story demonstrates the writer's awareness of the contradictions inherent in publishing his experiences of slavery, his condemnations of the Algerians, and his celebration of liberty in a country dominated by its own slave system. In some ways his avoidance of the issue is not particularly surprising, as despite his many ethnographic observations, he follows pre-independence Barbary narratives from the seventeenth

34 **CHAPTER ONE**

and eighteenth centuries in framing the conflicts primarily as a matter of religious rather than racial difference. Nevertheless, by the time Foss published his account, quite a few fictional Barbary texts had already insisted on exploring American hypocrisy regarding slavery. The most often studied of these early Algerine texts is Royall Tyler's *The Algerine Captive* (1797), in which the protagonist, Updike Underhill, sails on a slaving expedition only be reduced to slavery himself by Algerian corsairs. Almost immediately after his capture Underhill expresses an acute awareness of how the power dynamic has reversed, writing that "the treatment we gave the unhappy Africans . . . now came full into my mind." Through his experience as both a slaver and a slave, he comes to recognize that these Africans are his "BRETH-REN OF THE HUMAN RACE."[10] It seems entirely plausible that *The Algerine Captive*, published not far from Newburyport in Walpole, New Hampshire, may have conditioned the response to Foss's *Journal*. However, any reader expecting such grand declarations from Foss would have been disappointed.

As we have seen in my earlier discussions of race and fictionality, *The Algerine Captive* has often been held up as a model text for representing important trends at the end of the eighteenth century. To some extent the critical attention paid to Tyler's novel has overshadowed the broader print cultural response to white slavery that anticipated and responded to the unspoken contradictions of Foss's narrative in its opposition of American liberty and Barbary captivity. Pivoting away from the immensely popular accounts by captives like Foss and Tyler's well-known novel, below I survey several lesser known "minor" fictions of Barbary slavery that explore the parallels between white and Black slave narratives. The first two works I read, a mock slave advertisement and the two-canto poem *The American in Algiers* (1797), both of which circulated before returning American captives published their accounts, imagine graphic violence against white bodies as itself a form of publication.[11] The third work, the novella *Humanity in Algiers; or, The Story of Azem* (1801), appeared years after the first edition of Foss's *Journal* and rewrites the relationship between Foss and Jackson to make explicit the role of the enslaved African in the liberation of the white author.

Taken together, these minor fictions center on acts of inscription and address through which the voice of the slave enters the public sphere. Drawing on the interplay of body and text—blood and ink—they explore how the authorial and editorial power of the white slave mediates the engagement with the enslaved Black body while insisting on the primacy and universality of white suffering and the liberated white subject's "entry into history."[12] In other words, these works are about communicating the horrors of slavery to the public and how such accounts are translated into forms of social and political action within a structure of white supremacy that seeks to center white liberty and contain the radical power of Black testimony. In this chapter I begin this book's overarching work of developing narrative connections between the Barbary crises and the later antebellum period by making the case that, while situated in the late eighteenth century, these early abolitionist works demonstrate how white slavery served discursively to legitimate and authorize accounts of Black suffering, anticipating the framing of African American slave narratives as they evolved in the nineteenth century with the validation of white abolitionist editors.

MARKS ON THE BODY

For many early republican readers, particularly in the North, their most consistent exposure to the brutality of American slavery came through the local circulation of escaped slave advertisements, a genre centered on detailed descriptions of enslaved bodies. In some cases, the same paper that carried the desperate pleas for freedom from Barbary captives such as Richard O'Brien benefited financially from efforts to re-enslave the victims of the plantation system. Philadelphian Mathew Carey, in his pamphlet *A Short Account of Algiers* (1794), comments explicitly on this hypocrisy as he describes the slave markets of North Africa:

> For this practice of buying and selling slaves, we are not entitled to charge the Algerines with any exclusive degree of Barbarity. The Christians of Europe and America carry on this commerce an hundred times more extensively than the Algerines. . . . Nobody seems even to be surprised by a diabolical kind of advertisements, which, for some months past, have frequently adorned the newspapers of Philadelphia. The French fugitives from the West-Indies have brought with them a croud of slaves. These most injured people sometimes run off, and their master advertises a reward for apprehending them. At the same time, we are commonly informed, that his sacred name is marked in capitals, on their breasts; or in plainer terms, it is stamped on that part of the body with a red hot iron.

For Carey, descriptions of branded bodies—bodies printed and printed upon—undercut any claim the American public might have to moral superiority over North Africans. He concludes the passage by commenting simply, "Before therefore we reprobate the ferocity of the Algerines, we should enquire whether it is not possible to find, in some other regions of the globe, a systematic brutality still more disgraceful?"[13] David Waldstreicher has explored the importance of escape slave advertisements in legitimizing and restoring confidence in the slave system in response to the failure represented by the runaway.[14] Carey turns this complicity in the slave system on its head, marking both northern editors and reading publics as implicated in the same violence they condemn in Algiers. Notably, he frames his antislavery sentiment as an objection against the ways in which foreign texts intrude on local and national means of circulation. Among scholars today, Carey is most often noted for his firsthand account of the 1793 yellow fever epidemic in Philadelphia, the origins of which were blamed on French refugees from Saint-Domingue.[15] In the passage above, he describes a different kind of infection of the national body through print, while also remarking on how the Black bodies in turn are imprinted by slavery, made into texts of their enslavement.

Carey's *Short Account* provides a brief window into a complex hemispheric choreography of white figures arriving and Black figures escaping, leaving their mark on both the body and the newspaper page in Philadelphia. These themes would be taken up again within the genre of the escaped slave advertisement that same year, as newspapers in Philadelphia, New York, and Boston ran a parody of just such a "diabolical" slave advertisement. The piece begins with an imitation of the headlines and rhetoric commonly attached to these advertisements, announcing:

FORTY ZEQUINS REWARD.
Stop the ungrateful Villain!

RAN-AWAY from the Subscriber, an American slave; he is an incorrigible infidel, and all the hardships of constant labor, coarse and scanty food, nakedness and the severest application of the lash and the bastionado, have failed to make this stubborn dog renounce his Christian errors, or believe in our holy prophet.[16]

As with many longer runaway slave advertisements in the period, "Forty Zequins" offers a window into the life of the enslaved, here heightened for the purposes of satire. Like Foss's later account, the piece begins by framing the conflict in religious terms, invoking the theme of "turning Turk" common to earlier Barbary captivity narratives like Cotton Mather's "The Glory of Goodness" (1703). In that sermon, perhaps the earliest American Barbary captivity text, the minister sees God's "goodness" in the fact that none of the captives from New England in Algiers "proved *Apostates*, from our Holy Religion, when they were under so many *Temptations* to Apostasy."[17] In this case, the article both satirizes American hypocrisy in tolerating slavery and celebrates the resilience of Americans themselves, able to resist calls to defection. At the same time, that faithfulness is deeply ironic; by "playing Algerian," the writer themself engages in what Peter Reed terms "creative renegado acts," while the satire's critique of American slavery ultimately suggests that there is no real difference between Muslims and Christians, at least as slaveholders.[18]

While the thrust of the satire presents itself to the reader almost immediately, the mock advertisement does not stop with the conventional reversal of white slave and African master.[19] Rather, it continues on to make a point about the liberatory power of print. The slave owner, identified at the end of the advertisement as Ibrahim Ali Bey, describes an insidious (and entirely fictional) mode by which American captives have escaped from Barbary slavery: "I fear he has adopted a mode of escaping now often attempted, and I am informed has sometimes succeeded, and which scarcely admits detection. This is to procure the certificate of *redemption*, given some of the tribes of American infidels, admitted in redemption, and liberated by our courts of *justice*, and taking the name of the persons therein mentioned upon himself, passes under the sanction of the seal of office, unmolested, no one doubting but that the bearer is the person recognized in the certificate." The piece plays on the shifting relationships of texts, identities, and bodies, and on forms of passing. In North Africa, white names and white bodies are interchangeable, made "blank" in their foreignness. With print, identities are translated from body to body through means by which, as Ali Bey worries, the redeemed Americans might "liberate half the slaves in Algiers" and collapse the entire system. The piece accordingly offers a spin on what Waldstreicher calls the "rhetoric of pretense" common to escaped slave advertisements; at a time when Foss was still furtively recording his experiences nightly in his jail cell, white slaves in this satire wielded print as a means to "pretend to be free."[20] One might also easily compare this moment with the well-known episode later described by Frederick Douglass in which he gains his freedom through the use of a "sailor's protection."[21] In this case, however, the captive need not impersonate the patois of the American sailor—assuming the captive himself is a sailor who must present his body as proof of national belonging. The evidence lies in whiteness itself.

Despite the success of the American slaves' almost comical shell game, the final section of the satire, which takes up a significant portion of the paper column, asserts the limits of the text's liberatory power. The piece ends with a graphic description of the escaped slave's scarred body:

> The slave is about five feet eight or nine inches high, about 35 years of age, marked with a slip in his right ear, and a hole bored through his left, branded on his forehead and on his breast with the initials of my name—he has a large scar on his left cheek, occasioned by a wound with a scimitar; both his ancles are much bruised and wounded by his chains which, he found means to disengage himself from when he went away, his neck and shoulders bear the evident marks of having worn an iron collar, and his back the marks of having been well scored with the lash, and the soals of his feet of the bastionado, for his stubbornness.[22]

The advertisement confronts the audience with what Hortense J. Spillers describes as the distinction between "body" and "flesh." Commenting on descriptions of the torture and branding of enslaved Black bodies, she writes, "These undecipherable markings on the captive body render a kind of hieroglyphics of the flesh whose severe disjunctures come to be hidden to the cultural seeing by skin color."[23] It attempts to create unease in its audience by turning what Donna Haraway calls the "conquering gaze" on the white body, "the gaze that mythically inscribes all the marked bodies, that makes the unmarked category claim the power to see and not be seen, to represent while escaping representation."[24] The inability of the body to escape representation means that the white body becomes subject to a kind of publication. Like the descriptions of enslaved bodies that Carey decries above, this advertisement notes the branding of the slave—the body-made-text—as a key signifier of enslavement, to which he adds the "evident marks" of chains and a collar. Ultimately, injury takes the place of race in rendering the body visible and legible.

In his analysis of anti-Black satires that translate the cause of abolition as "Bobalition," Corey Capers deploys the term "public blackness" to describe the "contested material-semiotic figure created in and through practices of publicity."[25] The "Forty Zequins" piece certainly offers its own form of racial minstrelsy in its performance of the violent and frustrated Algerine slave master, but more significant and more subversive is its foregrounding of a "public whiteness," around which the advertisement translates an American reading public into an Algerian one concerned with maintaining the legitimacy of North African slavery. The piece complicates not only the moral superiority of an American public condemning Barbary slavery while complicit in its own system of racial violence but also the ideological move that imagines a nationally bounded public through print circulation and address. The piece posits instead a trans-Atlantic system by which slaveholders can identify a common cause in the circulation of enslaved bodies, Black and white. Whether America or Africa, masters and slaves are all the same. In the section below, I examine how a few years later *The American in Algiers* built on both these concepts of public whiteness and trans-Atlantic translation, this time from the perspective of the enslaved.

BLOOD AND INK

In February 1797, the first advertisements for the two-canto poem *The American in Algiers; or, The Patriot of Seventy-Six in Captivity* were published in New York City papers. Across the Atlantic, Joel Barlow and David Humphreys were concluding a treaty with the dey of Algiers, having already finalized the ransom of the captive Foss and his compatriots. Only days before the poem first appeared, *The Diary* of New York reported that the first freed captives had arrived in Philadelphia on a Swedish barque, and in the issues that followed, the paper ran a comprehensive list of American vessels and crewmen captured over the previous decade with asterisks next to the names of those who had died. A line near the bottom of the list totals: "13 vessels—132 captives—died 31." A final note in the column remarks, "By the information of several of the captives, we find that their treatment was uniformly cruel at Algiers. . . . It will be found with what becoming fortitude they bore their sufferings—by their feelings on witnessing the satisfaction of their fellow-citizens yesterday—they proved themselves no less worthy of their country and of Liberty."[26] This commentary draws a direct connection among the sufferings of the captives listed, their enduring connection to their "fellow-citizens," and their right to reclaim their freedom. It celebrates the reunification of a fractured American public facilitated by the captives' fealty to the nation and republican virtue. It is within this context that the anonymous poet behind *The American in Algiers*, recalling a crisis now over, challenges the rhetoric of national unity and liberty with the intervention of an enslaved Black voice from the American South. In my reading of the poem, I focus on how the poet complicates the relationship around dueling appeals for freedom through the distinction between a poem voiced and one written and circulated. That distinction, overlaid on both the geographic distance between America and Algiers and the racial differences between enslaved bodies, offers insight into a work that ostensibly sought to construct sympathetic bonds across races but was nonetheless beholden to and complicit in the larger historical process of the racialization of print.

On its surface, this long poem in heroic couplets announces itself in the vein of any number of other works inspired by the Algerine Crisis, meditating on the meaning of liberty after the Revolution and drawing on national outrage over the enslavement of Americans in Algiers. The title's reference to "Seventy-Six" precedes a short epigraph from Philip Freneau's revolutionary-era poem "America Independent" (1778): "When God from Chaos gave this world to be, / Man then he form'd, and form'd him to be free."[27] The inclusion of these lines signals the poem's participation in emerging narratives of literary nationalism while also subtly referencing the Revolutionary War hero Ethan Allen, who chose the same verse for the title page of *The Narrative of Colonel Ethan Allen's Captivity* (1779), an account of his military service and capture by the British. As James M. Greene has argued, Allen's narrative utilizes the war hero's suffering at the hands of British officers, Tories, and Native Americans to embody a "burgeoning sense of continental nationalism" that transcends local circumstances.[28] The title page of *The American in Algiers* seems engaged in much the same project, placing its fictional North African narrative alongside other colonial and postcolonial accounts of captivity and liberation with deep investments in nation-building.[29]

The first canto of the poem fulfills the promise of its title page. The titular Patriot recounts his service in the Revolutionary War and later, after the Treaty of Paris, his capture and enslavement by Algerian pirates. His lament focuses on the complacency of a newly independent America, so willing to give up its recently won liberty to the tyrannical dey of Algiers.[30] By speaking directly to the body of the nation, the Patriot seeks to "rouse *Columbia* from her torpid dream, / And bid her every free-born son reclaim, / The fate of Slavery's hapless sons to scan / And haste the triumph of the rights of man." Within this broad invocation of natural rights the poem implores readers to recognize the suffering of their compatriots in North Africa and to contribute to their immediate relief, whether through the various ransom funds advertised in American newspapers or through direct military action, as suggested by the Patriot's own martial past. The image of Columbia's "torpid dream" depicts a national body drained of energy, recalling a passage in Carey's earlier *A Short Account of Algiers* that describes the failure of various committees in Philadelphia to raise ransom funds: "Humanity has to deplore, that a most unaccountable torpor has taken place of benevolence and charity on this trying occasion." In both deployments, the lack of public action translates into a form of corporeal disability. The Patriot reinforces this focus on the ill and injured body as he shifts to a direct address of the reading public, commenting that, "while you my countrymen each blessing share," the captive "[bends] beneath a tyrant's rod." He complains that the "birthright of Columbia's sons," for which they "drench'd their native soil in kindred gore," has been stolen from him.[31]

The image of "kindred gore" leads into an extended narrative in which the Patriot, a native of Boston, describes his participation in the Revolutionary War. Most notable in this description is its persistent focus on blood. At Lexington, the Patriot stood, "arm'd and mingled in the bloody fight." At Bunker Hill, the Patriot notes that there were "dying heroes strew'd upon the ground; / . . . And freedom's cause from every vein did bleed." During the Battle of New York, a regiment of Virginians' "blood e'en fertilized the barren sand." The narrator reiterates that "I saw the earth besmear'd with human blood," and that "these eyes have seen full many a hero bleed." After numerous references to the "crimson plain" of battle, the Revolution is finally won, and the Patriot at last purchases freedom "with . . . blood."[32] Among these many references, blood at different points represents the cost of freedom and freedom itself.

In the wake of the war, the Patriot settles down with his new bride, Rosina, "Resolv'd abroad, henceforth no more to roam." Tragically, the Patriot finds that his family's property has been stolen, leaving him destitute, while "splendor round the sunshine patriot reigns." Economic hardship forces the Patriot to find work on a merchant ship from Boston bound to Genoa. On the return trip, the narrative of bloodletting resumes as the Patriot's ship is attacked by pirates, with "the bloody Mussulman . . . / Alike for battle, and for blood prepared." After his capture, the pirates bring the Patriot to the ruler of Algiers, who gives him the opportunity to reclaim his freedom by converting to Islam. Refusing, he is then sold on the auction block.

The canto closes with the Patriot "urg'd by the driver, whose unfeeling lash / Extorts the blood that trickles from the gash."[33] This parting verse establishes the Patriot as continuously bleeding, even as the reader encounters his poem. Critically, this image of the bleeding wound bounds the Patriot's address to the national public temporally as well as geographically. This national exsanguination comes to represent both the sacrifice necessary for freedom and the betrayal of that sacrifice to a new African oppressor. In his analysis of George Washington's 1796 Farewell Address, Bruce Burgett draws on Ernst H. Kantorowitz's concept of the king's two bodies to argue that, "like the mortal body of the monarch, the 'thing-ness' of Washington's body threatens to disrupt the equation of the nation and the state, of the citizen and the subject. In contrast to the monarch's Christic body, however, Washington's patriotic body disavows that threat by linking popular sovereignty to state representation."[34] The Patriot's bleeding body in the poem offers a similar corporate "thing-ness" to the public, in this case representing not necessarily the state but rather the institutionalization of the Revolution and its continued resonance in the public sphere.

Only in the poem's second canto does the work's abolitionist message emerge with a vengeance. This canto replaces the perspective of the Patriot in North Africa with that of an African enslaved in the American South who identifies himself as the "Sable Bard." Utilizing the same poetic structure of the first canto, the second speaker directly confronts not just the Patriot's claim to freedom earned through struggle but also the hypocrisy of slave-holding revolutionary leaders such as Washington and Thomas Jefferson. It answers the poem's earlier appeal to natural rights with a biting condemnation of the carnage wreaked upon Africa by western colonial powers and offers the Sable Bard's personal account of his kidnapping, the middle passage, and the inhuman conditions of the southern plantation. Nowhere is this dramatic shift in perspective or theme anticipated on *The American in Algiers*'s title page or any of the work's other paratextual materials, raising the question of whether readers would have naturally drawn connections between slavery as it was practiced for centuries on the Barbary Coast and the American plantation system; how likely were readers to see the suffering of the Patriot and the Sable Bard as two sides of the same coin?

If the Patriot's canto imagines the ability of the poet to embody the nation in a way that allows direct address across the time and space of the Atlantic world, the Sable Bard reasserts that distance in the face of geographic proximity. In the opening lines of the second canto, the poem dramatizes the shift in the audience's focus as movement:

> From the piratic coast where slavery reigns,
> And freedom's champions wear despotic chains;
> Turn to Columbia—cross the western waves,
> And view her wide spread empire throng'd with slaves
> Whose wrongs unmerited, shall blast with shame
> Her boasted rights, and prove them but a name.[35]

Not only does the poetic voice of the piece shift from a white American captive to a Sable Bard but the narrator invites the American audience to view the United States from the position of Africa. However, this trans-positioning also suggests that there is little difference between these sites, as the terms used—"where slavery reigns" and "empire throng'd with slaves"—could describe either side of the Atlantic. Furthermore, these opening lines seem directly aimed at the voice of the Patriot, implying that the American's complicity in the nation's slave system renders his supposed purchase of freedom at least suspect, if not wholly invalid.

With the shift in speaker comes a shift in modality. The first canto consistently presents the reader with the conceit of the Patriot speaking directly to the audience; the sense of national crisis depends on the reader imagining the Patriot at that moment across the Atlantic being tortured by his African captors, even while the real-life captives had already returned home. In contrast, the turn to the narrative of an African in America begins,

> Now gentle reader, think thy task not hard
> Awhile to listen to a sable bard,
> Whose pen undaunted thus shall dare address
> A world of critics, and her thoughts express,
> Th' envenom'd source of every ill to trace,
> That preys incessant on his hapless race.[36]

The construction of the Sable Bard as a self-conscious literary figure laboring through his pen recalls the framing of Phillis Wheatley's work, and in particular the frontispiece of *Poems on Various Subjects, Religious and Moral* (1773), in which Wheatley seems to pause in thought at her desk, pen in hand. Going further, the choice of a "sable" pen-name, gendering of the pen as female, and the address to a "world of critics" all point to a connection with Wheatley, who wrote in "On Being Brought from Africa to America": "Some view our sable race with scornful eye, / 'Their colour is a diabolic die.'"[37] These allusions set the stage not only for the second canto's own middle-passage narrative but also for a shift in the poem's relationship to racial identity and textual production. Colleen Glenney Boggs argues that Wheatley's most famous poem posits the middle passage as a kind of translation in both the geographical and physical senses of the term, quoting the multiple definitions of "to translate" from Noah's Webster's 1828 *Dictionary*: "1. to bear, carry, or remove from one place to another. . . . 3. to transfer, to convey from one to another. 4. to cause to remove from one part of the body to another, as to translate disease. 5. to change. 6. to interpret; to render into another language; to express the sense of one language in the words of another 7. to explain."[38] We do not know for sure whether the anonymous poet of *The American in Algiers* drew directly from Wheatley for inspiration, but nevertheless they clearly play on the spatial, linguistic, and corporeal aspects of translation. Moving from the first canto to the second, the address to "you my countrymen" becomes "my reader," a move that distances the Black speaker from claims of national belonging and highlights a relationship structured entirely by circulation and reading practices. As Henry Louis Gates Jr. argues, "Black people could become speaking subjects only by inscribing their voices in the written word."[39] *The American in Algiers* seems to reflect Gates's observation while being remarkably aware of the social and political dimensions of orality and textuality. In fact, as I show, unlike the Patriot's identity as a bloodied body moving through the revolutionary era, the Sable Bard's character seems himself intertextually constructed, referencing frequently not only the tropes of Black representation in print but also the founding documents that undergird the American republic.

In contrast to the individualized history of the Patriot's participation in the national-historical struggle presented in the first canto, the second offers a broader world-historical critique not only of America but of European colonization globally. For riches and slaves, "old Europe's fleets first cross'd the flood, / And bath'd the coast of Africa in blood." Extending this history to North America, the poet catalogues,

> For these [treasures], Hispania's pious children hurl'd
> Death and destruction round the western world;

FIGURE 2. Scipio Moorhead, "Phillis Wheatley, Negro Servant to Mr. John Wheatley, of Boston" (London: Archd. Bell, September 1, 1773). —Courtesy Library of Congress, Washington, DC

> For these, Britannia loos'd the dogs of war,
> And pour'd her vengeance from Belona's carr;
> For these, French, Dutch, and Portuguese, and Danes,
> Have slaughter'd millions on Columbia's plains;
> And with our sable sons the place supply'd
> Of tribes less suited to sustain their pride.

While the first canto presents the Patriot as a personal witness to the carnage of American Independence and as a supplicant for the sympathy of his audience, the Sable Bard relates events on a dramatically different scale, offering a long history of global white aggression that "sluic'd the veins of half the human race," African and Native American. He makes clear that the Patriot's own sacrifice for liberty is only enabled by the death of nonwhite bodies before him.[40]

Having established this broader context of European imperialism, the poem again shifts to address America itself, which it carefully distinguishes from the colonial powers: "I pause to freedom's sons—my lays belong, / And hence to *them* I consecrate my song: / Rulers and rul'd in turn, shall share

my rhyme, / Well made, and suited to Columbia's clime." In the lines to follow the Sable Bard addresses the rhetoric of American liberty not through
his "fellow countrymen" but through the icons and documents of the
Revolution. Following the conceit of a poem written rather than spoken,
footnotes clutter the Sable Bard's account, elaborating on the historical and
philosophical concepts mentioned in the verse. Providing evidence for his
right to liberty, he even interpolates the Declaration of Independence into
his lines: "*We hold these Truths self-evident to be, / All men are equal and
created Free; / Endow'd with Rights, no Law can e'er suppress, / Life, Liberty,
Pursuit of Happiness.*" This moment of appropriation comes complete with
a footnote, presenting too the "precise words" of the passage, as if the Sable
Bard needed to present his evidence from the "true" texts of American freedom. From this appropriation springs a critique of the American Revolution,
within which the Sable Bard seems fully aware of the Patriot's complaint
in the previous canto. The Patriot specifically claims to have been present
during the war at the deaths of General Joseph Warren at Bunker Hill and
General Hugh Mercer at Princeton; the Sable Bard answers with the charge
that "in vain, Montgomery, Warren, Mercer fell." The poet thus asserts textual
control over the Patriot's narrative, revising the meaning of violence against
white bodies within a trans-Atlantic context. At moments the Sable Bard
also shifts into direct address, but rather than invoking the nation as the
Patriot does, he specifically targets George Washington, imploring him to
"look o'er your fields, and see them black with slaves," emphasizing again the
emptiness of the rhetoric of liberty within the larger context of European-
American slavery.[41]

When the Sable Bard finally turns to his own story of captivity, he begins
with a relation of his life before the middle passage. In contrast to the first
canto's hellish depictions of North Africa, West Africa is an idyllic Eden
where the poet was "nurs'd in the lap of luxury and ease."[42] Like the Patriot,
the Sable Bard finds himself in love with a young woman named Zephra,
"whose perfections ev'ry pen defy." In asserting his inability to capture the
beauty of his love through writing, the poet answers Jefferson's notorious
criticisms of Wheatley and Ignatius Sancho in the *Notes on the State of
Virginia* (1785): "Misery is often the parent of the most affecting touches in
poetry.—Among the blacks is misery enough, God knows, but no poetry.
Love is the peculiar oestrum of the poet. Their love is ardent, but it kindles
the senses only, not the imagination."[43] To this, the Sable Bard responds

parenthetically, "Nor here let scorn attempt the point to prove / That blacks ne'er feel the soft impulse of love; / If actions speak the feelings of the mind, / Whites have the bluntest of the human kind."[44] Unlike the Patriot, who can relate his own love story simply and without mediation, the Sable Bard plays on his awareness that he is contending with larger ideological and textual systems that deny Black humanity and Black authority.

The Sable Bard is set to wed his beloved when, just before the wedding feast, a group of slavers attack his village. Put in chains and brought to a slave ship, he describes entering the hold, where "groans of anguish, screams, and dismal cries, / Forth from the deep and noxious hole arise; / lashes, and oaths, and threats, and clanking chains, / Form the hoarse music of those curs'd domains."[45] The poet's description recalls Olaudah Equiano's account of the sounds and smells of the slave ship from *The Interesting Narrative*: "I was soon put down under the decks, and there I received such a salutation in my nostrils as I had never experienced in my life; so that with loathsomeness of the stench, and crying together, I became so sick and low that I was not able to eat."[46] If the Sable Bard's writing persona seems inspired by Wheatley, his story of lost paradise and the middle passage follows Equiano's abduction from Igboland and arrival in America before the Revolution, reinforcing the idea that the poet, in his intertextual construction, represents both Black bodies and Black texts as they circulate. The slave ship lands in Baltimore, where "Albion's flag in haughty triumph wav'd, / The proud insignia of a world enslav'd."[47] Philip Gould notes that, despite the thorough indictment of American hypocrisy, this passage suggests that Britain is ultimately at fault for imposing slavery on the United States and that the Sable Bard shares a common cause with the Patriot.[48] The poet's narrative ends shortly after he is sold at auction, skipping over the revolutionary period of the first canto, but the implication is clear: the Patriot's sacrifice was ultimately futile, as the country remains beholden to a slave system created by its former colonial masters.

As we have seen, the Sable Bard offers what may be a cutting critique of the Patriot's sacrifice, but *The American in Algiers* also literalizes the ways in which the white slave's pain precedes and structures the reader's engagement with the Black slave narrative. The Patriot's story makes possible the Sable Bard's entry—and by extension Wheatley's and Equiano's entries—into the public sphere. As the final lines of the poem make clear, such access remains heavily mediated by the processes of textual production.

In contrast to the bleeding body of the Patriot, the second canto ends, "Of Afric's race, I make the just appeal; / And leave the portrait which my pen has drawn, / A short, concise, and comprehensive one."[49] The return to the pen in these final lines reminds us both of Wheatley's frontispiece and of the critical distinction between handwriting and print. If, as Joseph Rezek argues, Wheatley's frontispiece purposely collapses media difference by inviting the reader of the printed work "to witness the slave girl's mastery of the technology of writing," I argue that *The American in Algiers* does just the opposite by articulating the racialized dimensions of the different forms of address between the two cantos.[50] The Sable Bard, after all, does not have the last word; the printer does. Similarly, we saw at the opening of this chapter how Foss sought to invoke the image of furtively scribbling his narrative nightly in his Algerian jail cell to attest to the truth of the events as recorded, but how he also asserted his control of the text as it was edited, printed, and received by the public. The Sable Bard's pen draws attention to the fact that other (white) actors must translate the poet's plea from handwriting to print, thereby stabilizing and authorizing the text. At the same time, within the Patriot's narrative, the immediacy of his bleeding body exemplifies the privilege he retains even as a slave. He can embody print in a way that the Sable Bard cannot. What makes *The American in Algiers* so exceptional is its critical understanding of these distinctions as they shape accounts of slavery and their reception.

To bring my reading of this poem to a close, I want to point to the ways in which the construction of the Sable Bard speaks to the challenges faced by African American writers in the nineteenth century. In his 1825 account of his life in slavery, the first such narrative written by a fugitive slave in the United States, William Grimes directly references the scars on his back in connection to the country's founding documents: "If it were not for the stripes on my back which were made while I was a slave, I would in my will leave my skin as a legacy to the goverment, desiring that it might be taken off and made into parchment, and then bind the constitution of glorious, happy, and free America. Let the skin of an American slave bind the charter of American liberty!"[51] In her analysis of this passage, Susanna Ashton asserts how it, and the memoir overall, "rendered visible the contradictions of a national ideology that could marry freedom and slavery."[52] Unquestionably the dueling narratives of *The American in Algiers* anticipate this critique, yet while Grimes's publication of his account fundamentally "challeng[ed] the sacred status of print," this earlier poem preserves publication and print as processes that ultimately uphold racial difference. Through the poem, then, we can read the role of Barbary texts in articulating the limitations that early American abolitionists placed on the circulation of the speaking slave in the public sphere.

SUBSCRIBING TO HUMANITY

As I argued in the previous section, the trans-Atlantic movement that structures the two cantos of *The American in Algiers* offers a somewhat straightforward inversion of white slave and African master that facilitates the more complex relationship between the Patriot's body and the Sable Bard's pen. In this section, I want to compare those parallel slave narratives with the reimagining of the white slave's authorial and editorial power in the later novella *Humanity in Algiers; or, The Story of Azem* (1801). Published after Foss's popular narrative and shortly before the Tripolitan War, *Humanity in Algiers* offers another iteration of a fictionalized Black slave narrative nested within a larger framework of white liberation. The story takes the form of an eighteenth-century oriental tale, set in Algiers and related to the reader by a former American captive. It follows Azem, a West African slave who gains his freedom through his virtue and builds a fortune as a trader. As suggested by the title, the novella seeks to humanize its African protagonist; however, as my reading demonstrates, this humanization comes part and parcel with Azem's role in liberating the white author who makes possible the circulation of his narrative. We can see in this work, even more explicitly than in *The American in Algiers*, how white slavery served to legitimate and authorize the suffering of Africans by mediating the public's access to it through print.

The preface of *Humanity in Algiers* offers a critique of American hypocrisy that would have been quite familiar to readers of Barbary works by 1801. Closely recalling Carey's language from *A Short Account of Algiers*, the author writes, "With the same impropriety on our part do we reprobate the Algerines. 'A vile, piratical set of unprincipled robbers,' is the softest name we can give them; forgetful of our former depredations on the coasts of Africa, and the cruel manner in which we at present treat the offspring of those whom we brought thence. When the Algerines yoke our citizens to the plough, or compel them to labour at the oar, they only retaliate on us for similar barbarities."[53] In some ways the author's condemnation of American hypocrisy goes a step further than the dueling narratives of *The American in Algiers*—here they present white slavery and the loss of liberty as fully justified revenge for the American slave system. In this sense, Africa, north and west, punishes the public for its misdeeds. Yet, while the author's causal claim makes more explicit the connections between American and African forms of enslavement, the narrative of *Humanity in Algiers* contests the critique of the earlier poem's Sable Bard by more completely asserting white textual control over African voices. To begin with, the white narrator of the work has already regained his freedom. If the Patriot's bleeding in the earlier poem was meant to convey the immediacy of trans-Atlantic violence against bodies, the title page of *Humanity in Algiers*, which describes the novella as "By an American, Late a Slave in Algiers," frames the work as coming *after* slavery, an idea reinforced by the final lines of the preface: "If any excuse for want of elegance of style should be thought necessary, the long and tiresome servitude from which the Author is just relieved, must be his apology."[54] The work offers an overt abolitionist message, but as we shall see, rather than centering on an appeal for action against slavery, the narrative sublimates the trauma of white enslavement through the objectification of the novella's protagonist, Azem.

The narrator elaborates on his personal history in the work's introduction. He describes embarking with Captain James O'Brian (*sic*) in 1785 for the East Indies. During the voyage, the ship is captured by an Algerian corsair and the narrator is then sold to a "rich planter" at the market in Algiers. Oddly, the captive American finds comfort in the fact that slavery exists too in America:

> Finding Heaven had ordained my future life to be spent in slavery, I endeavoured to reconcile myself to my condition. I considered my state no worse, if so bad, as that of thousands in my own country. My father, I knew, had a man and woman slave; and I had often heard him say they were happier than he was: and he would always be angry if any person appeared but to think he held them unjustly in bondage. "Have I not paid my money for them? And consequently they are of right my own," says my father. This same kind of right, I knew, my Algerine master had to me. I was determined, therefore, to serve him with the utmost fidelity. By these means I gained his affection, and he often spoke in my praise to others.

Verging on a parody of the narratives of Foss and others, this comical moment offers an undoubtedly softer critique of American slavery, attacking not the barbarity of the institution but the assumption that only Africans are fit for enslavement. This much more moderate view contrasts sharply with the condemnation of American "barbarities" described in the preface. Interestingly, that earlier section is signed "The AUTHOR," while the writer of the introduction is identified as "AN AMERICAN," suggesting a split between the authorizing presence of print and the national identity of the suffering slave.[55] This split, whether imagined in the same figure or not, emphasizes the text, and specifically the story of Azem that makes up the narrative proper, as embedded within multiple authorizing discourses. Additionally, the detail that the writer of the introduction was captured on O'Brien's ship, the *Dauphin*, signals his participation in a real national crisis, even if this is an obvious fiction.[56] Like the Patriot of *The American in Algiers*, the narrator's authority rests on his direct experience of an American historical narrative.

Little scholarly work exists on this novella, but what we do know contextualizes its less urgent antislavery rhetoric. In their prefatory comments to the edition of *Humanity in Algiers* for *Common-Place*'s "Just Teach One" program, Duncan Faherty and Ed White identify the text as having circulated primarily among moderate abolitionist congregations in New York, Vermont, and western Massachusetts that tended to favor a gradualist approach to abolition, a viewpoint reflected in the novella.[57] The American's fidelity to his master, rather than his resistance to enslavement, ultimately leads to his liberation. After nine years of obedient servitude on a plantation outside the city, the narrator describes finding and caring for a Muslim traveler who had fallen from his horse. That traveler then offers to free the American, having the "disposal of a legacy, which, once in every year, was to purchase the freedom of some honest slave." The American is redeemed and brought to Algiers, where the dey signs a certificate that frees him. Newly liberated, the American becomes interested in his benefactor, the now deceased former-slave-turned-prosperous-merchant Azem, and sets to collecting the details of Azem's life from "persons of note" around Algiers.[58]

More conventional than *The American in Algiers*, the primary narrative of *Humanity in Algiers* conforms to the generic expectations of the oriental tale, with the narrator fulfilling the role of Orientalist scholar collecting and organizing the fragments of eastern narrative and gradually revealing the truth about his object of study. Azem enters the story as a child with mysterious origins. He is enslaved by an Algerian family after having been captured in battle, but nothing is known about his past until much later in the novella. He works faithfully for years until he earns his freedom. After his manumission, Azem becomes a trader in West Africa, where he discovers his long-lost mother and pursues a fellow slave he fell in love with during his servitude who turns out to be his sister. The story ranges between North and West Africa, with a brief sojourn in Arabia, yet the actual geography remains obscure. Despite the many firsthand accounts of Algiers available in the years before the publication of the novella, the North African place names cited in the story are fictional, beginning with the "plains of Natola" and "the beautiful river Tenun." The choice of Algiers as the setting for much of the work would seem almost entirely arbitrary except for its connection to the preface and to the captive member of Captain O'Brien's crew, which offers the reader a fixed position within national space-time in relation to the Algerine Crisis. In the final pages of the novella, Azem builds his fortune in Algiers, only to have his loved ones die in a plague. His final act is to request that a family friend named Arramel ensure that half his fortune go to freeing one "honest slave" each year. In the final paragraphs the narrator reemerges to comment that it was Arramel who had fallen from his horse in the frame story, and that "his name, with Azem's, has ever continued to dwell on my enraptured tongue and, while remembrance of my relief from past misfortunes continues, they shall never cease to be adored."[59]

As Ros Ballaster argues, the central features of the oriental tale genre involve a narrator "whose survival rests upon the continuing production of textual credit" as they engage in "acts of transmigratory identification, projecting [themself] into the place of the eastern interlocutor."[60] In *Humanity in Algiers*, that "transmigration" works as a kind of translation that operates between the frame story, which announces itself in the tradition of abolitionist slave narratives, and the tale of the narrative proper. The novella presents a kind of hybrid genre that superimposes an Orientalist power structure on the relationship of the enslaved white and Black bodies. In turn, we can see again the privileging of the authority of the editor in their mastery of the slave's story. As in the case of John Foss's relation of Scipio Jackson's death in the first section of this chapter, *Humanity in Algiers* showcases how the white narrative voice, embodying a distinctly American identity, processes the appeal of the enslaved for its white audience. In this case, the framing of Azem's story anticipates the circulation of American slave narratives in the nineteenth century "folded into white authored forms and framed by white-authored evidence and analysis."[61] Here, the fictional white slave functions akin to William Lloyd Garrison's introduction to the *Narrative of the Life of Frederick Douglass* (1845) and Lydia Maria Child's editing of Harriet Jacobs's *Incidents in the Life of a Slave Girl* (1861). Of course, what distinguishes *Humanity in Algiers* is that the Barbary context creates a situation of nested slave narratives that makes visible the instrumentality of Black bodies in articulating and securing white freedom within the wider Atlantic world. In other words, to the extent that the primary narrative seeks to prove the "humanity" of Azem in order to indirectly evoke sympathy for enslaved African Americans, that humanity is contingent on the frame story of white liberation and narrative mastery.

THE PERILS OF TRANSLATION

My readings of *The American in Algiers* and *Humanity in Algiers* demonstrate how the lens of the Barbary was used to imagine and interpret the voices of the enslaved in the United States during and after the Algerine Crisis. In chapter 5 I explore at length the continued circulation of Barbary texts within discussions of slavery into the mid-nineteenth century, but to bring this chapter to a close I want to briefly consider here one such later narrative that takes up the tropes of writing, translation, and publication I have discussed above. The article in question is a short piece that appeared in the *Christian Advocate* in 1825 describing the discovery on a North Carolina plantation of an enslaved man, identified as Prince Moro, able to write in Arabic script. Moro's name, the Spanish translation of the word "Moor," seems to associate him with Morocco and the Barbary, yet in reality Prince Moro was Omar ibn Said, who had lived in Futa Tooro in present-day Senegal until his capture and enslavement in 1807 at age thirty-seven. Six years after this first account of Prince Moro circulated, Ibn Said wrote an autobiography in Arabic that was later forwarded to and translated by members of the American Ethnographic Society but not published until almost a century later in 1925. Given this complicated history of circulation and translation, I argue that we might compare the Prince Moro of 1825 who exists only in others' translation to the Ibn Said who is able to exercise his own voice in Arabic. The former, I would suggest, is a "Barbarized" version that reflects, however faintly, the tropes of the Barbary archive I have discussed above and their enduring connection to emergent varieties of American fictionality.

54 **CHAPTER ONE**

In the 1825 article the writer speculates that Prince Moro must have been from "far in the interior of Africa—perhaps Tombuctoo or its neighborhood," placing his origins somewhere near the border between North and sub-Saharan Africa.[62] In this period Timbuktu retained a semi-mythical status; a decade earlier the publication of *The Narrative of Robert Adams* (1816), a Barbary captivity narrative related by an African American sailor, caused a sensation in Europe as Adams claimed to have been carried to Timbuktu, making him the first westerner to visit the city. Following its publication, however, the narrative was often dismissed as a fabrication, particularly in the United States, where the *North American Review* in 1817 remarked that the falsity of the account "to us . . . has appeared so obvious, that we should not think it worthy of an serious examination, had it not excited so much interest, and gained universal belief in England."[63] While the narrative may perhaps have been a fraud, its dismissal was certainly motivated in part by Adams's race. In the case of Prince Moro, it is unclear why the writer speculates about Timbuktu, although this claim seems to garner more credit than afforded to Adams precisely because Prince Moro is enslaved and unable to speak (or publish) for himself. Just as importantly, we might speculate that the impulse of the writer to misidentify Moro's origins suggests an enduring association of Islam and even literacy itself with North rather than West Africa. The account of Prince Moro's "discovery," quoted from another publication, begins, "'The following paper,' says the Christian Advocate, 'was put into our hands by a friend, who received it from a friend in Fayetteville in North Carolina, by whom it was drawn up. Such cases we believe are not uncommon. We have heard of several instances of learned Mahomedans among the slaves in the Southern States, who were princes or priests in their native country.'" The piece proceeds to describe Moro as a "man of slender frame and delicate constitution" who wandered off of his plantation and was later jailed in Fayetteville. No master claimed him from the jail because "he appeared of no value," but that assessment changed when Moro revealed himself to be literate: "The boys . . . [fit] up a temporary desk of a flour barrel, on which he wrote in a masterly hand writing, from right to left, in what was to them an unknown language."[64] Despite the fact that the education of enslaved people had been prohibited in North Carolina for several years, Moro's literacy is not seen as threatening because it is in an indecipherable Arabic. He can write, but not in a way that is readily translated by his white masters, and therefore not in a way that can contest their narrative.

Later in the piece, Moro's "masterly" command of Arabic contrasts with his meek and playful demeanor: "His dignified deportment showed him of a superior cast—his humility, that of a peaceful subject, not a despot." Ironically, they assume Moro to be royalty because he seems to be the ideal servant, and his education justifies his acceptance of his enslavement. The article ends with Prince Moro's affirmation of a number of common pro-slavery arguments:

> His good master has offered to send him to his native land, his home and his friends; but he says "No,—this is my home, here are my friends, and here is my Bible; I enjoy all that I want in this world. If I should return to my native land, the fortune of war might transport me to a country where I should be deprived of the greatest of all blessings, that of worshipping the true and living God, and his son Jesus Christ, whom to worship and serve is eternal life."

The article itself perhaps inadvertently hints that this monologue must be viewed skeptically, as a footnote from the *Philadelphia Recorder* attached to the title mentions, "He speaks English more imperfectly than any African we have ever seen."[65] Nevertheless, the prince channels a newfound eloquence when rejecting offers of freedom and a return to Africa. In the hands of white editors and translators, Moro becomes grateful for his enslavement. However, Ibn Said tells a very different story in his own words. In the Arabic manuscript of *The Life of Omar ibn Said*, recently retranslated by Ala Alryyes, the writer reveals a very different understanding of his trans-Atlantic journey. In the final paragraph of the narrative, he writes,

> I reside in our country here because of the great harm. The Infidels took me unjustly and sold me into the hands of the Christian man (*Nasrani*) who bought me. We sailed on the big sea for a month and a half to a place called Charleston in the Christian language. I fell into the hands of a small, weak, and wicked man who did not fear Allah at all, nor did he read nor pray. I was afraid to stay with such a wicked man who committed many evil deeds so I escaped.[66]

Although Ibn Said notes that he is now in the hands of a "righteous" master who does not beat him, the closing paragraph makes clear the original injustice of capture, enslavement, and the middle passage. In contrast, the "Prince Moro" version translates slavery in America into freedom from the dangers and insecurities of Africa, where Moro could only be a victim of one or another inevitable form of re-enslavement.

So what do we make of the Barbary Prince Moro presented in this article, distinct from the historical figure who would write his own narrative? Circulated in religious periodicals such as the *Christian Advocate*, the *Christian Register*, and the *Christian Watchman*, the piece consciously obscures the continued enslavement of Moro by superimposing on it a narrative of the teleological progression from African Muslim Otherness to American Christian "liberation," facilitated by the discovery of Moro's handwriting as evidence of his capacity to be saved. Prince Moro's translation comes simultaneously within linguistic (Arabic to English), religious (Muslim to Christian), and territorial (Africa to America) registers, reaffirming the congruence of these modes of identity-making. However, this assimilation does not guarantee Prince Moro's access to a direct public voice; he is, instead, made a mouthpiece for the American slave system. Furthermore, the periodicals themselves as they circulate the story preface the work as passing from "friend" to "friend" and magazine to magazine. Moro's desire to stay among "friends" is also a desire to stay within a system of circulation that represents his body as that of the perfect enslaved subject.

To tie the strings of this chapter together, I want to suggest that the article on Prince Moro shares certain similarities to Foss's *Journal* as well as to *The American in Algiers* and *Humanity in Algiers*. These texts demonstrate the ways in which white authors sought to recognize, translate, and ultimate subsume Black suffering and Black expression within the dominant power structure, and in some cases to utilize the radical potential of Black literacy to reinforce the ideological structures of white liberty. Many readings of the Barbary archive focus on the trope of reversal—the African slave master and the white slave, as in the mock slave advertisement discussed above—yet the works themselves often play out the containment of this inversion through the authorial and editorial power of the white captive. In these texts, narrators use the Barbary framework to prioritize white suffering and to encode both the sympathy for and the instrumentality of Black bodies within abolitionist discourse. In the next chapter, Barbary figures in print take on a more active role in interrogating the efficacy and weaknesses of early American liberty and nationhood.

CHAPTER TWO

BARBARY(AN) INVASIONS

Americans, beware! Let nothing tempt you to come in the way of these people, for they are worse than you can imagine.

—"Public Letter from Three Captive American Captains in Algiers" (1785)

Glorious News!!" announces an issue of the *Impartial Herald* of Newburyport, Massachusetts, on August 30, 1794.[1] Citing European papers just arrived from Rotterdam on the ship *Mary*, the *Herald* reports on French advances in Belgium, detailing months-old battles across northern Europe. Yet, the *Mary* brought more to Newburyport than just belated news from a war on the far side of the Atlantic; near the bottom of this tightly packed column of newsprint appears a brief mention of two conspicuous visitors:

> Two Algerine gentlemen came passengers in the Mary: As various reports are in circulation respecting their visiting this country, for the satisfaction of our readers, we have obtained the following accounts from a gentleman who has conversed with them. Eight years since one of them commanded a frigate in the service of the Dey and being taken by three Neapolitan frigates, it was dangerous for them to return to Algiers; they have since been traveling in different parts of Europe, and have recommendations from very respectable characters there. They will in a few days proceed on to Philadelphia.[2]

The arrival of these two Algerian tourists at Newburyport had apparently caused quite a stir—an event that, in contrast to the wars raging in Europe, had both a geographic and temporal immediacy for readers of the *Herald*. The newspaper's report of the two gentlemen circulated as a timely and authoritative intervention into the public conversation. Although the piece does not elaborate on the content of the "various reports," they came at the height of the Algerine Crisis in the months following the rapid capture of eleven American ships and more than a hundred American sailors, including Newburyport native John Foss. Years later, in his account of his captivity, Foss would strongly condemn not only the Algerians but more broadly the "extreme cruelties . . . taught by the Religion of Mahomet . . . to persecute all its opposers."[3] However, at a time when Foss was still toiling in Algiers, the *Herald* offers a notably evenhanded account of the Algerian gentlemen in its own backyard. The gentlemen were, after all, recommended by many respectable people in Europe.

It is unclear whether these two Algerian visitors ever arrived in Philadelphia, but reports of them certainly did. On August 30, the *Gazette of the United States* in Philadelphia reprinted the *Impartial Herald*'s report. On September 22, it announced that the Algerian gentlemen had reached Boston and met with Governor Samuel Adams. The report describes them simply as "men of great size and dressed in Turkish habiliments."[4] Over a month later, the *Gazette* carried a report from Providence that names the two travelers: Sieur Ibrahim and Mahomed Ben Ali. It announces, "They are at present soliciting permission of the Dey to return home; it being dangerous for them to return after having been taken, although by a superior force." The article goes on to describe them as "gentlemen of respectable families," and that, should they return home, "they will be of service to our unfortunate countrymen now prisoners in Algiers."[5] Ibrahim and Ben Ali are described in various reports as being "Algerines," "Turks," and, in at least one instance, "Moors." These classifications were not arbitrary nor were they necessarily interchangeable, as Americans were frequently fascinated by the cultural diversity of North Africa. In his recent study of Barbary captivity narratives, Jacob Rama Berman argues that within American orientalism, comparisons of "Barbary types"—Arabs, Moors, Bedouins, Turks, and others—"allowed Federal-era readers to negotiate American racial classifications, the limits of American democratic inclusion, and ultimately the fantasy of America's exceptional difference through exotic proxies."[6] In this case, the actual presence of these Algerians on American soil tested the ability of these newspapers to define these figures and thus to define the borders of their reading publics. After Providence, Ibrahim and Ben Ali seemed to disappear, as no local Philadelphia paper apparently reported on their arrival in that city, despite how closely their earlier progress was tracked.[7] If they did complete their journey, they would have arrived in a city reeling from the recent spike in Barbary piracy. While readers of the *Gazette* in Philadelphia were anticipating Ibrahim's and Ben Ali's arrival, Susanna Rowson's play *Slaves in*

Algiers; or, A Struggle for Freedom opened at the Chestnut Street Theater and printer Mathew Carey published *A Short Account of Algiers*, both works seeking to contextualize the intensifying national crisis for an anxious public. We can only speculate as to how Philadelphians would have reacted to the appearance of two former corsairs on their doorstep.

In the previous chapter I focused on how Barbary slavery was used to highlight the suffering of the (white) slave body in ways that would frame and make legible for white audiences accounts of enslaved Africans. In this chapter I shift focus from the bodies of the enslaved to the disruptive bodies of the Algerines and Tripolitans themselves. Specifically, I examine instances in which American writers used North African Muslim figures in print to intervene in public debates and situate local issues within the punctuated temporality of crises both internal, in the form of political unrest, and trans-Atlantic, in the case of the conflicts with Barbary pirates. Many of these texts reference, directly or indirectly, American captives in North Africa, and some deliberately play on widespread fears that Muslim pirates would cross the Atlantic to raid American shores. Below I examine three satirical works across three different genres. The first is Benjamin Franklin's 1790 "On the Slave Trade," an article attacking pro-slavery arguments in Congress. The second, Peter Markoe's 1787 epistolary novel *The Algerine Spy in Pennsylvania*, concerns a spy named Mehemet sent by the dey of Algiers to observe the American government in Philadelphia during the Constitutional Convention. The third text is the Mustapha letters from *Salmagundi* (1807–1808), a series of letters allegedly written by a Tripolitan prisoner of war in New York City. These works offer three distinct examples of how Barbary figures in print circulated within ongoing debates over pressing issues such as slavery, state power, popular representation, and national security, critiquing the ideological assumptions of the republican public sphere and playing on anxieties concerning the weakness of a republic built on print within a wider Atlantic network of texts and bodies.

Barbary figures in these works—as pirates, slave-drivers, spies, or prisoners—challenged the elite fantasy of a disembodied republican public sphere, a concept exemplified in the period by the widespread use of pseudonyms, often classical, like Cato, Civis, and most famously Publius of *The Federalist Papers*. According to Michael Warner, pseudonymous authorship enabled "the virtue of the citizen by the very fact that writing is not regarded as a form of personal preference."[8] In other words, pseudonymous authorship allowed political elites to claim to speak for the anonymous masses and for the nation itself, rather than just for their own interests. As Eran Shalev observes, the popularity of classical pseudonyms worked to contextualize and stabilize political discourse in times of crisis by invoking the model of Rome as a precedent for the American republican experiment.[9] In the following, I demonstrate how Barbary figures were frequently deployed as a direct counter to this elite narrative and to figures like Publius, interrogating ideas of abstraction and embodiment by repeatedly recentering public debates on the (raced) body as a threat to the rhetorical integrity of the republic. Specifically, these texts registered an anxiety about the ability of print and language itself to serve as a coherent foundation for American nation-building. North Africa's place in antiquity made it, for classically minded republicans, a fitting site on which to project anxieties about political representation and language. As Paul Baepler notes, the scholarly consensus locates the derivation of the term "Barbary" from the same Greek and Latin root as "barbarian." In the classical era, "Africans were called 'barbarians' because they refused to communicate and were reluctant to cooperate."[10] As we will see, Barbary figures threatened not just national security but also the conventions of print and speech on which the republic rested.

To the extent that the Barbary invaders in the texts I explore in this chapter functioned as embodied figures who disrupted genteel public debate, they entered the public sphere through fictions of pseudo-translation.[11] All three works include the "discovery" of an Arabic source text translated for the reading public.[12] My readings demonstrate that this recurring trope serves two vital ideological functions. First, it marks the outer boundary of a text's capacity for public-making by distinguishing the American self from the barbarian Other. Second, much like the "found manuscript" trope that Lindsay DiCuirci explores in a variety of early American works, the "translated manuscript" trope signals both the text's fictionality and its alien origins.[13] Emily Apter points to pseudo-translation as "the premier illustration of a deconstructed ontology, insofar as it reveals the extent to which all translations are unreliable transmitters of the original."[14] The repeated trope of the Arabic original points to the inaccessible "foreignness" at the root of the national project, of origins rendered indecipherable and therefore subject to endless manipulation by those who control the discourse and define the boundaries of the American (re)public.[15]

Ultimately, I highlight these devices of fictionality—pseudonyms and pseudo-translations—to suggest that Barbary texts offered American writers an opportunity to play on their awareness that their notions of national solidarity were, as Trish Loughran argues, unsupported by the local material conditions of life in the early republic.[16] Such fantasies, however, were not without necessity in an era in which the country faced what it saw as a major threat from Algiers, Tripoli, and Tunis. Even as these Barbary figures challenged the foundations of deliberative democracy, they served as convenient antagonists against whom a sense of national belonging could take shape. To the extent that, as Warner argues, an early American national public was "constructed on the basis of its metonymic embodiment in print artifacts," figures in print like the Algerian gentlemen discussed above became metonyms by which communities could imagine their participation in larger national and transnational conflicts.[17] These circulating Barbary figures worked to both mediate and complicate the relationship between the competing claims of the *local* and the *national* within the early republic by way of the *trans-Atlantic*.

BENJAMIN FRANKLIN'S BODY

Taking my texts just a little out of chronological order, I want to start with Benjamin Franklin's "On the Slave Trade," mainly because of how important that author is to notions of early American publicity. "On the Slave Trade" is one of the best-known Barbary texts outside of the genre of the captivity narrative, and convenient to my overarching argument, Franklin himself is often cited as the exemplar of print ideology in the period. In Warner's study of the epitaph Franklin wrote for himself in 1728 at the age of twenty-two, he remarks on how the printer compares his body to "the Cover of an old Book" whose content will be "Corrected and amended / by the Author."[18] Warner locates the source of Franklin's cultural authority in his willingness to live entirely in print, "[repudiating] *personal* authority in favor of a general authority based in a negative relation to one's own person."[19] Yet, I argue that Franklin's "On the Slave Trade," the last work he published in his lifetime, can be seen as a very different kind of epitaph that offers an alternative understanding of how bodies and textual identities operated in the late eighteenth-century public sphere. "On the Slave Trade" appeared as an open letter in the *Federal Gazette* commenting on an ongoing debate in Congress over whether the United States should support efforts in Britain to ban the slave trade. Franklin, writing as Historicus, notes that a recent pro-slavery speech by Georgian congressman James Jackson resembles a historical speech given a century ago in Algiers by a member of the Divan named Sidi Mehemet Ibrahim and translated in "*Martin's* account of his consulship, anno 1687."[20] Despite his claim of recovering a century-old text, Franklin's choice of Algiers clearly references the American captives then held there; in 1790, Algiers still held surviving crew members from the two merchant ships captured in 1785. As I discuss in my introduction, Franklin himself had been rumored to have been captured by pirates and enslaved in Algiers just four years earlier.

While adopting a classical pseudonym for himself, Franklin casts his opponent as the threatening Muslim figure. In his speech, Sidi Mehemet Ibrahim runs through several pro-slavery arguments common in eighteenth- and nineteenth-century debates. Ibrahim argues that Algiers must continue to enslave Christians, or else there would be no one to do the "common labours of our city." There would be no reason to give in to the demands of the *Erika* (that is, Algerian abolitionists) because slaves in Algiers are well treated and ultimately better off than they were in their home countries. Christians cannot survive on their own in Africa, and it would only be a matter of time before they are re-enslaved by "Wild Arabs," so the Divan of Algiers has no reasonable course but to continue the current slave system.[21]

Of this pro-slavery speech, Historicus notes, "Mr. Jackson does not quote it; perhaps he has not seen it.—if therefore some of its reasonings are to be found in his eloquent speech, it may only show that men's interests and intellects operate and are operated on with surprising similarity in all countries and climates."[22] In effect, what Historicus emphasizes are the bodies at work—the embodied form of Jackson's oratory, the translated body of Sidi Mehemet Ibrahim, and most of all the white American bodies enslaved in North Africa and the Africans enslaved in America. As Malini Johar Schueller argues, "The North African Orient at this stage in USAmerican history . . . signified despotism and slavery, which, in turn, both validated imperial definitions of nation and marked the nation as a free body."[23] Yet, Franklin's satire does nothing to confront the actual logic or content of either Ibrahim's or Jackson's pro-slavery arguments; the piece seems to take an entirely cynical view of the role of rational deliberation to persuade.[24] Rather, the satirical thrust comes in the translation of an invisible white American body into that of an exotic and threatening North African. Franklin suggests that, for members of Congress, their pretension to disembodied abstract reason leads them to ignore the immediacy of the humanitarian disaster facing millions of African bodies crossing the Atlantic in slave ships. His solution to the problem of immediacy then involves re-embodying the debate by reversing at the level of discourse the trans-Atlantic exchange he argues against.

In short, contrary to the ideological narrative of self-negation, bodies proliferate, intervene in, and disrupt the rhetorical constructions of Jackson/Ibrahim within Franklin's article. Not the least of these bodies is Franklin's own, so close to death. In 1790, Franklin's authorship of "On the Slave Trade" was a poorly kept secret; in fact, several newspapers that reproduced this article added the heading "by B. Franklin," including fellow Philadelphian Mathew Carey, who reprinted the article several months later in his magazine the *American Museum*. This reprinted version became the basis for the article's inclusion in the 1806 *Complete Works* of Franklin. In fact, nineteenth-century abolitionists were quite eager to remind Americans that publication of this article was one of Franklin's very last public acts. In his famous 1853 speech on white slavery in North Africa, abolitionist Charles Sumner emphasized the work as the author's swan song: on the issue of the slave trade, "the last and almost dying energies of Franklin were excited." Sumner's summary of the article ends in similarly dramatic fashion: "With the protest against a great wrong, Franklin died."[25] For Sumner looking back, it is the martyrdom of Franklin's dying body that authorizes the text.

While his pseudonym is not particularly effective in hiding his identity, by writing as Historicus, Franklin plays on a common convention of public representation through which this disembodied voice lends him the authority to make claims on the bodies of Jackson and Ibrahim; however, the article raises inevitable questions about Historicus's reliability. Despite the pretense of his name, the history that Historicus offers and authorizes for the reader is an obvious fiction. Franklin completely invents *Martin's Account of His Consulship*, the alleged source of the original translation. While critics have traditionally located the satirical focus of the article in the character of Sidi Mehemet Ibrahim, they have often overlooked the ways that Franklin's fraudulent historian represents a critique of elite commentators who claim to speak for the people and in this instance for history itself. When one can hide behind a name like Publius or Cato and claim to speak for others, Franklin seems to suggest, one can make almost anything sound authoritative. The article ultimately places Historicus and Ibrahim in the same category, in effect demonstrating the unreliability of abstract debate divorced from the material conditions of the bodies of both citizen and enslaved.

"On the Slave Trade" demonstrates how references to North Africans and Barbary slavery in print were used to disrupt and expose the conventions of public debate. The rhetorical distance between Historicus and Ibrahim as identities in print is highly charged—filled with a complex choreography of speaking, moving, and laboring bodies that complicate the division between embodied presence and textual abstraction. Franklin's last work also typifies the ways in which abolitionists utilized this challenge throughout the period to expose how rhetorical distance obscures the actual violence perpetrated against bodies in the Atlantic world. In other words, against the notion of a disembodied print sphere, Barbary texts were deployed strategically to close the conceptual gap between the circulation of print and the circulation of bodies.

SPYING ON THE CONSTITUTION

While Franklin's "On the Slave Trade" located the threatening body of Ibrahim long ago and far away, other Barbary-era works played explicitly on public fears that the Muslim threat would actually cross the Atlantic. As my opening example of the two Algerian visitors demonstrates, the presence of North African Muslims on American shores, real or otherwise, was a pressing topic for public discussion. For example, in the May 3, 1785, edition of the *Pennsylvania Packet*, immediately following the Ship News, is an item with the simple heading "To the Printer." The item includes a short preface, signed by "Y.Z.," that announces, "The general concern of the following intelligence, which is just arrived by packet, induces me to request you will publish it without loss of time." What follows is allegedly an intercepted letter "By Al Koraschi Ebnallad, Sovereign and Supreme Dey of Algiers, Lord of the Algerine Territories and the Atlantic Ocean." This fictional dey writes that "North-America, having withdrawn themselves from a subjection to their masters, nearly as mild as that we inflict on our slaves, [has] not yet submitted to our prerogative or acknowledged our clemency, wherefore we have proposed to let loose our corsairs upon them." The dey's letter notes the vulnerabilities of postwar Philadelphia and outlines a plot to hold the city hostage and to demand, among other goods, "one fair and unblemished virgin" from each Christian sect found in the city. The letter closes, "And for the sake of [the Americans'] future happiness and tranquility, we shall communicate to them our decision, in order, that laying aside all controversies and disputes, which are fit for women only, they may live peaceable and serene as our own slaves."[26] The translator of the letter argues, as Thomas Jefferson at the same time was arguing from Paris, that a strong coastal defense, and even an attack against Algiers and the Barbary states themselves, would be the only way to secure American shores. The dey's letter was reprinted by a number of newspapers up and down the coast in the summer of 1785. Although the letter itself is an obvious farce, the idea of North African pirates abducting Americans was one that circulated widely in American periodicals throughout the late eighteenth century, spurred on by similar stories of Europeans plucked off the continent by Muslim corsairs. Paranoia over a possible Muslim invasion in 1785 even led Governor Patrick Henry of Virginia to arrest four Algerian visitors on suspicion of spying, an episode I explore at greater length in the next chapter.[27]

What is perhaps most interesting about these reports of a potential coastal invasion, credible or not, is how they anticipated similar national anxieties around the destabilizing potential of the Haitian Revolution. In one example of national paranoia, newspapers in major cities circulated rumors in 1802 that French frigates full of West Indian revolutionaries were traveling up and down the coast. Such dangerous cargo could escape at any moment to raid coastal communities and potentially radicalize the enslaved. As Duncan Faherty argues, the circulating reports of this common threat served to unite, at least temporarily, the disparate coastal cities of the North and South; from these rumors "emerged a temporally disjointed community united by paranoia, suggesting a sense of national cohesion imagined out of negation, disavowal, and a cathecting of racialized fear."[28] For early republicans, Algerines served much the same role as these Black revolutionaries: unassimilable racial Others threatening to dismember the national body by exploiting the fundamental weaknesses and contradictions of the country's foundational rhetoric of liberty and unity.

Into this period of national crisis came *The Algerine Spy in Pennsylvania*, written by antifederalist Peter Markoe in Philadelphia during the Constitutional Convention in 1787. In this novel, Mehemet, the titular spy, observes and critiques American society over the course of twenty-four letters addressed to various characters back in Algiers, ending not with the spy's return to North Africa but with his assimilation into the American public. Markoe reproduces many of the generic features of earlier European eastern spy/observer narratives, most notably Giovanni Paolo Marana's late seventeenth-century novel *Letters Writ by a Turkish Spy* (1682–1684) about a spy named Mahmut residing in Paris, while bringing them into the American present and the context of the Algerine Crisis.[29] The full title of the work announces the letters as written *From the Close of the Year 1783 to the Meeting of the Convention*, locating the text as circulating contemporaneously with the new Constitution itself and with commentaries by figures like Publius in New York and Centinel in Philadelphia. It is from these widespread debates over not just governing structures but also over the authority of print itself that the text draws its larger significance. As Sandra M. Gustafson has argued, the current perception of the Constitution as an "immutable, if ever-elusive, source of national meaning" is the result of a gradual process during which print was "in competition with other modes of national embodiment," including the "power of the voice."[30] *The Algerine Spy* offers an exploration of these forms of embodiment through the threat represented by the body of the spy and his circulation within republican Philadelphia.

The inspiration for Mehemet may have in part come from the author's own experiences as a recent immigrant to the United States. Published anonymously, *The Algerine Spy* was not consistently connected to Peter Markoe until well after the author's death.[31] We know little about Markoe himself; although he held the reputation as the "city poet" of Philadelphia, largely for his satirical poem "The Times" (also printed in 1787), he published only three works and a collection of poems before he died in 1792.[32] Unlike many other Barbary texts, *The Algerine Spy* has no clear abolitionist agenda, possibly because the Markoe family was deeply involved in the triangle trade, shipping sugar and rum to Philadelphia from the Caribbean. In fact, at the time the novel was published, Markoe had only lived a few years in the United States, having moved to Philadelphia from his family's plantation in St. Croix in 1785. Nevertheless, *The Algerine Spy* concerns itself with the very same issues of rhetoric and the body that drive the satire of Franklin's Historicus and with the linguistic construction of American identity. While one must always be careful about making biographical arguments on such thin evidence, I would suggest that Markoe possibly found inspiration for his spy's infiltration of America and eventual assimilation in his own insider/outsider position as a recent immigrant in Philadelphia trying to navigate the complexities of a new identity that might or might not quite fit.

Perhaps the most interesting feature of *The Algerine Spy* is its prefaces, which show how Markoe adapted his source material to the concerns of republican-era Americans. The novel's seventeenth-century precursor, *The Turkish Spy*, is notable for its complex history of "delirious transmission and circulation." That novel, which originally appeared in French and Italian, purported to be translated from letters written in Arabic that were found in an abandoned Paris apartment. Later English editions of the work add a further layer of translation to the process of transmission, resulting in "a destabilizing web of found manuscripts, translation, and secret information from various elsewheres."[33] *The Algerine Spy* retains much of this fictive framework, somewhat simplified, but with additional emphasis on the process of publication. The work includes two prefaces, with one focused on the translation of Mehemet's letters and signed only "S.T.P."[34] In this preface, not addressed to the public but to the printer "Mr. William Pritchard," the translator explains, "The letters, written in different languages, but chiefly in Arabic, were delivered into my hands, with a note, which contained a request that I should translate and publish them for the good of the United States." The translator remarks that the letters "were all without dates, which omission will be excused, when it is considered that they are but copies; but the principal facts mentioned in them are so notorious and recent, that dates seem unnecessary."[35] The omitted dates emphasize the presence of the letters within a timely archive of national lived experience, what I describe in the introduction as the early American iteration of the novel-news matrix. Thus, the current events contained within already offer a fantasy of national identity that self-consciously overcomes its own foreign origins.

Noteworthy in this preface is the text's insistence on its mediation. If the spy wrote the anonymous note, then he would seem perfectly able to translate the letters himself, yet that process becomes more visible as the letters pass from hand to hand. The second preface, addressed "To the Public," supposedly comes from the printer himself and further emphasizes the translatedness of the text. Pritchard describes finding the letters on his doorstep and recalls, "In the course of that day and the next I occasionally dipped into the papers; but as to sell books, not the criticize them, is my business, all I shall say is, that the style, if we consider that the work is but a translation, is tolerably smooth and easy; and the sentiments (due allowance being made for the disposition and education of an Algerine) are not unworthy of the public attention." While distancing himself from any role in interpreting texts, Pritchard nevertheless judges the work's "sentiments" to be of public interest. Despite his disavowals, Pritchard's preface establishes the roles of both translator and publisher in mediating the foreign text's relationship with the public. Pritchard adds to this picture the role of the critic, as he goes on to assert that "these states abound in critics equal to any in the world," and he invites these critics to send their remarks to him so that they may be appended onto the "third or fourth impression" in order to increase the value of work "by rendering it at once more bulky and amusing." The preface thus includes both a concession to and a deflection of future criticism, while depicting a text potentially weighed down by commentaries accrued through circulation. Immediately contradicting this image of the corpulent text, the printer reasserts the work as valuable precisely for its portability and mobility:

> I confess that, although a bookseller, I am not fond of large volumes. A huge folio has an imposing air of dignity, which is very apt to deter people from having anything to say to it, as my shelves can testify; but a snug little pocket volume, neatly bound and lettered, is like an easy good natured friend, who is ready to sit down with us near a good fire, or to take a walk on the commons. If we happen to be otherwise engaged, we part from the one, or pocket the other, without trouble or ceremony.[36]

Pritchard's characterization of the work suggests that the book itself takes on the character of a spy able to circulate in both public and private spheres. His image depicts not a body becoming a book but a book becoming a body. The book becomes readable—or, as Pritchard suggests, you can "say" something to it—through its ability to mimic corporeality. Taken together, *The Algerine Spy*'s dual prefaces create a thoroughly messy picture of a text authored, found, translated, found again, evaluated, printed, and finally critiqued. This unruly history of multiple mediations implicitly challenges the ideological assumptions of stability in print beyond the contingencies of social circulation.

The two prefaces of *The Algerine Spy* establish a narrative by which we can see the translation and publication of Mehemet's letters as inextricably linked with the disappearance of his body. The recirculation of the fictional

Arabic original in the form of an English epistolary novel comes hand in hand with the assimilation of the spy's otherness into the American public. To the extent that the prefaces establish a framework for the novel, Mehemet's letters explore and at times celebrate the ideological processes of translation and publication as central to the constitution of American nationhood; however, Markoe's use of the Algerian spy as his protagonist suggests that these processes are vulnerable to deception and transgression. Much in the same way that Franklin's satire draws attention to how the multiple bodies that inhabit the public sphere challenge the validity of abstract political rhetoric, the spy threatens the borders of that public and thus its coherence as a salient social and political formation.

The novel itself begins with Mehemet's description of his journey from Algiers to America, including a sojourn with the Jews of Gibraltar and Lisbon, with whom the spy stays as he awaits passage to Philadelphia.[37] During his travels, Mehemet disguises himself "in the character of a native of the south of France," remarking, "My knowledge of the French language, the predilection of the citizens of the new states for their allies, and the swarthiness of my complexion, induced me to follow this advice."[38] This single reference to Mehemet's appearance and the ruse that would allow him to circulate in European-American society announces the work as a kind of "passing" novel, evoking modes of difference that look back to earlier epistemologies—religious, cultural, climatological—rather than forward to the nineteenth century's ascendance of phenotypical racial categories. Most importantly, Mehemet's mastery of language, his knowledge of both French and English, gives him free access to the republic.

Even before infiltrating the United States, Mehemet offers several pointed critiques of the ideological assumptions of American republicanism. In one notable passage, he indulges in counterfactual history to critique America's "Roman" pretensions and figures like Publius. He writes that while "our imagination is highly delighted, when we read the histories of ancient Greece and Rome, . . . it might be entertaining, and perhaps useful, to trace the probable progress of Carthaginian power, if, in the last Punic war, she had subdued [Rome]." Mehemet goes on to speculate that Carthage would have set about expanding its commercial power, while conquest would be a "secondary object." Carthaginian navigators would explore the globe, establishing factories that would, "by happy contagion," spread their commercial empire. In contrast to Carthage, Mehemet writes that the Romans are the "barbarians"; Italy is the true Barbary Coast.[39] Notably, Markoe's spy's vision of a benign world conquest through what we call today "soft power" is quite similar to the millennial vision that ends Joel Barlow's *Visions of Columbus*, published the same year. Barlow describes how America will lead the world into perpetual peace when "For commerce arm'd the different Powers combine, / An heaven approving aids the blest design."[40] However, as pleasant as this vision is, the implicit comparison of the United States and Carthage in Markoe's text sets a historical precedent of invasion and destruction that again plays on fears of the vulnerability of American shores.

Importantly, Mehemet's invocation of Carthage not only refers to North Africa's distant past but the more recent history of the revolutionary era. As Shalev notes, Bostonians during the period of the Coercive Acts began to depict themselves as Carthaginians being ravaged by Roman Britain. After independence, antifederalists like Markoe frequently expressed opposition to the Roman model and an affinity for Carthage to express their fear of a strong executive power.[41] Carthage therefore became an icon of anti-imperial resistance and, by extension, a symbol for radical post-coloniality that diverged from and challenged European historiography. Mehemet offers (or perhaps threatens) to turn the world of classical republicanism on its head. Going beyond the standard opposition between republican freedom and oriental despotism that Timothy Marr identifies as the *raison d'être* of so many early American Islamicist works, Markoe's Mehemet constructs an alternate fantastical genealogy of African modernity in place of European imperialism.[42] This narrative too emphasizes Mehemet himself as a destabilizing, counter-historical presence, as an African traveling west not as a slave but as a menacing presence and, perhaps, as a conqueror.

Mehemet's Carthaginian speculations point to yet another precedent for his eventual infiltration of America. His eleventh letter opens with his arrival in Philadelphia: "I am arrived. I tread on the western continent. A native of Algiers is lodging under the roof of a Pennsylvanian. Yet the genius of the state seems unconscious of danger, and the unsuspecting crowd are as busily employed in their affairs or pleasures, as if I was at home extended on my sopha." Mehemet's arrival apparently goes unobserved by a Philadelphia society occupied with "the pursuit of wealth and pleasure."[43] Casting himself now as the European-Roman invader arriving in North Africa, Mehemet comments that "the cloud, which prevented the Carthaginians from perceiving Aeneas and Achates, those illustrious spies, was undoubtedly the hurry of business."[44] Unlike his previous invocation of Carthage, this references is undoubtedly ominous, making more explicit the connection between the United States and that doomed North African civilization. But more significant from a postcolonial perspective is how the vacillating identities of the United States and Algiers between Carthage and Rome reconfigure center-periphery relationality, imagining an antiquity that largely ignores Europe in favor of a new *circum*-Atlantic rather than a narrow trans-Atlantic orientation.

Alongside these broad critiques of American hubris, Markoe's Mehemet satirizes more mundane aspects of American and specifically Philadelphian society, often drawing on orientalist tropes to play the role of scandalized easterner. Typical of the oriental spy genre, one of Mehemet's chief targets of criticism are the women of America, whom he depicts as immodest and much too bold: "What shall I tell thee of a city, where women appear barefaced in the streets, and, what is still more extraordinary, the men behold them with insensibility. . . . Even in the churches they gaze on the men with undaunted eyes, nor have I, since my arrival, seen a blush on a female cheek. . . . Yet are they lovely in the extreme. Nature has profusely adorned them with charms, but a bad education diminishes the luster of their beauties."[45] This passage expressing Mehemet's surprise and horror over the effrontery of western women is fairly standard for the genre, recalling similar passages in *The Turkish Spy*. However, it takes on new meaning when compared to earlier descriptions of Mehemet's infiltration of the republic. Schueller points out that this passage "demonstrate[s] the significance of gender to conceptions of nationhood." She reads Markoe's satire as having a kind of disciplinary purpose: "The representations of frivolity are intended to wake women to the tasks of being chaste and virtuous embodiments of nation so that they can be guardians of the morality of the country."[46] The role of women as "embodying" the nation contrasts with Mehemet's ability to obscure his own body as he moves within the public sphere, yet in this gendered context, Mehemet describes himself as *seeing* and being *seen*. These women are problematic precisely because they retain a kind of corporeality, threatening again and again to pull men out of the realm of rational abstraction and Mehemet from his position as distant, objective observer. To Mehemet they represent, in Lauren Berlant's words, a femininity that "tends toward the erotic, the sensational, which hyper-emphasizes the visual frame," and therefore they threaten Mehemet's ability to "pass" in Philadelphia society and the security afforded by his mastery of language.[47]

During his stay in Philadelphia, Mehemet's musings range widely, from the state of education to the superiority of a unicameral over a bicameral legislature, but he reserves his sharpest critiques for the proceedings of the Constitutional Convention.[48] The spy takes direct aim at the participants in the event, mocking speakers who invoke the classical past as a way of claiming the voice of the people: "The republican form of government is extremely flattering to the pride of man. Orators, poets and philosophers, have sounded its praises, whilst the civilized part of the world has listened with rapture. Who is not soothed by the splendid dreams of Plato . . . ? Who is not roused by the thunder of Demosthenes and Cicero? But in all matters, which involve the welfare of nations, fancy should be restrained and judgment alone consulted." Mehemet concludes—somewhat out of character—that classical "fancy" obscures the true source of political power in the people. Just as Franklin would do a few years later in "On the Slave Trade," Markoe deployed the Algerian figure to contest elite claims not with argument but simply with its embodied presence. According to Mehemet, republican political rhetoric is too abstract and too preoccupied with its own classical antecedents to grapple with the true concerns of the public, including the very real issue, represented by the spy himself, of North African piracy and enslaved American sailors. Immediately after commenting on the "pride" of republican government, Mehemet presents the opposite extreme in Algiers and the Muslim world:

> I have often lamented the situation of our Deys. No sooner is one murdered, than another is elected by the murderers of his predecessor. Should he dare to decline the honor, his refusal is followed by instant death. To preserve life, he is obligated to act the tyrant, and reluctantly consent to murders, which the brutal soldiers demand and execute with rapture. . . . Has not Constantinople herself often beheld an emperor triumphant in the morning and a headless trunk at night.[49]

The emperor's "headless trunk" offers a nightmare vision of self-consuming political power mutilating the national body. In addition to warning against the dangers of tyrannical executive power, that violent image would have undoubtedly conjured for readers descriptions of the ongoing hardships and gruesome injuries of American captives discussed in my previous chapter, locating the real stakes of the convention's deliberations in the actual bodies of the citizenry.

Of course, Mehemet's critique must necessarily be suspect, as over the course of the letters that follow, he proposes his own scheme to disassemble the American national body. Observing Rhode Island's refusal to cooperate in the convention, Mehemet suggests to his master a scheme to bribe Daniel Shays to aid a revolt in Providence that would establish "an Ottoman Malta on the coasts of America" from which the country's "defenseless coasts, bays and rivers may be plundered [by pirates] without the least risque, and their young men and maidens triumphantly carried into captivity."[50] Here Markoe uses the controversy surrounding Shays's Rebellion to make explicit the existential threat of national disintegration. This speculative future, like the alternative past offered by Mehemet's earlier musing on Carthage, reverses the positions of Africa and the West. Although not mentioned in the novel, the Ottoman invasion of Rhode Island would create conditions on the American coast mirroring those faced by West Africans, repeatedly victimized by raids from slaving compounds on the coast. This proposed alliance of the Ottoman Porte and Daniel Shays's insurgency further ties anxieties over North Africa to fears of domestic antielite discontent. Jeremy Engels notes that the alarmist rhetoric surrounding Shays, stoked by elites during the protracted ratification debates, contrasted sharply with the ideal of rational public discussion trumpeted by both federalists and antifederalists. The reference to Shays in the novel connects Mehemet with what Engels calls the discourse of "enemyship," which describes the counter-revolutionary strategy through which political leaders in the early republic "name the enemy in order to achieve desirable rhetorical effects . . . including unity, hierarchy, and deference." The intent was to "encourage allegiance to the Constitution by trading obedience for protection."[51] Shays offers a domestic corollary to Mehemet's foreign, orientalized body and its opposition to the rational public sphere, suggesting that Shays too represents a corporeality that threatens rhetorical distance and the fantasy of disinterestedness.

If Mehemet's plot to invade Rhode Island potentially reinforced federalist calls for national unity and a stable hierarchy within the republic, a dramatic reversal at the novel's close suggests a rejection of the rhetoric of enemyship. In a plot twist that emerges in the work's last three letters, Mehemet undergoes a dramatic religious, political, and territorial conversion that Marr argues demonstrates Markoe's inclusive vision of American freedom.[52] Letters from allies on the other side of the Atlantic report to the spy that his wife had recently escaped to Spain with their Spanish slave and converted to Christianity, and consequently the suspicious dey of Algiers has exiled Mehemet from his home city. Rather than mourn this misfortune, Mehemet decides to embrace his assumed identity: "RUINED, did thou say?—No; I am preserved. I am free and delight in the freedom of others, and am no longer either a slave or a tyrant. At once a CHRISTIAN and a PENNSYLVANIAN, I am doubly an advocate for the rights of mankind." Mehemet declares himself free, and in a territorializing gesture, purchases "two extensive farms" where he will live with "the united blessings of FREEDOM and CHRISTIANITY."[53] Mehemet's ability to become American revises the understanding of national identity seen most prominently in J. Hector St. John de Crèvecoeur's *Letters from an American Farmer* (1782). In his chapter "What Is an American," Crèvecoeur writes, "*He* is an American, who, leaving behind him all his ancient prejudices and manners, receives new ones from the new mode of life he has embraced, the new government he obeys, and the new rank he holds. . . . Here individuals are melted into a new race of men."[54] Crèvecoeur's physical metaphor of "melting" rests on the possibility of the mutability of the body—the idea that a body can be deracialized in the process of nationalization. In contrast, Markoe's vision focuses on a declarative act that makes clear the discursive layering—linguistic, territorial, and religious—surrounding the process of assimilation. Importantly, Mehemet's body is not *melted*; it is *published* through a series of linguistic and economic acts that make possible the public's access to his letters.

Although the disappearance of Mehemet's North African body into the American public can be read as a reaffirmation of public-sphere abstraction stabilized by the textual authority of the Constitution to be ratified, the novel itself repeatedly challenges these processes and marks their limits. Arguably, the work is no more inclusive than any other novel of racial passing—if Mehemet gains access to the public, he does so only by translating himself into a white, Christian landowner under a name that is never divulged in the text. This conversion brings the plot full circle to the work's prefaces, where the spy completes the correlative processes of naturalization and publication by submitting his Arabic-language identity for translation into an English text "for the good of the United States."[55] As I have argued, Mehemet functions as the anti-Publius, challenging not just the centralization of federal power but also the ideological structures that allow elites to imagine that they to speak for the people. If the spy does ultimately succeed in leaving behind his body, he does so by offering himself to the public, rather than claiming to speak for it.

MUSTAPHA TAKES IN A PLAY

If *The Algerine Spy* reflected the anxieties surrounding the Constitutional Convention—the fear of external threat, the worries about government power, and the question of exactly who is represented by the phrase "We the People"—the Mustapha letters, published across several issues of *Salmagundi* years after the end of the Tripolitan War in the first decade of the nineteenth century, approached a new social and political moment but with a similar focus on how the Barbary figure disrupts the linguistic construction of public and nation. Rather than a spy, Mustapha is a prisoner of war captured by the American navy and let loose on the streets of New York. Authored by Washington Irving, his brother William Irving, and their collaborator James Kirke Paulding, these letters follow Markoe's earlier example by adapting the eastern observer genre for the American present, yet Mustapha occupies a very different position than Mehemet. In the following, I examine how the letters combine earlier republican-era critiques of print ideology with the emerging racial epistemology of the nineteenth century.

As I began to discuss in my previous chapter in reference to the novella *Humanity in Algiers* (1801), after the resolution of the Algerine Crisis and the return of the American captives in the late 1790s, print culture's engagement with North Africa and Islam began to foreground schemes of proto-imperialist mastery more consistent with cultural orientalism. In his survey of representations of the Muslim world in American periodicals at the end of the eighteenth century, Robert Battistini suggests that before 1800, American writers and audiences saw themselves as "members of an international community of individuals who, despite differences in color and creed, shared basic human preoccupations such as health, safety, religion, memory, and art." This perspective meant that they approached Islamic cultures with more curiosity than condescension. After 1800, however, Battistini observes that articles moved toward a rhetoric of authority and bigotry that dominated the nineteenth century's writing about Muslims.[56] To an extent, this transition represents a reorientation of what Edward Said calls "positional superiority" at the source of orientalist discourse.[57] In early conflicts with the Barbary States, political and economic turmoil meant that the young country had no naval resources to expend defending its shipping from pirates. That situation changed with the establishment of the U.S. Navy in between the Algerine Crisis and the Tripolitan War. As Battistini's survey shows, Barbary works provide a vital index of the shift in American self-conception that we might broadly characterize as moving between postcolonial and imperialist positions. Specifically, Stephen Decatur's and William Eaton's victories in Tripoli resulted in a surge of triumphalist narratives and a very different vision for the future of American Empire than we see in Markoe's invocation of Carthage. Eaton's and Decatur's successes erased the humiliation of previous enslavements and reaffirmed the superiority of American values and a rising sense of American racial identity. In Joseph Hanson's celebratory *The Mussulmen Humbled; or, A Heroic Poem* (1806), the poet crows that "if the audacious Tripolitans, expecting to see American citizens submit to their insults and impositions; the valorous conduct of your brave Tars, has taught them another lesson: and caused them to know, that on this side of the Atlantic, dwells a race of beings! Of equal spirit to the first of nations."[58] What emerges, distinct from the settler colonialism of western expansion, is a vision of empire as intervention, pacification, and regime change. In the final section of this chapter I demonstrate how this larger geopolitical and cultural shift registered in Barbary texts' critique of republican discourse and of public debate.

While the Mustapha letters reflect the larger shift toward orientalist representations of Muslims in the period, they also build on the critiques present in previous Barbary works by repeatedly satirizing the inability of American political rhetoric to process or metabolize the raced body of the oriental Other. In these terms my reading of *Salmagundi* below might usefully be understood in the context of Joseph Rezek's analysis of African American oratory in the same period. Rezek has explored how circulating orations surrounding the abolition of the slave trade in 1807 challenged the concept of a rational public sphere dominated by print ideology, invoking "voice, embodied collectivity, a delimited religious community, and the lived experience of a racialized and marginalized people."[59] Similar to the ways in which these orations contested the boundaries of print, the presence of Mustapha's body in New York exposed the limitations of political rhetoric.

Salmagundi's Mustapha and his letters are fictional, but the character was inspired by actual North Africans who were briefly held as captives in

New York two years earlier. In 1805, the final year of the Tripolitan War, the frigate *John Adams* returned from the Mediterranean to New York harbor carrying six Tripolitan prisoners. These prisoners of war created a sensation, and society responded as it usually does when confronted with strange and exotic visitors—it took them to the theatre. Few records exist of the Tripolitan prisoners' stay in the city, but newspaper advertisements indicate that they attended at least three separate performances in March 1805. On March 6, one paper announced that for an evening performance of *Blue Beard; or, Female Curiosity*, "the Stage Box will be occupied by the Turkish Officers, viz. MUSTAFFA, Captain of the Ketch; ABULLAH, Captain of the Gun Boat taken on the 3d of August, 1804; SALLEE, MUSTAPHA, ALLEE, MAHOMET, ACHMET, &c. Captives on board the John Adams Frigate."[60] Ironically, the play that Mustaffa and company were brought to see was an orientalized adaptation of the traditional French Blue Beard story. This version, set in Turkey, depicts Blue Beard as a strange character not just because of his facial hair but because he only marries one woman at a time. According to reports of the event, the real-life Muslim sailors attracted far more attention that night than the orientalist caricatures onstage. Theatre historian George Clinton Densmore Odell complained that the "atrocious taste of these proceedings is only equaled by the vulgarity of the audience that flocked to the show."[61] In a unique triangulation of spectatorial desire, the American actors of a British play adapted from a French story and dressed as Turkish aristocrats were watched by Tripolitan captives (who might or might not have been ethnically Turkish) who in turn were watched by an American audience hungry for authentic exotic spectacle—ironically, the presence of North African bodies thoroughly disrupted the representation of Muslim identity on stage. Little is known of the captives' response to this scene, except for a report in the *Chronicle* the next day that said, "The grand drama of Blue Beard was performed in a very excellent style, and the Turks appeared to find much satisfaction in the representation."[62] Prisoners of war far from home, Mustaffa and his crew were called upon to confirm (or at least appear to confirm) the veracity of popular orientalist performances.

The Tripolitan captives were taken to the theatre several more times while in New York. On March 11, an advertisement announced, "In order to gratify the earnest desires of many Ladies and Gentlemen, who were obliged to retire for want of places on Wednesday last, the Turkish Captives . . . will revisit the Theatre."[63] Regarding a third outing in late March, Odell comments, "On this occasion the exoticism of the show became occidental; the spectacle was Columbus, and the queer people were Indians, not Moors or Turks (or whatever the characters in Blue Beard were supposed to be)."[64] In one final outing on April 5, the captives were again treated to a performance of *Blue Beard* and left to return to North Africa shortly after.[65] What perhaps stands out most in these reports is the dearth of details about the captives themselves; they became, for the most part, theatrical props that facilitated public introspection.

The disruptive presence of the Tripolitans in New York two years earlier is thoroughly reimagined in *Salmagundi* as the narrative of Mustapha Rub-a-Dub Keli Khan's impressions of the United States. It is unknown whether either Paulding or the Irving brothers were present for any of the Tripolitans' theatrical outings, although evidence suggests that at least one of them attended a performance of *Blue Beard*. Mustapha's bizarre middle name, Rub-a-Dub, may be inspired by the refrain of the song that begins the second act of that play, which repeats "Rub Dub Dub" in imitation of a military drumbeat performed by Turkish soldiers. The change to "Rub-a-Dub" for Mustapha indicates the ways in which *Salmagundi* portrays this former corsair as comical and nonthreatening. The character of Sir Launcelot Langstaff introduces the first of Mustapha's letters in *Salmagundi*'s third issue:

> Among the few strangers whose acquaintance has entertained me, I particularly rank the magnanimous MUSTAPHA RUB-A-DUB KELI KHAN, a most illustrious captain of a ketch, who figured some time since, in our fashionable circles, at the head of a ragged regiment of Tripolitan prisoners. His conversation was to me a perpetual feast;—I chuckled with inward pleasure at his whimsical mistakes and unaffected observations on men and manners; and I rolled each odd conceit "like a sweet morsel under my tongue."
>
> Whether Mustapha was captivated by my iron-bound physiognomy, or flattered by the attentions which I paid him, I won't determine; but I so far gained his confidence, that, at his departure, he presented me with a bundle of papers, containing, among other articles, several copies of letters, which he had written to his friend in Tripoli.—the following is a translation of one of them.—the original is in Arabic-Greek; but by the assistance of Will Wizard, who understands all languages, . . . I have been enabled to accomplish a tolerable translation.[66]

Langstaff's preface contextualizes the translation of Mustapha's letters within a larger scheme of superiority, domination, and ultimately consumption. Rather than stumbled upon, the letters are offered up as food for the proto-imperial body—a racialized body that boasts an exemplary physiognomy. In contrast to Mehemet, who directly states his intention to benefit the country with his letters, it remains unclear why Mustapha gives his papers to Langstaff, suggesting he has little actual agency. That he writes in "Arabic-Greek" further reinforces his absurdity as a character as well as the power of Langstaff and Wizard to master him through their linguistic prowess.

Mustapha is presented as dominated by growing American military power and by white elites, yet his contributions contain some of the most biting satire in all of *Salmagundi*. It is not long into Mustapha's first letter that he begins to satirize Langstaff's arrogance: "The people of the United States have assured me that they themselves are the most enlightened nation under the sun; but thou knowest that the barbarians of the desert, who assemble at the summer solstice to shoot their arrows at that glorious luminary, in order to extinguish its burning rays, make precisely the same boast." Although the series portrays him as a clown and the object of condescension, Mustapha nevertheless offers several sharp criticisms aimed at the country's troubled relationship with language. Mustapha points out first and foremost that the republic's understanding of itself is always already the result of an act of translation or adaptation of a foreign language:

> Some insisted that it savours of aristocracy; others maintain that is a pure democracy; and a third set of theories declare absolutely that it is nothing more nor less than a mobocracy. The latter, I must confess, though still wide in error, have come nearest to the truth. You of course must understand the meaning of these different words, as they are derived from the ancient Greek language, and bespeak loudly the verbal poverty of these poor infidels, who cannot utter a learned phrase without laying the dead languages under contribution.

After observing the political system of the United States, Mustapha concludes that the country is, in fact, "a pure unadulterated LOGOCRACY, or a government of words." Much like Mehemet's indictment of classical "fancy," Mustapha satirizes the pointlessness of abstract rhetoric:

> But in nothing is the verbose nature of this government more evident than in its grand national divan, or congress, where the laws are framed; this is a blustering, windy assembly, where everything is carried by noise, tumult and debate; for thou must know, that the members of this assembly do not meet

together to find wisdom in the multitude of counsellors, but to wrangle, call each other hard names, and hear themselves talk. When the congress opens, the bashaw first sends them a long message, i.e., a huge mass of words—vox et preterea nihil, all meaning nothing.

Mustapha translates Congress from a republican institution to an instrument for orientalized oppression, much in the same way that Franklin translated Congressman Jackson's speech nearly two decades earlier. President Thomas Jefferson himself becomes the "present bashaw," guilty not of despotism per se but of rendering words meaningless.[67] Marr writes that Mustapha's satirical gaze "identifie[s] the petty debates of American politics as themselves a source of oriental excess."[68]

Yet, alternatively, we can read this problem of a pure logocracy—the disconnect between language and action or speech and the authorizing body—as signaling just the opposite of the corporeal excess that orientalized figures so often represent. Christopher Looby has noted the connection between political and social instability and the emphasis on language throughout the Mustapha letters. He asserts, "It would not be too much to claim that Irving's denomination of America as a 'logocracy' was meant to suggest that [during] the endemic legitimation crisis that beset the new nation . . . the *only* social institution readily available to the young republic was language itself."[69] I would add that the letters make evident too that language, and the republic itself, became institutionalized only through, and remained vulnerable to, acts of translation and reversal that could easily render it foreign to itself.

As in *The Algerine Spy*, Mustapha's critique of the logocracy directly invokes anxieties about the rhetorical construction of the public. Similar too is the way Irving's work plays on the crisis that arises when that logocracy must confront the problems of the body. Like Mehemet, Mustapha comments on the immodesty and freedom of American women who, "instead of being carefully shut up in seraglios, are abandoned to the direction of their own reason and suffered to run about in perfect freedom, like other domestic animals." While he attributes this untoward freedom to the American practice of "treating their women as rational being[s] and allowing them souls," when he focuses on their dress he falls back into the language of eastern excess: "The dress of these women is, if possible, more eccentric and whimsical than their deportment. . . . A woman of this country, dressed out for an exhibition, is loaded with as many ornaments as a Circassian slave when brought out for sale."[70] Building on her reading of Markoe's novel, Schueller argues that Mustapha's criticism of women's "frivolity" reflects a similar call to the chastity and virtue necessary to embody the nation; however, later in this letter Mustapha turns not to the profusion of ornament but to language as the enemy of embodied virtue.[71] Arriving in New York, "In vain did I look around me, on my first landing, for the divine forms of redundant proportions, which answer to the true standard of eastern beauty;—not a single fat fair one could I behold among the multitudes that thronged the streets; the females that passed a review before me, tripping sportively along, resembled a procession of shadows, returning to their graves at the crowing of the cock." Mustapha attributes this lack of corporeality to the logocracy, to "a peculiar activity of tongue" that "steals flesh from their bones and the rose from their cheeks."[72] While Mustapha concedes his mistake when he learns that the thinness of the women is, in fact, pursuant to western beauty standards, his theory of language eating away the body offers a startling image of the excesses of logocratic rule.

The problems of the body resurface again when Mustapha informs his friend that he, "the invincible captain of a ketch, is sadly in want of a pair of breeches!" When applying for new breeches, Mustapha is told that, as a prisoner of war, he must petition Congress for the necessary garments. Issues of the body become issues of public speech, and vice versa. Revisiting his earlier critique of "the grand national divan," Mustapha says, "this prolific body may not improperly be termed the 'mother of inventions'; and a most fruitful mother it is, let me tell thee, though its children are generally abortions." Here he directly compares Congress's empty language to deformed or dead bodies. Mustapha marvels at the situation in which "all the sages of an immense logocracy assembled together to talk about my breeches!"[73] One might accuse Paulson and the Irving brothers of going for the cheap laugh here, but Mustapha's petition nevertheless recalls a real-life event. While the actual Mustaffa was in New York City, citizens conducted a benefit performance aimed at buying new clothes for the Tripolitan captives. An advertisement in the *New-York Commercial Advertiser* on March 29, 1805, announces that "on Friday evening, March 29, (At the request of several gentlemen) A Benefit Will be given to the TURKISH CAPTIVES on board the Frigate John Adams, for the purpose of accommodating them with additional cloathes: they have at present no other apparel than what they had on at the time they were made prisoners of War."[74] The Mustapha letters' direct reference to this episode suggests that the needs of the body continue to intrude on rational discourse within a nation constituted largely of words and texts.

Beneath the humor of this scene is a sharp satire aimed at how race is understood in the American logocracy. Mustapha's lobbying of Congress in writing reveals how othered bodies are afforded or denied recognition and status through political rhetoric and the circulation of texts. That it is a pair of breeches that are under debate in Mustapha's letter may well be a reference to Michel de Montaigne's well-known essay "On Cannibals." Mustapha's observations throughout the series seem aimed at reminding the reader of what Montaigne argues concerning American natives: "I do not believe, . . . that there is anything barbarous or savage about them, except that we all call barbarous anything that is contrary to our own habits."[75] In his essay, Montaigne argues that the "barbarians" are no different from Europeans, except for one final note in the last words of the piece, when he mentions that "they do not wear breeches."[76] If breeches for Montaigne signify the comparatively inconsequential sartorial differences between European and barbarian, Mustapha's letters go further to show how the logocracy cannot process the challenge of a racial Other who requests breeches.

As I have suggested throughout this chapter, it is no coincidence that the writers of *Salmagundi* use the perspective of the Barbary figure to character- ize the republic as an empty and ineffective logocracy, helpless to account for the demands of the body. In each of the works above, American conflicts with North Africa threatened not only the economy and national security but also the language that constituted representative government. However, while in Markoe's earlier work Mehemet can ultimately submit himself to publication and assimilation, *Salmagundi*'s Mustapha is irreconcilably oth- ered, a shift that is particularly evident in the description of translation in the later text as a process of consuming the body and asserting mastery. This dis- cursive othering, however, does nothing to solve the problems of the body and its presence within national space. The shift from spy to prisoner of war in the figuration of the North African in print makes manifest the evolving conceptualization of American nationhood from post-revolutionary classical republic to assertive, proto-imperial power in the Atlantic world. Yet, these Barbary figures on American shores also expose and play on underlying anxieties that the linguistic borders of the national public were inherently vulnerable to the threat of foreign-speaking bodies, and that its foundations in rational debate were perhaps not worth the paper they were printed on.

If the shift between *The Algerine Spy* and *Salmagundi* marks the emergence of a more stable, racialized narrative of post-republican publicity that decisively places the Tripolitan captive on the outside of American identity, other Barbary figures maintain a more complex positionality. In the chapter to follow, I explore the ways in which Barbary works represented Jews as capable of both aiding and hindering early American ambitions in the Atlantic. In that analysis I expand my engagement with the concept of logocracy. If Mustapha mocks the proliferation of inconsequential and impotent language in the republic, the Barbary Jew—in its racial mutability and lack of stable territorialized identity—presents the reader with the threatening image of the indecipherable page.

PART TWO

THE BARBARY AND THE JEWISH ATLANTIC

CHAPTER THREE

"A VAGUE RESEMBLANCE TO SOMETHING SEEN ELSEWHERE"

To be a Jew outright won't do at all—
But not to be a Jew will do still less.

—Gotthold Ephraim Lessing, *Nathan the Wise* (1779)

A brilliant skin is not hers; nor elegant proportions; not majestic stature; yet no creature had ever more power to bewitch.

—Charles Brockden Brown, *Arthur Mervyn* (1800)

As I briefly mentioned in the previous chapter, in 1785, just months after Algiers first declared war on the United States, Governor Patrick Henry of Virginia arrested three Algerian visitors in Norfolk on suspicion of spying. The arrivals had, according to the brief report circulated up and down the coast, disembarked from an English ship and had given "very inconsistent accounts of themselves."[1] These three strangers, two men and one woman, were transported to Williamsburg and finally to Richmond, where they were questioned by physician and former mayor William Foushee. This interrogation seems to have raised more questions than it answered. Foushee commented in a letter to Governor Henry that "they deny being Algerines, but say they are Moors," coming from England for an unknown purpose. In addition to finding funds "borrowed from a Jew in London," Foushee discovered several Hebrew documents that allegedly would "admit them to places of worship." He could not read these documents, nor could the prisoners read and vouch for the English travel papers they carried, which led to the speculation that they perhaps originated from Morocco. In closing his letter, Foushee noted that the visitors were "much distressed" that they would be returned to Norfolk rather than allowed to continue to their destination, which was apparently Philadelphia.[2] Nothing was conclusively determined, and Governor Henry eventually gave orders to deport the alleged spies back across the Atlantic, although their actual fate is unclear, as they were reportedly sighted in Charleston, South Carolina, early the next year.[3]

This anecdote opens the first chapter of Robert J. Allison's *The Crescent Obscured* (1995), a vital history of the Barbary crises that inaugurated a new wave of scholarship focused on early American relations with the Muslim world. While Allison rightly sees the imprisonment and supposed deportation of these alleged spies as reflecting the widespread paranoia provoked by the Barbary menace, he stops short of considering the implications of the Hebrew documents carried by the visitors. Where did they get these papers, and for what purpose? Why were they traveling to Philadelphia? There was no significant Jewish community in Norfolk at the time, but by 1785 Philadelphia boasted a small but thriving congregation anchored by the Mikveh Israel synagogue, constructed in 1782.[4] Was it this place of worship that the travelers intended to access? Why would these "Moors," assumed to be Muslim, travel all the way across the Atlantic to visit a synagogue? Is it possible that Foushee misunderstood the visitors, labeling them Moors when they may have been Sephardic Jews from North Africa? On its surface, this incident has much in common with the reports of the two Algerine gentlemen with which I opened the previous chapter, but the Hebrew documents provide an extra complication. In this case, the racial identity of the travelers and the documents they carried were equally unknowable and indecipherable to authorities.

We will likely never unravel the confusion surrounding these mysterious visitors, but behind the conflicting identities and contradictory stories looms the shadow of a trans-Atlantic Muslim-Jewish conspiracy that early Americans often viewed as an existential threat to the country. The Hebrew documents clearly did not allay the Virginians' suspicions of Barbary espionage; on the contrary, Governor Henry and Foushee no doubt thought it entirely plausible that Jews in the United States and Europe might collude with Algerians to infiltrate the republic.[5] Two years later, Peter Markoe wrote of just such a conspiracy in *The Algerine Spy in Pennsylvania*, and he was by no means the only writer to associate Jews with North Africa and Barbary piracy. In fact, when American writers in this period represented modern (as opposed to biblical) Jews, they did so most often in relation to the Barbary. In his landmark survey of Jews in early American literature, Louis Harap, overlooking Markoe's novel, identifies Royall Tyler's *The Algerine Captive* (1797) as the first work of American fiction to include a modern Jew. In drama, for the period from 1794 to 1823, Harap lists three Barbary plays— Susanna Rowson's *Slaves in Algiers* (1794), James Ellison's *The American Captive* (1812), and Jonathan S. Smith's *The Siege of Algiers* (1823)—as among the six known productions to include contemporary Jews.[6] These works were inspired not only by incidents such as the appearance of the mysterious Algerines in Norfolk, Virginia, but also by reports coming from negotiators in North Africa working with powerful Jewish banking families such as the Bacri and Busnach to ransom American prisoners. Several American diplomats were deeply skeptical of the motivations of their Jewish counterparts, with some, like Tripolitan War hero William Eaton, even accusing them of obstructing the process out of malevolence and greed.[7]

Jews are everywhere in the fiction of the Barbary archive, and yet very few critics have explored the implications of the consistent association of Jews with Islam and Barbary piracy in the early republic.[8] In this chapter, I argue that, just as Muslim pirates and spies challenged the conventions of republican debate, early representations of orientalized Barbary Jews frequently functioned as a test for republican notions of naturalization and citizenship based on the stability of racial categories.[9] As recent works in the field of early African American print culture by Derrick R. Spires and Christopher James Bonner have explored, the country's founding documents left the definition of citizenship ambiguous, providing space for writers and activists to negotiate the boundaries of that concept for themselves.[10] In the 1790s, for example, Spires argues that Black community leaders Absalom Jones and Richard Allen developed a "social theory of citizenship as a practice of neighborliness" around their defense of African Americans' conduct during the 1793 yellow fever epidemic in Philadelphia.[11] For Jews in this same period, however, the Barbary archive relocates questions of civic participation and inclusion from the streets of New York and Philadelphia to a trans-Atlantic *elsewhere*, highlighting questions of assimilation and naturalization. The nearest thing to an articulation of the requirements of citizenship came, in fact, in the 1790 Naturalization Act, which limited the process to "free white person[s]."[12] Such requirements necessarily raise questions around the racial status of Jews, questions that often played out on stage and page.[13] For example, in his review of Richard Cumberland's philosemitic play *The Jew* (1794), critic William Dunlap celebrates the arrival of a "kind of white Shylock" on the American stage, suggesting the performative and behavioral dimensions of Jewish racialization in the period.[14] Are Jews white enough to be good Americans? For early republicans, the associations of the Sephardic diaspora with the Barbary Coast further complicated this already complex question.

As we will see, many Barbary works feature trans-Atlantic Jews either facilitating the infiltration of the republic or desiring to immigrate themselves, highlighting questions of Jewish racial identity, national loyalty, and related concerns over Jewish *futurity*: the possibility for Jews to become good citizens. Reading across the novels *The Algerine Spy* and *The Algerine Captive* and Susanna Rowson's drama *Slaves in Algiers*, I emphasize how these works manifest American anxieties over the racial ambiguity of diasporic Jews while diverging from more traditional antisemitic stereotypes represented by popular Anglo-Atlantic figures like Shakespeare's Shylock.[15] From there, I consider how, taken together, these narratives of the Algerine Crisis offer a powerful lens to interpret the mysterious and groundbreaking character of Achsa Fielding in Charles Brockden Brown's *Arthur Mervyn* (1800–1801). In the final section of this chapter, I briefly examine two later Barbary dramas to demonstrate how post–Tripolitan War narratives celebrate rising military power by ritually casting off the Jewish diaspora.

The fact that contemporary Jews in the period were so frequently depicted as coming from the Barbary raises further questions about how Jewish communities within the United States were understood. Many of the writers I discuss, including Markoe, Tyler, and Rowson, would have had little if any direct contact with Muslims, but they were far more likely to encounter Jews in their day-to-day lives on the streets of Philadelphia or New York. Did they associate these American Jews with the mysterious, orientalized figures who allegedly plotted with the dey of Algiers to exploit the republic? What notions of Jewishness in the public imagination would emerge from, in Julie Kalman's words, "a combination of this type of imagining and the reality of encounters"? In her study of representations of European and African Jewish identities in the context of France's relations with Algiers in 1830, Kalman asserts that "the history of the Orientalized Jew is a history of a middle space in relations between Jews and non-Jews, where contact, interchange, idealization, hatred and even ambivalence could play out." In the following, I build on Kalman's notion of a Jewish "middle space"—"a space of contact, complexity, and fluidity" embodied by Jews both at home and abroad—as it reflects early American perceptions of the Atlantic as a space on which to project both existential fears and imperial ambitions.[16] Barbary Jews cross borders, both racially and geographically. In the context of the Algerine crisis, they are often depicted as controlling, and in some sense representing, the trans-Atlantic circulation of texts and bodies, making them both a grave threat and a powerful resource for the early United States.

The notion of the Jewish diaspora as both a threat and an opportunity for the country manifests in a number of Barbary works in the fact that Jewish characters frequently come in pairs. As Aamir R. Mufti observes in relation to nineteenth-century European debates over Jewish emancipation, "Abstract citizen subjectivity and national belonging constitute moments in the dialectic of modern selfhood, with the figure of the Jew coming to mark the inherent limit of *each* moment of identification, to mark the disruption of the categories of identity, becoming in the process the site of crisis and its attempted containment." Mufti elaborates on how these disruptions generated a split view of the Jew as, on the one hand, "slavishly bound to external law and tradition, ritualistic and irrational, and incapable of . . . enlightened, modern subjectivity," and on the other, "a figure of transnational range and abilities, [raising] questions about deracination, homelessness, abstraction, supra-national identifications, and divided loyalties." In the works I read below, these contradictory representational demands appear as the persistent doubling of the Jew. *The Algerine Spy*, *The Algerine Captive*, and *Slaves in Algiers* all present the opposition of "good" and "bad" Jews, leaving open the question of how a true American may possibly emerge as synthesis from the "crisis in the *minor* practices, narratives, and locations of Jewish existence."[17] Within these works, the stakes of that emergence involve not just the inclusion of Jews in the republican public sphere but more vitally the liberty of the white American subject to move and act in the Atlantic world.

Finally, to tie this chapter back to previous chapters' discussions of race and print, I want to draw attention to the ways in which complications surrounding Jewish identity are so often tied to textual exchange. In his analysis of mid-nineteenth-century African American print, Jonathan Senchyne has explored the extent to which the "black/white binary of print" functioned as "an analogue of the black/white binary of race." As he observes, "Reading print relies on making meaning out of the difference between black and white," and therefore "the black/white dualism underwriting print legibility further naturalized black/white racial dualism by implying the possibility of 'reading' bodies in relation to one another."[18] Recalling my opening anecdote, we can see how the failure to read the bodies of the "Algerines" together with the texts they carried was emblematic of the ways in which these figures threatened the sharp contrast necessary for print legibility. As I argue throughout this chapter, the racial ambiguity of Barbary Jews, closely tied to the trans-Atlantic circulation of texts both written and printed, provoked a crisis of indecipherability and untranslatability for the republic in print.

TRANS-ATLANTIC NETWORKS

Kalman's concept of orientalized Barbary Jews as inhabiting a "middle space" derives directly from the French experience of using powerful Jewish banking families such as the Bacri and Busnach as diplomatic and financial points of contact with the regimes of North Africa. These powerful and wealthy families, "not quite Algerian and not entirely European," functioned as "professional go-betweens" who helped shape France's relationship with foreign Muslim rulers and with its own empire.[19] Leaving aside the very different geopolitical positions of France and the United States in the period, American negotiators faced many of the same limitations and frustrations as their French counterparts. Prominent Jewish Algerians not only facilitated lines of communication between diplomats and the dey of Algiers but also provided funds for consular activities and ransom.[20] As a result, diplomats and the American public at large often blamed Jewish bankers for the failure of negotiations, characterizing their greed and perfidy through the oft-deployed Shylock trope.[21] At the same time, Americans seem to have been quite aware of the oppression of Jewish communities in North Africa; newspapers appear to have gone out of their way to report on violence against the Jewish minority in Algiers. One typical article, dated November 1785, reported that five Jews were strangled in Algiers for "defrauding an English merchant of a great sum of money and a quantity of merchandize," and three additional culprits were tortured with one hundred bastinadoes and sent into "perpetual slavery" the following day.[22] Another report a months later described two Jews in Algiers "burnt alive upon the spot" after being apprehended and charged with "stealing bags of dollars."[23] The public was well aware of the paradoxical status of Jews in North Africa as both wealthy and influential figures and suffering bodies alongside the American captives. This tenuous position undoubtedly reinforced the perception of Jews as being eternally displaced, inhabiting but not quite belonging on the Barbary Coast.

For several writers in the Barbary archive, the seemingly unsustainable position of Jews in North Africa raised pertinent questions about Jewish particularity and its relationship to the new republican order. As my reading of Peter Markoe's *The Algerine Spy in Pennsylvania* in the previous chapter shows, the novel's arc and resolution can be read as a narrative of the Muslim spy's territorialization and "passing" into deracialization through the processes of publication. Mehemet's conversion and assimilation, while seemingly so abrupt in the final letter of the work, develop throughout the story as the spy becomes increasingly acculturated to the ideology of the republic. What I only glossed over in my previous reading, however, are the ways in which these processes are witnessed and facilitated by the Jews of the Sephardic Atlantic. During his sojourn in Spain, Mehemet stays with a Jewish merchant named Solomon Mendez, who agrees to help the spy infiltrate Philadelphia and provide him with credit to fund the mission. Even more, Mehemet's host provides him with insights into the "manners and amusements of the Nazarenes," knowledge the merchant collected during his own visits to America, ensuring that the spy will remain undetected in Philadelphia.[24] Mendez's firsthand knowledge of North America and his connection to Jewish communities there make possible Mehemet's successful infiltration. As he benefits from this Muslim-Jewish alliance, Mehemet muses that Jews will show loyalty to any country that protects them, and a liberal state will benefit from their ability "to collect intelligence of all the designs of foreign cabinets." Noting that even Britain restricts Jews from owning land, Mehemet suggests that a Jewish merchant is ultimately more "useful" than a Jewish farmer would be, as the former can demonstrate his patriotism by "advancing the credit of his nation" and "depressing that of the enemy."[25] Markoe indulges in conspiratorial rhetoric, remarking on the potentially dangerous power and influence of the Sephardic diaspora, albeit to argue for the benefits of an open and liberal society.

After befriending Mendez, Mehemet encounters the other side of the Jewish diaspora when he travels to Lisbon. There he lodges with another

94 **CHAPTER THREE**

Jew named Isaac D'Acosta, whom he judges to be a "tractable being" who "has not entirely recovered from the dread of the inquisition." The spy's encounter with less savory Jews prompts him to dedicate an entire letter to predicting the future of the Jewish diaspora, musing, "It may be reasonably supposed, that the genius of the Hebrews, which for ages has been oppressed by the rude hand of fanaticism, will now spread and flourish anew. Every nation, which protects them, is entitled to their exertions."[26] The context of Mehemet's mission suggests that the benefits of liberality are accruing not to the Christian West but to the Muslim world and the Ottoman Porte.[27]

Mehemet does not seem to have encountered any Jews on the streets of Philadelphia, but Markoe undoubtedly did. Although smaller than communities in New York and Charleston, the Philadelphia Jewish community was well established by the time of the Revolution. The majority of Jews in the city were Ashkenazi, although the city's first synagogue, Mikveh Israel, following the example of New York's Congregation Shearith Israel, conducted Sephardic services. In fact, during the time Markoe was writing *The Algerine Spy*, Congregation Mikveh Israel was led by hazzan Jacob Raphael Cohen, who was born on the Barbary Coast, although his exact city of origin remains unknown.[28] Furthermore, it seems likely that Mehemet's description of the Jewish banker who "by a few strokes of his pen creates fleets and armies" and the character of Solomon Mendez are direct references to Philadelphian Haym Salomon, a Sephardic immigrant from Poland who acted as one of the primary financiers of the Revolution.[29] Despite his support of the war effort, political opponents in the early 1780s attacked Salomon as having "worse than a Shylock's temperament."[30] Although Mehemet praises Mendez as largely free of "those vices too generally attributed to his degenerate nation," he does so in notably transactional terms. He faults D'Acosta for a resentment of past wrongs—a lack of commitment to the potential of Jewish futurity—while the notion that a liberal state might be "entitled to [the Jew's] exertions" suggests a relationship more extractive than inclusive.[31]

The Jewish characters, good and bad, fade to the background once Mehemet arrives in Philadelphia, but the novel's climax comes with Mehemet's discovery that the Sephardic Atlantic is a double-edged sword. In the only letter in the work written by someone other than Mehemet, Mendez informs the spy that an unnamed rabbi from Portugal has turned the dey against him, providing the catalyst for the Algerian's defection and assimilation. In sharp contrast to the opportunistic, spiteful rabbi, whose motives remain unclear, Mendez selflessly pledges his assistance, declaring, "My house, my purse, my credit, are at thy service. Can I do less for a man, who thought me worthy of his confidence, not only in pecuniary matters but even in an affair on which his life depended?"[32] It is to Mendez, then, as the only character to complete a trans-Atlantic dialogue, that Mehemet declares himself an American and a Christian, and it is Mendez's handling of the funds that facilitates the new republican's purchase of a Pennsylvania farm; as the othered half of a dialectical process, the Jew can witness the acts of naturalization and territorialization but must remain apart from them.

Markoe ultimately suggests in *The Algerine Spy* that *some* Jews have the potential to be good and loyal republicans, just not yet. The Jewish characters in *The Algerine Spy* conspire with the Barbary States but remain, until the novel's resolution, morally ambiguous and unpredictable, a pattern repeated throughout a number of Barbary works, including Tyler's *The Algerine Captive*. Previously I briefly discussed how the enslavement of that novel's protagonist, Updike Underhill, fosters sympathy for and comparison to the enslavement of Africans in America. In the following section, I emphasize how, for Underhill, his ultimate positioning within the geography of slavery and freedom depends on his relationship to Barbary Jews who occupy an ambiguous middle ground. Within a section of the novel imitating the descriptions of Algerian society seen in contemporary pamphlets and travelogues, Underhill turns his attention to the city's Jewish population. In a chapter entitled "Of the Jews," with an epigraph taken from *The Merchant of Venice* ("For sufferance is the badge of all our tribe"), Underhill observes in grand fashion that "this cunning race, since their dispersion by Vespasian and Titus, have contrived to compensate themselves for the loss of Palestine 'by engrossing the wealth, and often the luxuries of every other land.'" Like Mehemet before him, Underhill offers a sweeping, global history of the Jews. Noting their political power, he remarks, "The Jews transact almost all the dey's private business. . . . The Jews are also the spies of the dey upon his subjects at home, and the channels of intelligence from foreign powers."[33] Contrary to Mehemet's description of Jewish efforts producing a surplus to benefit the just and inclusive nation, Tyler portrays the diaspora as a drain on the country's wealth that nonetheless enables the despotic government of Algiers.

Near the end of the novel, in the chapter immediately following the reference to Captain Richard O'Brien that I discussed in the introduction, a

96   **CHAPTER THREE**

prominent Jewish merchant in the city recruits Underhill to cure his son of a "violent ague." The merchant, Adonah Ben Benjamin, in gratitude, befriends the captive and pledges to help him gain his freedom. The merchant agrees to secure Underhill's earnings as a physician and to enlist the help of another prominent merchant to raise funds for his ransom. Ben Benjamin also agrees to deliver the captive's letters to his family in New Hampshire and to the American consul in Spain, reconnecting Underhill to a trans-Atlantic network of exchange through the Sephardic Atlantic. Like Mendez, Ben Benjamin is characterized as a faithful Jew who runs counter to the Shylock stereotype. Notably, Underhill refers to his friend as "the benevolent Hebrew," likely a direct reference to British playwright Richard Cumberland's philosemitic play *The Jew; or, The Benevolent Hebrew*.[34] Answering the popularity of the Shylock stereotype, Cumberland's drama begins with a scenario very similar to that of *The Merchant of Venice*: a young man borrows a large sum from a miserly Jewish banker named Sheva to pay the debts of his beloved, whom he had married in secret against his father's wishes. Cumberland's plot ends very differently, however, as rather than calling in the unsustainable debt, the aging Jew instead makes the bride and her brother his heirs after discovering that they are the children of the man who rescued him from the Inquisition in Cadiz. Originally performed in London in 1794, *The Jew* debuted the next year in Philadelphia, New York, and in Boston's Federal Theatre, managed by Royall Tyler's brother. Tyler's novel gestures at a theme in common with Markoe's earlier novel and Cumberland's popular play: kindness to and protection of the Sephardic diaspora yields strategic, and most of all financial, dividends.

Again like Markoe's Solomon Mendez, Tyler's Ben Benjamin maintains connections on both sides of the Atlantic. Even as he agrees to work with Underhill to pay the ransom, he confesses that he is part of the reason why the sum is so high in the first place. Underhill relates, "He told me, in much confidence, that soon after I was taken, a Jew and two Algerines made a tour of the United States, and sent home an accurate account of the America commerce." The dey of Algiers was so impressed by American prosperity that he raised the cost of ransom for all American prisoners. The novel thus lends credence to the anxieties that the country's attempts to secure the freedom of its citizens were being stymied by secret Jewish intelligence. Ben Benjamin also requests a favor from the captive, entreating Underhill, once ransomed, to carry his letters to "a Mr. Lopez, a Jew, who, he said, lived in Rhode Island or Massachusetts, to whom he had a recommendation from a relation who had been in America."[35] At least some of Tyler's New England audience would have recognized this reference; Aaron Lopez was at the time of the American Revolution the most prosperous merchant in the Sephardic Jewish community of Newport, Rhode Island. Lopez fled Newport for Leicester, Massachusetts, when the British occupied Newport during the war. Sadly, Ben Benjamin's information was a few years out of date. Aaron Lopez was killed in a cart accident in 1782, six years before *The Algerine Captive* supposedly takes place. Nevertheless, the novel suggests that the diaspora and its connections with the Barbary offer Jewish figures a privileged position of mobility in the Atlantic world. It is unclear why Ben Benjamin would need Underhill to carry his letter to Lopez, since the Jew had already agreed to pass along Underhill's correspondence. The strangeness of the request points to a level of access to the nation that Underhill can leverage and that Ben Benjamin, as an extranational figure, cannot.

Critic Jared Gardner has suggested that Ben Benjamin, whose repetitious name labels him as the son of Benjamin, becomes a stand-in for Benjamin Franklin, who Underhill meets briefly in Philadelphia before setting sail for Europe and Africa.[36] Through hard work and frugality, Underhill and Ben Benjamin collaborate toward the former's freedom. Their scheme collapses, however, with the Jewish merchant's sudden death. At Ben Benjamin's passing, Underhill expresses true sentiment, claiming to be "as sincere a mourner as the nearest kindred," a display of cross-racial and transnational sympathy that leaves him vulnerable and exploitable. When Underhill visits the late Ben Benjamin's home, he finds that the merchant's son pretends to know nothing about the plan or about the money that was entrusted to his father. Underhill despairs of his inability to enforce the agreement he had with Ben Benjamin: "If I had been a Mussulman I might have attested to my story; but a slave is never admitted as an evidence in Algiers, the West Indies, or the Southern States."[37] As in the case of his reversal of fortune earlier in the novel, Underhill empathizes with the West Africans he formerly enslaved, while the Jew shifts quickly from the captive's accomplice to his oppressor.

A number of critics have noted the reassertion of the Shylock stereotype late in *The Algerine Captive*, but none to date has acknowledged how the sudden turn in Underhill's fortunes constitutes a specific challenge to Cumberland's *The Jew*. Tyler draws attention to the fact that the play's happy ending depends entirely on Sheva's lack of Jewish heirs. Early in the play the banker announces, "I am a solitary being, a waif on the world's wide common."[38] The absence of Jewish descendants makes possible the white Christians' inheritance of the miser's wealth. Ben Benjamin, on the other hand, has an heir, and while the father embodies virtue and loyalty, the son does not. Ultimately, the problem is not Jewish greed, Jewish espionage, or Jewish perfidy but Jewish futurity. Even if a Jew can embody the republican ethic of an iconic figure like Franklin, there is no guarantee that such virtue will pass to the next generation. With the end of Ben Benjamin's ambition to become American, Tyler offers the opposite of the nationalizing and territorializing narrative in which Markoe's Mehemet expresses faith; for Jews, loyalty does not accrue across generations, and the son can just as easily turn away from western virtue as turn toward it.[39]

The still unnamed son becomes the principal villain of the final chapters of the novel, shifting the plot from a struggle with Algerine slavery to a struggle with Jewish deceit.[40] With Underhill's plan to escape from Algiers foiled, the novel ends with the captive traveling with his Algerian master to Medina, Mecca, and then to Scandaroon in Turkey. There, he meets again Ben Benjamin's son, who has again fallen ill. The son confesses to his earlier deception in Algiers and begs the doctor to treat him once more, which Underhill does. In the novel's penultimate chapter, including an epigraph from *The Merchant of Venice* and an argument that states simply, "The Gratitude of a Jew," the son offers to pay Underhill's ransom and is ready to transport him back to America in gratitude for saving his life twice. However, once again the captive fails to properly read and understand the true intentions of the Jew. Instead, the son betrays the captive on the beach and sells him to a new master in Tunis.

Underhill finally achieves his freedom when, while sailing to Tunis, his master's ship is captured by the Portuguese. Mirroring the reversal that begins the novel as Underhill goes from slaver to enslaved, he finds sympathy for his former enemies: "I must confess that this reverse of fortune made me feel for the wretched mussulman. . . . I could not refrain from endeavouring to prevent the Portuguese from avenging himself for the cruelties he had suffered under this Barbarian."[41] As Sarah Sillin argues, "Compassion allows Underhill to signal his own virtue" by allowing him to distance himself from the slavers, East and West.[42] This final expression of pity ends a long arc in which a white slaver finds empathy for both West and North Africans. The last chapter of the novel translates Underhill's sympathy for his former

North African slave masters to a national sympathy that can tie together the interests of northern free states and southern slave states, declaring, "BY UNITING WE STAND, BY DIVIDING WE FALL."[43] If sympathy can connect the disparate peoples of the Atlantic world and ultimately lend coherence and stability to the nation, North African Jews are notably absent from this picture; only in their case is racial and national difference reinforced by the end of the novel. Sillin suggests that Tyler's novel ultimately expresses skepticism concerning the value of a "global sympathy" that extends beyond the borders of the nation, yet "[Underhill's] expressions of sympathy suggest a purposeful effort to redefine US identity in the global sphere, even as fellow feeling exceeds his control."[44] The final chapters of the novel locate the dangers of excess sympathy not on the Barbary Coast or West Africa but in the Jewish diaspora as the treacherous Other of national and transnational sentiment.

In *The Algerine Spy* and *The Algerine Captive*, we can see how these Barbary works depict the free, nationalized subject emerging from the dialectical opposition between liberty and slavery, America and Africa. Imminent to and facilitating this ideological process, however, is the further dialectical opposition of the "good (white) Jew" and the "bad (non-white) Jew," the outcome of which diverges into two very different understandings of Jewish futurity across those works. Where Markoe sees the guarantee of rights as creating the conditions for future Jewish citizenship, Tyler suggests that such extranational bonds of sympathy cannot but threaten American independence. Notably, a very similar dynamic appears in another early novel that only tangentially engages with Barbary captivity: James Butler's picaresque *Fortune's Foot-Ball* (1797). The first mention of a Jewish character appears in the work's first volume, when Mercutio, the novel's British protagonist, learns that his beloved must marry a wealthy broker named Ephraims, "of the old Jewry." Ephraims never actually appears in the novel, but Mercutio repeatedly condemns his "damned avarice." The novel's second Jewish character plays a slightly more significant role in the plot of the second volume. When Mercutio's friends are captured by a Turkish pirate, they are brought to the slave markets of Constantinople. A wealthy Jewish merchant by the name of Aaron Levy swiftly pays their bond, freeing the captives; the narrator comments that "by the timely assistance of Levy, these people, who but a few hours before, reduced to a situation similar to the barbarously-treated Africans, having been exposed as objects of traffic, were now in the full enjoyment of personal freedom."[45] While previously in the novel Mercutio himself had been captured by Barbary pirates and enslaved in Algiers, only in association with Levy does the narrator connect such captivity to North American slavery. Butler's pair of Jews again reflect the risks and benefits of the diaspora. Ephraims, the Jew "at home," embodies a stereotypical Shylockian greed that threatens Mercutio's future as an English gentleman. The Jew abroad, on the other hand, can protect the white European-American subject from the barbarities of the Muslim world and ensure both freedom and mobility.

Returning to *The Algerine Spy* and *The Algerine Captive*, it is worth noting that both Jewish villains, the rabbi in Markoe's text and Ben Benjamin's son in Tyler's, remain unnamed, suggesting a further ambiguity and indecipherability to their characters. On the surface they seem to reflect the Shylockian stereotype in their greed and opportunism as well as in their all-consuming bitterness in the face of discrimination, but seen another way, they represent just the opposite. Shakespeare's character never lies; his fault is in his merciless insistence on the letter of the law and his entitlement to a pound of flesh. The Jewish villains of the Barbary archive, on the other hand, freely lie and break contracts, betraying the trust that underlies any rational form of global exchange, including the purchase of captives' freedom. Reviving the questions of textual authority in the previous chapters, we can see how, as Mufti writes, Jews become "a site for the elaboration of the constitutive narratives of modern life" in the context of republican print.[46] I want to suggest that Solomon Mendez and Ben Benjamin, in their honesty and fidelity, and in their roles carrying the letters of the spy and captive, respectively, represent the stability of text itself, while the anonymous rabbi and son constitute antitexts that challenge, like the threatening bodies of the Barbary pirates and spies themselves, the ideological underpinnings of the public sphere.

ROWSON'S GOOD JEW

In drawing these connections between Jewish figures in early American novels, I momentarily set aside the Jews that populated early American Barbary dramas, including, most notably, Susanna Rowson's *Slaves in Algiers; or, A Struggle for Freedom*. *Slaves in Algiers* centers on a daring escape attempt by American and British captives from the tyrannical dey of Algiers Muley Moloc and his renegado subordinate Ben Hassan, a Jewish convert to Islam. Early in the play Frederic, the leader of the Americans, plots with Ben Hassan to facilitate his escape, but he is soon betrayed. Fortunately, the Americans are aided by Ben Hassan's daughter, Fetnah, and the Muley Moloc's daughter, Zoriana, who are influenced by their American servants, Rebecca and Olivia, respectively. Both Fetnah and Zoriana become converts to the American cause, the former to avoid becoming the dey's latest wife and the latter for love of one of the captives. Along the way, Rebecca discovers that her British husband (and Olivia's father), Constant, is also a captive in Algiers. They are reunited, and the play ends with the new unified group of American and British captives storming the dey's palace, capturing both Muley Moloc and Ben Hassan, and forcing them to free all the slaves in the city.

While Markoe's and Tyler's Jews play small (but pivotal) roles in their respective novels, Ben Hassan looms as the principal antagonist of Rowson's play; he is, in Harap's estimation, an "unmitigated villain," more than willing to scheme with and then betray the desperate captives.[47] Fetnah, on the other hand, yearns to escape from Algiers and emigrate to America, actively aiding the slaves and even attempting a romance with one to ensure her future access to the republic. At first glance, Ben Hassan and Fetnah seem to follow closely the model of Shylock and his faithless daughter Jessica, a connection that few theatregoers in the early republic would fail to make. Several critics, however, have pointed to the more complicated genealogies behind these characters, especially Ben Hassan. Heather Nathans, for example, locates the renegado within a trans-Atlantic stage Jew tradition that includes not only Shylock but more contemporary characters such as Mordecai in Charles Macklin's *Love à la Mode* (1759), the second most recognizable Jewish role in the period. Nathans's reading points to the politics of Jewish masculinity in the late eighteenth century, emphasizing Rowson's "unmanning" of her Jewish villain, who resorts to crossdressing late in the play to escape the anger of the dey after the captives' escape.[48] Elizabeth Maddock Dillon's reading of the play points more directly at the racialization of the Jewish figures who, against the exotic background of Algiers and its Muslim natives, help to shore up both American national identity and trans-Atlantic white solidarity among the American and British characters a decade after the end of the Revolutionary War.[49] While Nathans and Dillon have provided considerable insight into these first modern Jews in American drama, the focus on Anglo-American relations has long overlooked the distinct tropes surrounding Jewish identity that characterize American Barbary works across genres. In the following section, I examine how Rowson's Jews reproduce a similar dialectic seen in Markoe and Tyler, while foregrounding the problems of text and body that I explored more thoroughly in previous chapters.

Rowson's play, which debuted in Philadelphia and was later performed in Baltimore, New York, Boston, and Charleston in subsequent years, was the first American drama to depict scenes from the United States' conflicts with the Barbary, yet even before 1794 the country's nascent theatre culture was involved in the Algerine Crisis. In several cases, acting troupes held fundraising events to provide support and even ransom for captives in Algiers. One such performance, held in Philadelphia in 1787, featured an address by theatre manager Lewis Hallam Jr. that turns on familiar notes connecting the enslavement of Americans in Algiers to a betrayal of the ideals of the Revolution:

> Behold! The barbarous triumphs of Algiers,
> See Christian blood, bedew the burning plains,
> And, friends to freedom languishing in chains! . . .
> Those veterans perhaps, whose patriot toil,
> Gave independence to their native soil,
> Lost in the sad vicissitudes of fate,
> Call on their country to repay the debt.

Repayment, according to Hallam, must come in the form of a "glitt'ring bribe," whereby "freedom from benevolence proceeds."[50] The rhetoric of the speech, circulated widely in newspapers, points to the theatre's role in performing solidarity with the faraway captives. In her book *New World Drama*, Dillon deploys the phrase "intimate distance" to describe the embodied performances of colonial culture that create intimacy "across great distances such as that between the colony and metropole, or that between Africa and the slave quarters of the New World plantation."[51] Hallam's entreaty to "behold" the blood-soaked plains of Algiers, like the appeal of the Patriot in *American in Algiers* discussed in chapter 1, creates a sense of temporal and geographic immediacy for the audience, collapsing the distance between Philadelphia and Algiers. The short speech is also noteworthy for its reframing of the very-recent war within the context of peacetime transnational capital and the slave trade; the debt of freedom can be paid, literally, in cold, hard cash.

The above performance was an early example of the kind of grassroots funding effort that became more common in the 1790s as the public became increasingly frustrated with the government's lack of progress in diplomatic negotiations.[52] In March 1794, Rowson's theatre troupe held just such a benefit night that included a "pantomimical dance" she authored entitled "The Sailor's Landlady." Less than a week before, the Philadelphia papers had printed several letters from Captain James Taylor, whose brig the *George* had recently been captured by pirates. Those letters, according to the *Philadelphia Gazette*, "ought to excite the pity, and call forth the immediate exertions of every citizen; so that our countrymen in captivity may find relief."[53] In response to that call to action, the benefit raised about nine hundred dollars after expenses.[54] As part of the program, Rowson's pantomime celebrated the bravery and generosity of American sailors, with a refrain of "To America, commerce and freedom."[55]

Slaves in Algiers premiered in Philadelphia three months after this benefit performance, and while one can never be certain of direct influence, Rowson undeniably embedded her play within a theatrical culture that saw itself playing a vital role, like the sailors of the song, in supporting "America," "commerce," and "freedom" with its involvement in the Algerine Crisis.[56] In the play's prologue, Rowson echoes Hallam's earlier call, asking, "What then behoves it, they who help'd gain, / A nation's freedom, feel the galling chain? / They, who a more than ten year's war withstood, / And stamp'd their country's honour with their blood?" While the preface to the printed play states the goal of the piece as to "call forth the tear of sensibility," the prologue establishes a more direct connection to the play's performance and the ransoming of the captives, beseeching that "each ear must listen to their distant cries; / Each hand must give, and the quick sail unfurl'd / Must bear their ransom to the distant world."[57] The repetition of "distant" emphasizes how the play imagines itself creating intimacy—sanctified by the blood of the patriot—back and forth across the Atlantic with the direct exchange of the captives' pleas and public ransom funds.

As Dillon has argued, Rowson's celebration of a "nationalist-branded commerce and liberty" in the play, connected with attempts to redeem the captives, finds its antithesis in Ben Hassan's greed and self-interest.[58] Like the Barbary Jews of the novels discussed above and the many stage Jews that came before him, Ben Hassan is primarily a money man, yet the play opens with him purposely obstructing the trans-Atlantic exchange of funds that should buy the freedom of his American house slave Rebecca. Ben Hassan is introduced into the play as he attempts to comfort and then seduce Rebecca, who laments that the ransom money she requested from her friends in the United States still has not arrived. Ben Hassan pleads with Rebecca to forget her ransom and agree to marry him; it is only when she leaves the stage that the audience learns in a short monologue that the captive's ransom, along with funds for the redemption of six other slaves, has already arrived and was pocketed by Ben Hassan. It is not, then, his commercial vocation that marks the Jew as the villain but rather his refusal to assent to a rational scheme of trans-Atlantic exchange. Even more than the dey of Algiers, Ben Hassan stands as an obstacle to white liberation through commerce.

Because Ben Hassan reveals his treachery to the audience early in the play, there is never any question about his status as a villain. As Rebecca leaves the stage, another American slave, Frederic, arrives to discuss his plot to purchase a vessel through Ben Hassan to escape the city. Even as the characters negotiate the price for the financier's involvement, Ben Hassan, in a series of gratuitous asides to the audience, admits his own plan to betray Frederic and his fellow captives. Several of these asides come midsentence, as Ben Hassan assures the American of his cooperation and then turns to the audience to reveal his true motives. In one typical example, he condemns the Moors as "uncharitable dogs," stating, "I feels very mush [sic] for the poor Christians; I should be very glad (aside) to have a hundred or two of them my prisoners."[59] One can imagine how awkward this dialogue would have been on stage, and the character's blatant duplicity was undoubtedly played for comic effect. In some ways, Ben Hassan seems a throwback to an earlier, almost clownish version of Shylock that was disappearing from the American stage by the end of the eighteenth century.[60] He relates his sordid past as a usurer and later a forger in England to Frederic in response to the latter's question of what prompted him to "put on the turban" (convert to Islam):

> Next to try my luck in the alley I vent,
> But of dat I soon grew tir'd and wiser;

Monies I lent out at fifty per cent.
And my name was I. H. in the Public Advertiser.

The next thing I did was a spirited prank,
Which at one stroke my fortune was made;
I wrote so very like the cashiers of the bank,
The clerks did not know the difference, and the monies was paid.

So, having cheated the Gentiles, as Moses commanded,
Oh! I began to tremble at every gibbet that I saw;
But I got on board a ship, and here was safely landed,
In spite of the judges, counsellors, attorneys, and law.[61]

As an Anglo-Jewish Muslim forger, would-be seducer, and financier to Barbary pirates, Ben Hassan is a veritable archive of early national literary villains, but beyond his comic excesses, he raises deeper questions about national and racial identity. Nominally a Muslim and a subject of the dey, he nevertheless seems out of place in Algiers, a point made evident in the fact that, among the multinational cast of characters from three continents, Ben Hassan is the only one to speak in dialect, replacing "w" with "v" and "s" with "sh" in the manner of a stereotypical British stage Jew. As a forger, his relation to his own identity and to textual authority are automatically put into question. Along these lines, his confessional monologue and asides in his first scene manifest his status of inhabiting two distinct and seemingly mutually exclusive frames, both Muslim and Jew, both East and West. Within this scheme, Rowson renders Jewishness as itself a kind of dramatic irony—an indelible mark of duplicity at the level of race that cannot be overwritten by conversion.

Ben Hassan's Jewishness manifests a kind of negativity of identity that limits his ability to assimilate to either the East or the West.[62] Despite supposedly embracing Islam, he cannot be more than, in Frederic's words, a "little Israelite."[63] His daughter Fetnah, however, strives for the hope of future assimilation (and for women's rights) afforded by republican rhetoric. Like her father, she remains disconnected from the cultural context of Algiers. She is the first character in the play to speak, and she does so lamenting having been chosen by the dey to be his latest wife. She complains that "he is old and ugly, then he wears such tremendous whiskers; and when he makes love, he looks so grave and stately, that I declare, if it was not for fear of his huge scymetar, I shou'd burst out laughing in his face." In a thinly masked double entendre, Fetnah is repulsed and threatened by the body of the despot. Fetnah's servant Selima wonders how Fetnah "conceived such an aversion to the manners of a country where [she was] born," at which point Fetnah reveals her past: "You are mistaken.—I was not born in Algiers, I drew my first breath in England; my father, Ben Hassan, as he is now called, was a Jew. I can scarcely remember our arrival here, and have been educated in the Moorish religion, tho' I always had a natural antipathy to their manners."[64] Fetnah is effectively homeless, distant from her birthplace and detached by "natural antipathy" from the Barbary. However, she soon relates to Selima that her "natural" inclinations were in fact taught to her by an American slave brought into her household. While Rowson clearly sets her up to be the good Jewish/Muslim character in opposition to her father, the depiction of Fetnah leads one to wonder whether she has any identity at all. Like Ben Hassan, Fetnah's Jewishness expresses itself as a kind of national/territorial negativity—a lack of belonging that sets her apart from both East and West in the play.

As Frederic's escape scheme and Ben Hassan's betrayal take their course, the plot of *Slaves in Algiers* begins to cohere around the story of several potential marriages, one of which is between Fetnah and Frederic. Throughout the play it is made clear that Fetnah merely sees this potential alliance with an Anglo-American man as an avenue through which she can escape the harem. Unwilling to submit to the dey's licentiousness, she is nevertheless willing to use her body to gain access to the republic. Desiring the rhetoric of America more than any specific American, Fetnah says, "I do wish, some dear, sweet, Christian man, would fall in love with me, break open the garden gates, and carry me off." During a chance encounter with Frederic in the garden of the dey's palace, she wastes little time on courtship: "*(Aside.)* Oh dear! What a charming man. I do wish he would run away with me." Frederic is already primed to accept her aggressive advances, having found a packet of love letters he assumes were addressed to him. Fetnah soon learns that these are Zoriana's love letters for another American slave, but she immediately takes ownership of them to further her own romance plot. In another aside, she schemes, "He takes me for some other, I'll not undeceive him, and may be, he'll carry off.— Yes, sire; yes, I did write to you."[65] Dillon argues that Rowson mocks Fetnah's romantic desires as "too politically (rather than personally) scripted," but more than simply scripted, we can read this as a wholesale appropriation or forging of republican rhetoric through a performative romantic attachment that emphasizes the artificiality of Fetnah's "natural inclinations."[66]

"A VAGUE RESEMBLANCE TO SOMETHING SEEN ELSEWHERE" 107

Unlike her father, Fetnah is not a villain, yet she does not fit as easily into the Manichean dialectic of Markoe and Tyler. Her overriding ambition to escape a future in the dey's harem makes her a sympathetic character, and even after she flees the city, she seeks out a group of escaped slaves and implores them to rescue Rebecca from her father's house. She also utters the closest thing in the play to an antislavery message, declaring, "It does not signify, that word slave does so stick in my throat—I wonder how any woman of spirit can gulp it down."[67] Nevertheless, throughout the play she remains trapped between the contesting forces of oriental embodiment and republican abstraction, body and text. Her first encounter with Frederic, with her numerous asides and blatant deception, mirrors the earlier scene between the captive and her father. Despite the fact that he is unaware of her heritage, Frederic refers to her as a "little infidel," echoing Ben Hassan as the "little Israelite." She may not be a forger, but she is more than willing to claim authorship of another's words for personal gain. Furthermore, her escape from Algiers involves disguising herself as the dey's son, literally putting on the turban just as her father does symbolically. In the end, the "bad" Jew and the "good" Jewess are two sides of the same coin; neither Ben Hassan nor Fetnah seem to *belong* anywhere, but both characters seek to ground themselves through a mixture of political expediency and sexual desire. In a broader sense, the differences between the two mark a contrast between British and American performances of Jewishness. Ben Hassan, with his accented speech and his stereotypical greed, echoes the British stage Jew tradition, whereas Fetnah's claiming of the letters and her desire to "dress" in republican rhetoric, just as her father "put on the turban," reflect an American anxiety over the inability to stabilize race and national identity in print. In other words, if the play overall focuses on the reconciliation of Anglo-American relations after the Revolution, as Dillon argues, Ben Hassan and Fetnah represent the demons that each side must exorcise to make possible that cultural reunification.

Rowson's play concludes with Ben Hassan's riches lost and the triumph of western freedom, represented by the reconciled Anglo-American family, over oriental despotism. Despite Frederic's freedom and his offer to take her home with him, Fetnah's romance with the American ends when she decides to remain in Algiers to take care of her now-impoverished father. Ultimately, Ben Hassan and Fetnah remain ashore in Algiers, never to threaten the coasts of America again. The daughter's decision to care for her father is repeated across characters at the play's resolution, with the American Olivia reasserting her own role as a good "daughter of Columbia."[68] Dillon argues that these parent-child reunions offer "a version of American political identity for women that does not involve breaking bonds with British parental authority and that enables a republican daughter to be both virtuous and American."[69] In contrast, Fetnah ultimately chooses blood and race over politics and liberty. The demands placed on her by the broken body of her Shylockian father foreclose the possibility of a Jewish future in America and her participation in an Anglo-American genealogy of liberty in the Atlantic world.

The same year that Rowson's play opened in Philadelphia, Absalom Jones and Richard Allen, two leaders in the city's Black community, were formulating their own claims to citizenship around the heroic work of African Americans to aid their fellow Philadelphians during the 1793 yellow fever epidemic. Derrick R. Spires argues that in their account of the epidemic, Jones and Allen theorized "neighborly citizenship as the proactive engagement with the suffering stranger."[70] Rowson's Jews, in their manipulation of the captive Americans, render themselves unworthy under this criterion for citizenship. The play ultimately reassures its audience that such figures, proven unfit for naturalization, would remain on their own side of the Atlantic.

"TAWNEY AS A MOOR"

As we have seen, Barbary Jews represented a large proportion of all contemporary Jews in republican-era literature and drama. Arguably it is not until Achsa Fielding in Charles Brockden Brown's novel *Arthur Mervyn* (1799–1800) that we see a major Jewish character in fiction with seemingly no connection to North Africa. Fielding, a wealthy British Jew who converted to Christianity before the events of the novel, has long been a mystery to Brown scholars, appearing seemingly out of nowhere and having only a vague connection to Jewish identity. In the following section, I argue that her character and sudden appearance late in the second half of the novel makes more sense when we consider the anxieties surrounding the ambiguities of Jewish racial identity represented by earlier Barbary Jews, particularly Rowson's Ben Hassan and Fetnah. As discussed, Jews conspiring with Barbary pirates and those who were Muslim or at least "Moorish" like

Ben Hassan and Fetnah raised questions not only about the trustworthiness of Jewish bankers in North Africa but also about the essential content of Jewish identity. In Rowson's play, Fetnah states that in England, Ben Hassan "*was* a Jew," while in her first encounter with Frederic she states decisively, "I'm not a moriscan." She never tells the American who she is, nor does he recognize her Jewish heritage or relation to Ben Hassan.[71] Fetnah places her father's (and by extension, her) Jewish identity in the past; nevertheless, the play itself seems to argue throughout that once a Jew, always a Jew in the new trans-Atlantic racial order.

The Barbary context allows us to see how Brown experiments with these same racial dimensions of citizenship. He might have had characters like Fetnah in mind when, in an 1800 article for the *Monthly Magazine and American Review*, he pondered the question of what defined a Jew. Is it a creed? A race? Do children inherit Jewishness according to the principle of hypo-descent? Brown offers few answers, but his analysis leads him to conclude that Jews are defined by "opinion," by "descent," or by some combination of the two: "If opinion and descent together make a Jew, then it is impossible to ascertain the genuineness of a Jew. If definite pedigree be not necessary to make a Jew, what number of generations must pass before he acquires all the penalties and privileges annexed to this people? Are they five, ten, fifteen, or twenty generations? And where is to be found the tree of any Jew's pedigree?"[72] Failing to reach a decisive answer to the question, Brown shifts the issue to one of Jewish futurity and, ultimately, to assimilation. The unasked question in the final lines of the essay might as well be, how long does it take a Jew to become a good white citizen, like us? As Brown's unanswered question demonstrates, Jewish ambiguity represented not only a concern for national foreign relations but also a challenge to emerging scientific taxonomies of race such as those developed in Thomas Jefferson's *Notes on the State of Virginia* (1785) and further codified at the turn of the century through works such as British physician Charles White's *The Regular Gradation of Man* (1799).[73] It is within the context of "the incipient arrival of scientific racism as a tactic for containing class and gender insubordination" that critics have read Brown's query and connected it to Fielding's introduction in part 2 of *Arthur Mervyn*, published just two months before the essay.[74]

Fielding's late introduction into the narrative complicates an already fractured text that extends across two distinct sections published a year apart. The first part of *Arthur Mervyn*, published in 1799 and subtitled *Memoirs of the Year 1793*, follows the titular protagonist as he leaves his family home in rural Pennsylvania and arrives in Philadelphia just before the yellow fever epidemic of 1793. Mervyn meets a thief, forger, and murderer named Welbeck, who has seduced and deserted a rich Italian woman named Clemenza Lodi. After confronting Welbeck over the pregnant Lodi and her stolen money, Mervyn ends the novel's first part sick from the fever. He collapses on the street, where he is found and nursed back to health by a friend, Dr. Stevens. *Arthur Mervyn*'s second half, which Brown himself described not as a simple continuation of the story but as a "sequel," extends the chronology past the yellow fever epidemic and into 1794. The plot picks up where the first left off, with a recovered Mervyn setting out to rescue Lodi and Eliza Hadwin, a young woman he meets in a farm outside of the city whose family had died of the fever. While searching for Lodi in a bordello, he first encounters the mysterious Achsa Fielding. Mervyn finds himself entranced by Fielding, a friend of Lodi, learning only later that she is a British divorcee hiding her Jewish heritage. Over the course of the last quarter of the novel, Mervyn describes his enchantment with Fielding as he learns more about her background. In the final pages, he proposes to Fielding, and the novel ends with the now engaged Mervyn planning to travel abroad in Europe with his soon-to-be wife.

Critical readings over the last two decades, focusing mainly on the plague narrative of the first half, have explored the novel's articulation of race and the connections it draws between the yellow fever and Black communities both in Philadelphia and in the Caribbean. Sean X. Goudie, in his influential essay on specularity and racial taxonomy, argues that, within the novel, "West Indian and Anglo-American cultures and commodities clash and cohere in ways that resist hegemonic attempts to domesticate West Indian figures within their discursive constructions of a resolutely *white* empire."[75] In another vital reading, Michael J. Drexler points out how the yellow fever provides a metaphor for critiquing a country "infected by foreign ideas" from the Caribbean and revolutionary France.[76] Many critics cite an incident in which Arthur Mervyn is knocked unconscious by an assumedly Black worker collecting the bodies of plague victims as a commentary on white American reactions to the ongoing interracial violence of the Haitian Revolution.[77] While there are variations within these readings, recent scholarship has cohered around the work's hemispheric racial commentary, within which the fever operates allegorically as the irrational violence underlying colonial hierarchies.

In contrast, readers have long been puzzled by the abrupt shift in the novel's plot in its second part. In his biography of Brown, William Dunlap, a close friend of Brown, comments that the second half suffers from "every species of fault which a man of Mr. Brown's talents could be guilty of," and that "the reader is soon convinced that the work has no plan." The biographer uncharitably concludes that, "both as a continuation of a preceding work, and as a work of itself, the reader is subjected to continual disappointments."[78] While Dunlap's short assessment of the novel does not comment on the character of Fielding, other critics have wondered why Brown chose to suddenly introduce a Jewish character as Mervyn's love interest. As Goudie puts it, the novel's resolution has "disturbed generations of readers" with its "unfathomability."[79] Harap states bluntly, "We know no reason why Brown should have created Achsa as Jewish." Even as he celebrates the character for being perhaps the first Jew in either British or American literature to thoroughly defy common Jewish stereotypes, Harap notes that there seems to be little positive meaning to Fielding's identity, concluding that, "to be sure, Achsa is not a 'Jewish' Jew. But neither is she a stereotype."[80] Interestingly, to make his case that Brown's Fielding breaks from the popular image of the Jew (largely drawn from British novels and dramas), Harap has to define the character by its negativity: an un-Jewish Jew. Perhaps because of the apparent lack of content in Fielding's Jewish identity, critics have attempted to incorporate her into the novel's larger discussion of Black and mixed-race identities. Shapiro, for example, repeatedly describes Fielding as "exotic" and suggests that Fielding "may be using the unverifiable claim of her southern European Jewishness as a passing cover story for her (Caribbean) mixed race." Ultimately, Mervyn's marriage to Fielding "conveys the claim that the traumatic history of Atlantic slavery and white fear of black agency can be removed in a time of revolutionary action."[81] Similarly, Samuel Otter argues that Fielding's complexion, described at one point as "dark and almost sallow," "links her visually with the African Americans who served during the epidemic."[82] In the absence of a clear rationale behind Fielding's Jewishness, critics have naturally assumed that it stands as an encoding of or proxy for Blackness.

I argue that such readings that seek to position Fielding's exoticism within a more familiar Black-white binary are, in light of the Barbary archive, unnecessarily reductive. The most common single piece of textual evidence cited in proof of her possible mixed-race heritage involves Dr. Stevens's less than flattering description of her appearance: "She is unsightly as a night-hag, tawney as a moor, the eye of a gypsey."[83] In his article cited above and in the notes for the 2008 edited edition of *Arthur Mervyn*, Shapiro identifies "tawney as a moor" to be "a period code for blackness," an assertion echoed by Carroll Smith-Rosenberg, who claims that the phrase represents Fielding as "unmistakably black."[84] In support of this reading of Fielding's Blackness, several critics have cited Brown's use of the term "tawney" to describe the skin of the earlier assailant who ambushes Mervyn and knocks him unconscious.[85] The term "tawney," however, had a far more varied usage in the period than to just refer to sub-Saharan or mixed-race heritage. In between the publication of the two halves of *Arthur Mervyn*, Brown described the "tawny and terrific visage" of one of the Native American raiders in *Edgar Huntley* (1799).[86] Early in the eighteenth century, Benjamin Franklin, in an essay about preserving the "lovely White and Red" of American skin colors, used the term to refer specifically to North African, Arab, and South Asian peoples, observing that "all *Africa* is black or tawny. *Asia* chiefly tawny."[87] While undoubtedly signaling some form of nonwhiteness, it cannot necessarily be assumed that the term refers to mixed-race or Black heritage.

Importantly, Dr. Stevens describes Fielding not only as tawney but tawney as a *moor*. While critics again have tended to equate "Moor" with "Black," we know from the Barbary archive that Americans at the end of eighteenth century knew quite well that Moors were just one of many different peoples inhabiting North Africa, distinct from West and Central Africans. In *A Short Account of Algiers* (1794), Mathew Carey identifies "swarthy" Moors as one of the principle peoples of Algiers but associates them specifically with Arabs, commenting that the terms "Moor" and "Arab" "appear to be synonymous."[88] Throughout 1799, Brown reprinted in the *Monthly Magazine* excerpts from Mungo Park's *Travels in the Interior Districts of Africa* (1799) that drew a clear distinction between North African "Moors" and sub-Saharan "Negroes," frequently noting how the former exploited the latter.[89] Writing years after the return of the surviving captives from Algiers, Brown may have encountered an early account such as John Foss's *A Journal, of the Captivity and Sufferings of John Foss* (1798), in which he describes the many variations in skin color in Algiers, including Moors as having "a very dark complexion, much like the Indians in North America," and the mixed-race offspring of Moorish mothers and Turkish fathers as having "a more tawney complexion" than Turks in general.[90] Given that the Algerine Crisis had ended only a few years before, Brown would have had many opportunities to encounter descriptions of Moors as Moors and not simply as coded African American and Afro-Caribbean figures.

Commenting on the vastness and ambition of the novel, Drexler writes, "From rural Chester County, Pennsylvania, to the streets of Philadelphia, from Charleston, South Carolina, to Baltimore, and from France to England and Revolutionary Saint-Domingue (soon to become Haiti), the geography of *Arthur Mervyn* is global."[91] Africa is notably absent from this span of territories and interconnections within the novel; acknowledging the Moorish hue and Egyptian/gypsy eye of Fielding's Sephardic Atlantic identity offers a link to North Africa and a very different geography of liberty and slavery that complicates the racial dynamics of republican Philadelphia in 1794, the year that Ben Hassan and Fetnah first mounted the stage of the Chestnut Street Theatre as well as the year Carey first published his *Short Account*.[92] Fielding's puzzling qualities become more explicable when we can read her not just as a response to more general Anglo-American stereotypes of Jewishness with their origins in *The Merchant of Venice* but rather as a more direct answer to the distinctly American concerns over trans-Atlantic mobility, assimilation, and Jewish futurity raised in the context of the Algerine Crisis.

From her introduction in the story, Fielding appears embedded within "the mysteries of the Orient."[93] Mervyn first encounters her when he visits Mrs. Villars's brothel in search of Lodi. Hearing her voice through the door, Mervyn describes its "accents . . . as musical as those of Clemenza, but were in other respects, different." Her voice contains a subtle strangeness that marks her as akin to another Mediterranean character, yet she retains an indeterminate quality only explained much later in the novel with the revelation of her Jewish identity. As Mervyn enters the room, he encounters two women in a scene that closely recalls descriptions of seraglios and harems popular in the period. He observes, "Two females, arrayed with voluptuous negligence, in a manner adapted to utmost seclusion, and seated in careless attitude, on a sofa, were now discovered."[94] In depicting this "temple of voluptuousness," Brown may have had in mind an article printed in the *Monthly Magazine* in August 1799 that described the "Condition of the Female Sex at Constantinople." Detailing the lives of the women in the sultan's seraglio, the author notes, "They depend entirely upon their female slaves for amusements, which have any thing like gaiety for their object, recline on their sofas for hours, whilst dancing, comedy, and buffoonery, as indelicate as our vulgar puppet show, are exhibited before them." The article mentions later that "all the Levantine women, from their mode of sitting on their sofa, stoop extremely, and walk very awkwardly."[95] This emphasis on the effect of the sofa on the body of the "Levantine" women, an adjective that occasionally but did not always signify Jewishness, sheds light on Dr. Stevens's observation later in the novel that Fielding is "low in stature, contemptibly diminutive, scarcely bulk enough to cast a shadow as she walks, less luxuriance than a charred log, fewer elasticities than a sheet pebble."[96] The punchline of the scene finally lands when Mervyn and the reader learn that Fielding was unaware that the Villars house was a bordello, casting her character as a seemingly paradoxical mix of oriental excess and innocence.

The scene of Fielding's first appearance in the novel offers multiple parallels to the moment in *Slaves in Algiers* when Frederic meets Fetnah in the dey's garden. Both women are surrounded by oriental opulence that they ultimately reject. Fetnah has been sold to the dey by her father, while Mervyn mistakes Fielding for a prostitute. Both women are displaced, but in neither case does the American love interest recognize their Jewishness (neither has a Jewish name)—that Fielding is later described as Moorish recalls Fetnah's only direct statement about her own identity, that she is "not a moriscan." Both are ready for the virtuous American to rescue them from the excesses of the seraglio. Timothy Marr writes that, in the context of Islamic excess, the civilizing project of republicanism "worked to transmute the unregulated freedom of sexual desire into virtuous female action, often in the service of patriotic ends." In both works, foreign women are trapped by the lust of the "Turks" around them, awaiting the American hero to "cleanse libidinous desires of sensual excess by sublimating its thrills into a moral economy of national virtue."[97]

After the initial scene in Mrs. Villars's house, Fielding returns to the novel as Mervyn visits her to ask for her assistance with Eliza Hadwin. This time, Mervyn finds himself in far less "voluptuous" surroundings: "I was admitted to Mrs. Fielding's presence without scruple or difficulty. There were two females in her company, and one of the other sex, well dressed, elderly, and sedate persons. . . . They talked of fleets and armies, of Robespierre and Pitt, of whom I had only a newspaper knowledge." Rather than orientalized sensuality, in this scene Fielding embodies a kind of knowing and circulation within the larger trans-Atlantic world. Mervyn feels unable to participate within this cosmopolitan circle because he recognizes his own understanding of European events as mediated through an inefficient exchange of print and thus lacking the immediacy of experience. The way Fielding embodies knowledge in opposition to print here foreshadows the later scene in which Mervyn discovers the truth behind her identity. In a moment of racial recognition that seems to undercut the uncertainty surrounding the category of the Jew in Brown's later article, Mervyn stops Fielding mid-conversation to remark on something he has suddenly seen:

> One evening, she had been talking very earnestly on the influence annexed, in Great Britain, to birth, and had given me some examples of this influence. Meanwhile, my eyes were fixed steadfastly on hers. The peculiarity in their expression never before affected me so strongly. A vague resemblance to something seen elsewhere, on the same day, occurred, and occasioned me to exclaim, suddenly in a pause of her discourse—
>
> As I live, my good mamma, those eyes of yours have told me a secret. I almost think they spoke to me; and I am not less amazed at the strangeness than at the distinctness of their story.
>
> And pry'thee what have they said?
>
> Perhaps I was mistaken. I might have been deceived by a fancied voice, or have confounded one word with another near akin to it; but let me die, if I did not think they said that you were—*a Jew*.[98]

I quote this passage at length because both the context and the rendering of this revelation are steeped in the racial and print ideologies that underlie the novel. Within this dialogue "birth" becomes a signifier that highlights the difference between British and American cultures. Mervyn disrupts and replaces Fielding's discussion of birth in the context of socioeconomic class with one of racial identity. At the same time, this sudden moment of recognition comes from an unexplained event in Mervyn's own circulation around Philadelphia—something seen elsewhere that day—rather than from his "newspaper knowledge." Fielding's racial identity becomes legible through the geographical referent of an unexplained and unlocated "elsewhere." For Mervyn, direct bodily experience is needed to unmask the Jewish figure.[99] While, as Michael Warner argues, "Brown implicitly identifies his writing with the validity of the public sphere," print alone is ineffective in unmasking and translating Fielding's strangeness.[100] Mervyn's odd metaphor of the eye that speaks suggests what print is, or should be but is not. Just as she entered the novel as a voice that is "musical" but "different," her "gypsey" eyes allegedly speak to Mervyn in order to betray her "secret." Jewishness defies legibility, and Mervyn must have recourse to a fantasy of spoken authenticity, even if it is just a metaphor that replaces the importance of print in the novel to this point.

With this sudden revelation from Mervyn, Fielding confesses her secret: her father was a Portuguese-born Jew who settled in England. Yet, if she herself is a Jew by birth, her description of her life evacuates this Jewishness of any particularity. In discussing her father, she actually confirms antisemitic stereotypes: "He had few of the moral or external qualities of Jews. For I suppose there is some justice in the obloquy that follows them so closely." While marking her father as the exception, she reinforces the connection between external and moral qualities inherent in racial ideology. As she relates her own history, she also makes clear that there is no specific religious dimension to her Jewish identity. She describes her education as "purely English," and that, unable to understand the difference between herself and her peers, she "grew more indifferent, perhaps, than was proper to the distinctions of religion." On falling in love with a young aristocrat named Sir Ralph Fielding, she readily converts to Anglicanism. Her marriage and conversion ultimately save her from poverty after her father's bankruptcy and suicide. Strikingly, Fielding's relationship with her father inverts the earlier model of Ben Hassan and Fetnah. While Fetnah's flaw is a filiopiety toward her nonwhite father, Fielding readily abandons her Jewish identity: "My own heart having abjured my religion, it was absurd to make any difficulty about a formal renunciation." Furthermore, she admits to being influenced by the "disrepute and scorn which the Jewish nation are every where condemned."[101]

Unlike earlier representations, Fielding has no "bad Jew" counterpart within the novel. Instead, she can be read as a synthesis of previous characters. In one sense, Fielding operates as a kind of sequel to Fetnah: she married, converted, and embraced a non-Jewish future, yet like Ben Hassan, she retains a mark of difference that ensures her enduring outsider status. The content of that difference remains unarticulated, as Brown never seems to explain what about Fielding is Jewish. What actually signaled to Mervyn her Jewish past? Goudie argues that Fielding constitutes the final test of Mervyn's ability to "'fix' and classify racial others," and his success rewards him with access to the wider world, where he can continue to develop his intellectual faculties.[102] Within the novel, Achsa Fielding's race necessarily complicates the taxonomies that the emerging urbanite attempts to stabilize. This lack of fixity translates to Mervyn's greater dissatisfaction with print itself. Shortly after this pivotal scene, Mervyn begins to complain of the "lifelessness" of books, and he celebrates Fielding's "discourse" as "so versatile; so bending to the changes of occasion; so obsequious to my curiosity, and so abundant in that very knowledge in which I was most deficient, and on which I set the most value, the knowledge of the human heart."[103] In contrast to the stability and autonomy of print, the voice and body of Fielding represent a highly mutable and accommodating discursive field.

Mervyn brings his narrative to a close as he prepares with his future wife to leave America for Europe. The novel ends with Mervyn accessing larger trans-Atlantic networks of circulation and understanding through the body of the Jew. In this sense, Fielding's identity serves a similar purpose to Jewish figures in Markoe's, Tyler's, and Rowson's texts. Like in *Slaves in Algiers*, sexual desire and the Jewish body are associated with the Atlantic crossing. Yet, the Mervyn-Fielding relationship in some ways reverses Rowson's less successful pairing of Frederic and Fetnah. In Brown's novel, it is the young republican who pursues the Jewish "secret" in order to access alternate epistemologies of embodied knowledge beyond the ideology of republican print. Mervyn "rescues" Fielding from her initial scene in Mrs. Villars's house of oriental mystery and excess, a move representative of what contemporary critics have theorized as Brown's mission to rehabilitate the image of the Jew. Ultimately, however, the novel's resolution brings us back to questions of Jewish ambiguity and futurity raised by Tyler and Rowson. Brown does break from Shylockian tropes in his representation of Fielding, but he plays on a distinctly American stereotype of the doubled Jew, manifest here in the split between her hidden Jewish past and more proper Anglo-Atlantic present. Fielding's identity inhabits a vague middle ground between culture and body that very much reflects the ways in which Jews challenged the rhetorical and racial stability of citizenship just as they complicated the nation's projection of power abroad. As the ending of the novel makes clear, rather than providing a synthesis of the dialectic discussed across multiple works of the Algerine Crisis—of good and bad Jew and of body and text—Brown fails to (or declines to) imagine a future for Jews in America. Jewish futurity must be "seen elsewhere."

LATER BARBARY JEWS

Barbary Jews were often depicted as playing a significant role in the Algerine Crisis, but the situation in North Africa was somewhat different during the period of the Tripolitan War from 1801 to 1805. Jewish power and influence declined across the region, with tensions between Jewish communities and Muslim leaders exploding in 1800 and 1804 into widespread pogroms.[104] Meanwhile, the construction of new American frigates to protect the country's shipping meant that there was less to fear from a Muslim-Jewish conspiracy. In the wake of William Eaton's expedition in 1805 and the settlement with Tripoli, triumphalist Barbary dramas continued to include Jewish characters, but primarily to demonstrate how the country had outgrown its dependence on the Sephardic diaspora for control of trans-Atlantic exchange. Take, for example, James Ellison's *The American Captive; or, Siege of Tripoli* (1812). If Rowson's earlier play, as Dillon argues, celebrates the power of virtuous American commerce against the greed and selfishness of Ben Hassan, Ellison's play lauds the ability of American military power, through "the magnanimous conduct of our brave countrymen, Commodore PREBLE and General EATON," to surpass the reach and influence of Jewish brokers. The setup of the play seems drawn directly from a major plot point in *Slaves in Algiers*: an American captive held in Tripoli falls in love with the exiled former bashaw's daughter, Immorina, who then schemes with a Jewish banker named Ishmael to facilitate the American's escape. Ishmael, the lone Jewish figure in the play, is one of only two characters to speak in dialect, the other being the African American cook Juba. Juba appears only briefly on stage to prove to a Tripolitan slave master that there is no slavery in the American North—although, ironically, he calls the white sailor "massa."[105] Ishmael and Juba are only minor characters, but their distinct speech points to a shared undercurrent of racial otherness located elsewhere from both America and Tripoli.

In Ellison's story, Ishmael is no mastermind. Ishmael first appears in the play counting his money and cackling to himself about how remaining unmarried allowed him to preserve his fortune. Unlike the lecherous Ben Hassan, Ishmael is wholly consumed with his wealth to the detriment of his future. When Immorina approaches him about smuggling the American captive out of the city, he refuses but must eventually consent after she blackmails him with a debt that he owes her father. After a short dialogue in which Ishmael instructs the American to sneak away from the city as part of a departing caravan, Ishmael falls out of the action entirely. Notably, part of the plan has the American disguise himself as a Jewish merchant—in this play, the "good Jew" is just a white American appropriating the powers of Jewish mobility. Ishmael has no role in the plot to follow, as the escaped American joins Eaton's expedition then approaching to reinstall Immorina's father. Meanwhile, Commodore Edward Preble arrives by sea to threaten the city. Far from pulling the strings, Ishmael operates as a minor plot point, and the freedom he facilitates for the American captive means little, since the city would soon be conquered anyway.[106]

A similar, almost ritualistic dismissal of Barbary Jews occurs in Jonathan S. Smith's later play *The Siege of Algiers* (1823), composed years after the American victory in the Second Barbary War of 1815 and the effective end of the crises period. Smith reduces his Jewish character to a tragic figure doomed before the curtain even rises; the play's dramatic personae lists the character David Brokereye as "a Hebrew money changer of great note, decapitated by the Dey, through the intrigues of his Prime Minister."[107] Harap remarks that Brokereye seems to have been directly inspired by the Algerian Jewish Bacri family.[108] The play's description of Brokereye includes clear markers of Jewish identity but resists the characteristics of physical degradation common to stereotypical depictions: "A man of middle stature, well set, black beard, penetrating eye, and commanding countenance—he wore a blue tunic, petticoat trousers, black silk scull cap, and iron bound slip shods."[109] To the extent that he seems to embody moderation and understatement, he resists orientalization, although this in itself does not afford the character any sense of belonging. Like Ishmael, he finds himself ultimately marginalized by the larger movements of the plot. Sadly, Brokereye's end comes halfway through the play, as one of the dey's servant's indebted to the banker accuses the Jew of exposing the Algerian court's secrets to the Christian world through letters to newspapers in Europe. Once again, the North African Jewish character is accused of spying, yet Brokereye reverses previous representations by aligning more with the West than the East. Even so, he plays a vanishingly small role in the overall plot, which here involves the British consul scheming with the dey to undermine the United States. Overall, the trajectories of Jewish characters across these two later plays suggest that national and imperial relationships finally supplant the powerful and potentially treacherous Sephardic diaspora.

In this chapter, I outlined how the opposition between good and bad Barbary Jews across print and performance diverged from British Shylockian models but provoked larger taxonomic problems of race and citizenship during the Algerine Crisis. More than defying stereotype, these Jewish characters subverted the discourse of "type" itself, inevitably provoking anxieties over questions of national inclusion. However, as we can see in Ellison's and Smith's later plays, the Jew returns in triumphalist narratives after the Tripolitan War only to be rendered impotent. No longer able to mastermind the Barbary menace, the Jewish character becomes a degraded relic or fragment, signifying little aside from its otherness to both western and eastern cultures. In the next chapter, I tell the other half of this story, as I consider how one Jewish writer, Mordecai Manuel Noah, wrote back against the "Barbarization" of American Jewish identity to develop his own authorial and performative identity in the post-crises period.

CHAPTER FOUR

PERFORMING DIASPORA IN NOAH'S TRAVELS

"Malack, Muley." See Noah, Mordecai Manuel.

  —Entry in *American Authors, 1600–1900* (1938)

To this point I have primarily explored the impacts of the late eighteenth-century Algerine Crisis on early republican debates over race, slavery, and the public sphere, with each chapter offering a glimpse of how those discussions shifted during and after the Barbary Wars in the nineteenth century. In this chapter, I set up the second half of this book's focus on the post-crises period with an in-depth look at a long-neglected later Barbary text: Jewish American author Mordecai Manuel Noah's *Travels in England, France, Spain, and the Barbary States* (1819), his account of service as the American consul to Tunis from 1813 to 1815. I single out this particular text for the way it responds to many earlier representations of Barbary Muslims and Jews while setting the stage for how the crises would be reinterpreted through the lens of antebellum racial politics. In other words, I examine the *Travels* as a case study for how our reading across the Barbary archive can help us develop narrative linkages between the literary and theatrical cultures of the early republic and later nineteenth-century modes of racial representation and performance. By doing so, I also work to recover a vital text in the early development of Jewish American identity that expands our understanding of minority authorship in the period.

Relatively unknown to critics until recently but now the subject of a growing body of scholarship within both theatre studies and Jewish American literary criticism, Noah was a major player in the literature and politics of New York City in the 1820s and 1830s. He was most likely the most prominent Jewish public figure in the country up to the Civil War. As a playwright, he composed a number of very popular melodramas and would edit several widely read and influential New York newspapers, including the *National Era* and the *New-York Enquirer*. In 1836, the *New-York Mirror* identified Noah among twelve other writers, including Washington Irving, James Fenimore Cooper, and William Cullen Bryant, as part of America's flourishing "literati."[1] As a diplomat and politician, in addition to his consulship, he served briefly as the sheriff of New York in the early 1820s and would become a leading figure within the Tammany Hall political machine later in that decade. Today, however, he is most well-known among scholars for his attempt in 1825 to establish a Jewish colony—Ararat, the City of Refuge—on the Niagara River outside of Buffalo, New York. Ararat itself was never actually settled, but the failed venture stands as one of the most interesting public events in early nineteenth-century American Jewish history.

Among critical studies of Noah, the spectacular failure of Ararat has unquestionably overshadowed the significance of the earlier *Travels*.[2] The work narrates Noah's misadventures traveling to Tunis in the midst of the War of 1812, his work in the city during the Second Barbary War, and finally his dramatic dismissal from his post. Noah embarked for Tunis on the schooner *Joel Barlow* in 1813, but while crossing the Atlantic, he was captured by a British warship and taken to London, where he was held for nine weeks. After his release, Noah traveled to Spain and then through France to finally arrive at his post in Tunis. During his trip he would attempt to carry out secret instructions given to him by then–secretary of state James Monroe by hiring a Maryland native, Richard Keene, to travel to Algiers and ransom the Americans held in the city at the time. After serving in Tunis for little more than a year, he was unceremoniously removed from his post in a letter from Monroe delivered by Tripolitan War hero Stephen Decatur. Historians have suggested that the reason for Noah's abrupt dismissal was the poor performance of Keene, who thoroughly botched the negotiations with Algiers. As biographer Jonathan D. Sarna suggests, "There is no mystery as to why the President recalled Noah."[3]

If Noah had been dismissed explicitly for his lack of judgment in hiring Keene, there likely would have been little controversy; however, the reason given by Monroe in his letter to Noah offered a very different rationale:

"At the time of your appointment, as Consul at Tunis, it was not known that the religion which you profess would form any obstacle to the exercise of your Consular functions. Recent information, however, on which entire reliance may be placed, proves that it would produce a very unfavorable effect."[4] Historians have frequently expressed confusion as to why Noah's dismissal was framed this way. As Noah pointed out, it was precisely his Jewish identity that led previous diplomats such as Joel Barlow to recommend Noah for the post in the first place with the hope that he could be effective in negotiating with the rich Jewish banking families in Algiers. In his correspondence, Barlow noted that David Bacri, the head of the powerful Bacri family, "has more influence with the Dey than all the Regency put together."[5] The stated rationale for Noah's dismissal prompted calls for an explanation from a number of prominent American Jews, offering a valuable moment of solidarity across the country's small but growing Jewish communities. However, equally important here is the way that, as Lotfi Ben Rejeb observes, the State Department deployed North African Muslims as a scapegoat for expressing its own dissatisfaction with Noah's performance.[6] Whatever the actual motivation, the stated reason for the dismissal shaped Noah's account of his consulship and its triangulation of Jewish, American, and Muslim North African identities throughout the *Travels*.

On its surface, Noah's *Travels* reads as part modern political memoir, aimed at rehabilitating his career after the disgrace of his dismissal, and part traditional travelogue, with its exhaustive observations on European and North African society. Central to both, I argue, is the way Noah constructs himself as a character in his narrative. As James Clifford has argued, the ethnographer is fundamentally "a character in a fiction," and we can see that throughout his ethnographic ramblings in the *Travels*, Noah engages in forms of "cultural *poesis*," "the constant reconstitution of selves and others through specific exclusions, conventions, and discursive practices."[7] These acts of self-fashioning, however, are uniquely complicated by his need both to balance his American and diasporic Jewish identities and to respond to the stereotypes surrounding orientalized Jewish identity on display in so many representations of Barbary Jews. Along these lines, the text can be read productively in the context of the writer's theatrical career. Even before assuming his post, Noah had established himself as a promising young playwright in his native Philadelphia, having already written the play *The Wandering Boys* (1812). In 1819, the same year he published the *Travels*, his most successful play, *She Would Be a Soldier*, opened at New York's Park Theatre. The fact that critics of the *Travels* derisively referred to the work as a "performance" speaks to Noah's reputation principally as a playwright.[8] Accordingly, I argue that the text can be read as itself a performance history, a record of moments or set pieces in which Noah, as an agent of an aspiring proto-imperial state, performs "American-Jewish symbiosis" in the presence of American, European, and African audiences.[9] The work ultimately seeks to contest the stereotypes of Barbary Jewish identity I explored in the previous chapter by positing new performative notions of minority citizenship that reconcile national and transnational claims to identity.[10]

As a landmark Jewish American text, the *Travels* constitutes not only the most thorough denunciation of antisemitism from a Jewish writer in the period but also a vital record of the emergence of forms of Jewish diasporic performance culture that most historians and critics locate much later in the nineteenth century.[11] Going further, the text exemplifies too the problematic history of Jews locating their racial identity within the Black-white binary—of Jews "becoming white" by channeling racial antagonisms. Extensive scholarly work has been done to examine Jewish anti-Black racism and its ties to performance culture; critics such as Michael Rogin and Lori Harrison-Kahan have explored Jewish Blackface minstrelsy and what the latter calls the "Black-Jewish imaginary," but they have done so exclusively within the context of the twentieth century. Those narratives focus primarily on how appropriations of Blackness served to "shore up" whiteness, even as these performances might trouble discrete racial dynamics.[12] Throughout my analysis below, I explore how Noah navigates a similar dynamic as he seeks to decouple the historic association of Jewish figures with Muslim North Africa. In short, Noah's *Travels* allows us to recover the forgotten Barbary history of Jewish racialization in the United States and how that process spawned new forms of Jewish American performance.

MULY MALAK IN THE HOLY CITY

Noah's effectiveness as a transitionary figure emerges from the ways in which he grounds his account of his misadventures in Europe and Tunis in republican-era literary and theatrical cultures. Born in Philadelphia in 1785, Noah came of age reading many of the works I explored in previous chapters, and their influence on his career can be seen even before he embarked for Tunis. In 1812, as Noah waited to receive his appointment, he relocated temporarily to Charleston, South Carolina, where he launched his career as a political journalist writing articles for a local newspaper, *The Times*. These short articles included a series of fictional letters under the headline of "Oriental Correspondence," written by a Turkish observer named "Muly Malak," who reports on social and political developments in Charleston to his master in Aleppo. The first installment of the series appeared on April 15, 1812, with the heading: "Copy of a Letter from Muly Malak, Agent for the House of Sadi Hamet at Aleppo, to Caled the Elder, Aga of the Janizaries; Giving a Description of Charleston, the Manners and Customs of the Inhabitants. (Translated from the Arabic)." As I explored in chapter 2, the oriental spy/observer genre has a long trans-Atlantic history, with Peter Markoe reaching back as far as the seventeenth century for inspiration for *The Algerine Spy in Pennsylvania* (1787). The most obvious immediate source for Noah's Muly Malak letters, however, would have been Washington Irving's Mustapha letters, published just a few years earlier. It is easy to see Irving's influence on Noah, who had already previously attempted to imitate *Salmagundi* in a publication started by him and his friends in Philadelphia entitled *The Trangram; or, The Fashionable Trifler*.[13] Although the periodical was short-lived, Noah clearly drew from Irving as a model for his own emerging career in political journalism.

"Oriental Correspondence" is heavily indebted to the Mustapha letters in both structure and content, but Noah adds a subtle Jewish American twist to this already somewhat outdated genre, drawing on his own insider-outsider position. As Sarna points out, Noah chose the name Muly Malak because of his first two initials, M. M., perhaps parodying the longstanding accusations of a Muslim-Jewish conspiracy.[14] But the name too has a long history in Anglo-American performance culture. The name Muly Malak, spelled a variety of different ways, refers to the historical Mulai Abd el-Malik, the king of Fez and Morocco between 1576 and 1578. This king provided the inspiration for several Muslim monarchs on stage, including Mully Molucco in George Peele's *The Battle of Alcazar* (1589) and Muley-Moluch, the emperor of Barbary in John Dryden's *Don Sebastian, King of Portugal* (1689).[15] Noah may have been aware of this older British theatrical tradition, but the most obvious inspiration for this pseudonym is the character of Muley Moloc, the dey of Algiers from Susanna Rowson's *Slaves in Algiers* (1794), a play that Noah undoubtedly would have been familiar with as a young theatre enthusiast in Philadelphia.[16] My reading of that play in the previous chapter focuses almost entirely on the character of Ben Hassan. In contrast to the wily and deceptive Jewish renegado, Rowson's Moloc is both more straightforward and more physically (and sexually) threatening, and Noah's adoption of this persona signals both his defiance of the stereotypical Jewish diminution—Ben Hassan as the "little Israelite"—and his power as a social critic.[17]

Unlike his predecessors in the Barbary archive, Malak arrives in the United States from Aleppo, not the Barbary Coast, yet the letters seem unavoidably entangled with Noah's preparations to assume his post in North Africa. In this sense, the series can provide some insight into Noah's consideration of his own identity in relation to the Muslims with which he will soon be negotiating and the Christian Americans he will be representing. As a performance, Noah's turn as Muly Malak presents multiple potential readings that offer layer upon layer of critique; even more so than the oriental spy/observer narratives of Markoe and Irving, Noah plays on the superimposition of the exotic eastern body on his own identity. Malak offers a stage from which Noah can exercise what Stuart Hall calls the multiple "positions of enunciation" assumed by the writer in diaspora. As Hall writes, "Though we speak, so to say, 'in our own name', of ourselves and from our own experience, nevertheless who speaks, and the subject who is spoken of, are never identical, never exactly in the same place."[18] Muly Malak figures this disconnect as a way to work through Jewish liminality and make visible the multiple and even contradictory positions of the author: as a political actor in the republic, as a writer in the still-nascent American literary tradition, as a Jew writing for a primarily Christian audience, and, not the least significant, as a northerner observing southern society. Like Ben Hassan, Malak's Jewishness works as a kind of dramatic irony, or as Henry Bial puts it, "double coding": "the specific means and mechanisms by which a performance can communicate one message to Jewish audiences while simultaneously communicating another, often contradictory message to gentile audiences." Forms of double coding allow for "supplemental readings" that "arise from a shared awareness between the writer/performer and the audience, a mutual act of memory that is intrinsic to performance itself."[19] Noah's authorship of "Oriental Correspondence" was well known, and so his readers would have understood the complex layering of identity that the writer performs here, allowing them to read his persona as both insider and outsider, both Jew and Muslim at the margin of Christian society.

In his first letter, Malak describes his mission to offer "a description of the Infidels that inhabit the luxurious South." Noah's subtle critique here presents the orientalist caricature of the licentious Turk who, in this case, revels in the excesses of southern society. While the letters retain a light and somewhat whimsical tone throughout, Noah from the start plays on his own position outside mainstream, Christian society. Early in the first letter, Malak describes "stray[ing] . . . into one of their houses of devotion" and hearing "an eulogy on a dead Chief, whom the world agreed to call '*Father of his Country*.'" From Malak's outsider perspective, this incident points to a potentially troubling intersection of civic and religious worship that implies a connection between Christianity and Americanness. Noah's playful tone in these passages softens his critique—that Malak finds himself at home among the luxurious South's "mosques," surrounded, as he observes, by "Janizaries," connecting American Christian nationalism and theocracy as practiced by oriental tyrants. At the same time, Noah's critiques of southern society throughout his letters are notable for what they leave out—the presence of enslaved labor in the city—excepting one minor reference. In a passage on the women of Charleston, Noah writes, "The Ladies are fond of dress and ornament, yet never appear gaudy or fantastical. . . . They ride much in small machines driven by bare feet Ethiopians, (these are plenty here) in which they pay morning calls, or visit the Bazars."[20] Given Noah's reliance on his southern audience, the fact that he offers no further descriptions or critiques of slavery here is not surprising. However, in this brief moment, cloaked in parentheses, we see the familiar trope of white womanhood literally supported by enslaved labor.

Noah frames the early Muly Malak letters as a one-sided correspondence with a master identified as "Caled the Elder"; in the June 6 issue of *The Times*, Caled finally responds. Noah's biographers are split on the question of whether Noah too authored Caled's letter, although its forceful attack on Malak as an intruder in southern society suggests that one of the writer's political opponents may have intervened. Caled writes, "It appears that, the Infidels, among whom you sojourn, have treated you with politeness and civility, have admitted you to their places of amusement, and allowed you to indulge the curiosity of a stranger, and, if you had been so inclined, the liberality of a Turk, and, in return, you have abused and ridiculed them." Noting Malak's description of a public debate in the previous letter, Caled reminds him that "it was a law in Athens, to punish with death, every stranger who intermeddled with the public concerns; and was thus guilty of usurping their authority." The letter ends with a clear jab at Noah himself, stating, "By the Prophet Noah, write me not again." Caled draws on Noah's own orientalist conceit to portray him as an outsider in Charleston society and politics.[21]

With the intervention of Caled, whose letter Malak suspects to be a forgery, the series becomes a tangle of different characters writing back and forth. The final installment of "Oriental Correspondence" appeared on June 20, just two months after Noah invented Muly Malak. This final letter, written by Yusef Kahn, the "Chief Cook of the Aga of the Janizaries," to Malak's servant Selim, sets aside many of the political conflicts of earlier letters to express "astonishment" at the extent to which "the climate and customs of an Infidel Country had produced such a change in true Mussulmen." Recalling the final letters of Markoe's *Algerine Spy*, Kahn scolds Selim and Malak for assimilating to life in America and asserts that they would no longer be welcome in Aleppo. At the same time, he warns them that, as their letters have "crept into an Infidel Newspaper," they have "much more to fear from the indignation of these infidels."[22] Whether by design or from boredom, Noah leaves Malak suspended between East and West, having alienated both sides of the Atlantic, much like Rowson's earlier Ben Hassan.

A minor episode in Noah's early career, these letters have received very little attention from Noah scholars and the writer's few biographers.[23] Nevertheless, "Oriental Correspondence" offers valuable insight as a preface to the *Travels*. As I argued in chapter 2, Irving's Mustapha satirized the primacy of rhetoric within the American "logocracy." This critique, however, is mediated by its reference to the historical Mustaffa and by a framework of translation that denotes Mustapha's text as an oriental object for consumption by Irving's American characters, Sir Launcelot Langstaff and William Wizard. Noah's series, while imitating in many ways the Mustapha letters, complicates this ideology of mastery over the textual other. As orientalist texts, they participate in the emerging imperialist project of the United States in the early nineteenth century. Yet, Noah's references to his own insider-outsider status, along with his willingness to embody Muly Malak in his public personae, point to his extension of Irving's critique to emphasize not only the textuality but the performativity of national identity and otherness. To put it another way, the series points to how the Barbary archive offers a space for experimentation that allows a semi-marginalized figure like Noah to imagine forms of textual engagement with the public that are both participatory and subversive. In this sense, although published eight years earlier than Noah's travel narrative, we can read "Oriental Correspondence" as an introduction to his later work.

Furthermore, Noah's participation in the oriental spy/observer genre holds even greater significance when we consider it within the early history of racial masquerade and minstrelsy. The Muly Malak letters were the first draft for Noah's much later cross-racial performances as an editor and political figure in New York. In the 1820s, Noah, as the editor of the popular newspaper the *National Advocate*, became embroiled in a series of conflicts with the free African American population of the city, likely stemming from efforts to extend the franchise to all free Black citizens. Noah printed several articles mocking the first Black theatre in the city, the African Grove, that showcased thick Black dialect and buffoonish characters. Theatre historian Samuel A. Hay, in his work on African American theatre in the nineteenth century, has argued that Noah's frequent use of these racist stereotypes in his writings in fact inspired an entirely new form of performance: "The English actor Charles Mathews first brought Noah's words to the stage in 1824, making Noah . . . the father of Negro minstrelsy. . . . It was with Noah, then, that [W. E. B.] DuBois [*sic*] battled to recast the African American as a human being worthy of full citizenship."[24] Noah's adoption of orientalist caricatures, first explored here and expanded on in the *Travels*, functions as the precursor to later forms of anti-Black performance that, again, defined the whiteness of the Jewish figure against the otherness of another marginalized people.

Noah's career thus offers a direct line of influence from the discourse of the Barbary archive to the rise of minstrelsy later in the nineteenth century.

THE IMPORTANCE OF BEING SEEN

By reading Noah's exploration of his minority position in the "Oriental Correspondence" as the first act of the author's performances in the *Travels*, we can see the complex ways in which he triangulates Jewish, Muslim, and American identities. Following his controversial dismissal from his post, this triangulation became an even more difficult balancing act, as the writer responded to both the charges against him and the stereotypes of the Jewish diaspora explored in the previous chapter. As a direct answer to representations of Jews as ambiguous and indecipherable, Noah stakes a claim in the work's preface to a distinctly American perspective and outlines what he sees as his contribution to the nation: "I do not know that I have presented any thing new or extraordinary in this work, or that I shall have advanced science, or promoted useful learning; yet [this book] may add to the stock of American literature." Further on, he complains that the American public is "too apt to receive erroneous impressions through foreign sources; . . . if every citizen who travels in countries which are seldom visited, would give his ideas of men and things, would describe people, habits, and manners, in his own way, free from alloy or bias of other writers, we should be more independent, and in time establish a permanent literary character of our own."[25] In this sentiment, Noah comes close to Ralph Waldo Emerson's desire, expressed almost two decades later, to end "our day of dependence, our long apprenticeship to the learning of other lands."[26] In fact, the *Mercantile Advertiser* of New York used the publication of Noah's *Travels* as an occasion to express "the just pride which we feel in the rising literature of our country." Noting the number of American works being republished in Britain, the paper declared, "Our country is thus rapidly advancing to take its proper station among the nations of the earth."[27]

In framing his narrative, Noah strategically positions himself as a key figure in this nation-building project. Nevertheless, he balances these expressions of territorial-national identity throughout the work with a stated concern for the condition of the Jewish diaspora in North Africa. From the first chapter he acknowledges his motivation to "[obtain] the most authentic information, in relation to the situation, character, resources, and numerical force of the Jews in Barbary."[28] Noah presents himself as both an agent of emergent American imperial ambition in the Atlantic *and* as a Jew concerned for the welfare of other Jewish communities in the diaspora. Despite—or perhaps because of—the controversy surrounding the end of his diplomatic career, he does not hesitate to explain these parallel motivations to his audience. His willingness to express these dual if not directly conflicting associations, one fundamentally national and the other transnational in scope, suggests the work he intends to perform in this narrative to articulate the multiple positions of the American Jew.

Along with his preface, Noah includes an author portrait opposite the title page. The *National Register*'s mocking review of *Travels* as a performance describes the likeness as "at once lively and literary," poking fun at the presumption of the image.[29] Even as it potentially attracts criticism, the arresting figure of Noah seems particularly significant in the context of many less flattering images of Jewish men circulating in the period. As Janine Barchas has argued, author portraits not only "[signal] literary status" but also "[offer] visual clues to the interpretation of an individual text."[30] In this case, we can read through Noah's portrait several aspects of his self-fashioning project as it unfolds over the course of the *Travels*. Most strikingly, Noah's face is just slightly turned from the viewer, with his gaze directed outward from the page. While throughout the eighteenth century Anglo-American author portraits often provided a profile view to allow the audience to admire the figure's physiognomy, Noah's nearly straight-on gaze prevents such an analysis. Specifically, it denies the viewer a clear picture of his nose, a feature often exaggerated in stereotypical portraits of Jews.[31] Additionally, Noah's features are only lightly shaded, and his hands disappear at the margins of the portrait, emphasizing the lightness of his skin in contrast to the common descriptions of Jews as "sallow" or "tawney."[32] Perhaps intentionally, the color of much of his skin is the color of the page itself, offering a visual manifestation of his claims to white American identity. The title page opposite the portrait notes Noah as the "Late Consul of the United States for the City and Kingdom of Tunis" and a "Member of the New-York Historical Society, &c." The image invites the reader to imagine the clearly busy Noah at that very moment engaging within a larger narrative of mainstream American politics and history. The portrait presents his authorly persona not as assumed or fully formed but as perpetually in the act of textual production. It may very well have been Noah's background in the Chestnut Street and South Street Theatres in Philadelphia that inspired him to present his body in action, acting out the narrative he hoped to convey.

Even as he subtly evades a reading that would reinforce antisemitic stereotypes of Jewish bodies, Noah presents himself as knowable and decipherable, foregrounding his own image as a means of controlling his racial identity and public personae. In doing so, he models a kind of participatory white citizenship anchored in the embodied performance of authorship. With pen in hand, Noah's portrait signals both his contribution to the comparatively short history of American literary production and the author's mastery of the (national) text. On one hand, the image functions as the work's first response to the circumstances of Noah's dismissal, presenting him as like any other aspiring authorial figure in the period. On the other, given the history of Jewish associations with Barbary piracy seen in so many earlier American

132 CHAPTER FOUR

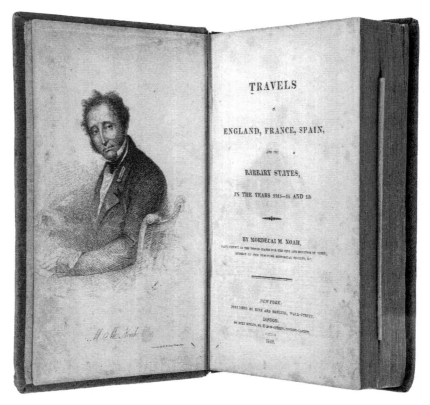

FIGURE 3. Frontispiece and title page of Mordecai Manuel Noah, *Travels in England, France, Spain, and the Barbary States, in the Years 1813–14 and 15* (New York: Kirk and Mercein, 1819). —Courtesy American Antiquarian Society, Worcester, MA

works, the frontispiece, located outside the text, distances Noah from the African figures depicted and analyzed within. Only two other illustrations are included in the *Travels*, one of which is a study of a "Merchant, Slave and Arab," assumedly in Tunis. With the caption proclaiming the figures "drawn from nature," the three Africans stand idly by in contrast to the dynamic author portrait that prefaces the work. The frontispiece serves not only to triangulate the relationship among the "reader, the author, and the work's narrative persona," as Barchas argues, but also to establish an authorial space for Noah separate from both the bigoted depictions of Jews outside his text and the exotic North Africans (including Tunisian Jews) contained and classified within it.[33] The portrait signals how Noah's claims to a white American

FIGURE 4. "Merchant, Slave and Arab," from Mordecai Manuel Noah, *Travels in England, France, Spain, and the Barbary States, in the Year 1813–14 and 15* (New York: Kirk and Mercein, 1819), 300. —Courtesy American Antiquarian Society, Worcester, MA

literary identity are rooted in and routed through his status as a producer of orientalist texts and images.

In short, the opening portrait of Noah speaks to the author's understanding of print as an increasingly racialized medium in the nineteenth century; he seems fully aware of the burden placed on his book as representative of his race and nation.[34] The portrait is symbolic of why I argue the *Travels* is so useful to literary scholars, as the author's active role in shaping racialized readings of the text make visible the shifts in what print meant in relation to evolving racial ideology between the late eighteenth and mid-nineteenth centuries.

In several other ways too Noah's *Travels* makes visible the shift between eighteenth- and nineteenth-century ways of thinking about race, identity, and the public sphere. Pere Gifra-Adroher, in his study of Noah's writing about Spain in the *Travels*, describes the narrative's positioning between Enlightenment and Romantic modes of travel writing, or what Mary Louise Pratt characterizes as the "scientific" and the "sentimental" perspectives, respectively. In her work on Mungo Park's African narrative, she notes the tensions between the "landscanning, self-effacing producer of information, . . . associated with the panoptic apparatuses of the bureaucratic state," and the "sentimental, experiential subject [who] inhabits that self-defined 'other' sector of the bourgeois world, the private sphere—home of desire, sex, spirituality, and the Individual."[35] Long passages of the *Travels* are taken up with straightforward, encyclopedic descriptions of places, peoples, and customs that characterize so many eighteenth-century travel narratives and earlier works like Mathew Carey's *A Short Account of Algiers* (1794). These passages, in which Noah himself seems to disappear, alternate with moments in which the writer emerges as a character embodying American Jewish identity as an unstable combination of the familiar and the Other, the national and the diasporic. Such episodes build toward the climax of Noah's dismissal, beginning with his account of his capture by the British. While describing his time as a prisoner aboard a British warship, he punctuates the narrative with an episode of performative Americanness not unlike his earlier performances of oriental excess as Muly Malak. On the Fourth of July, Noah laments that he is unable to celebrate that "day of jubilee, . . . when every citizen . . . toasted the heroes of our independence, and united in a solemn convocation for the preservation of our rights and liberties."[36] The ship's captain answers the captive's complaint by offering him his cabin, where Noah and his fellow captives enthusiastically celebrate the holiday. Whether or not this actually occurred, the scene emphasizes Noah's devotion to the forms of national identity, turning on its head the stereotype of Jews as "slavishly bound to external law and tradition, ritualistic and irrational."[37] His performance attempts to engender a kind of intimacy with his audience as compatriots facing common foes, British and Barbary.

After finally arriving in England and before attaining his release, Noah goes sightseeing in London. Turning his ethnographic gaze to the English, Noah largely concludes that there is little difference between Londoners and Americans, asserting that "they are only distinct in peculiarities; national feelings, and the etherial spirit, may be said to be more fully enjoyed by the Americans than by the English." While noting the similarities in ways of life between London and America, Noah is sure to add, "To an American, . . . after visiting the principal objects of curiosity, this city ceases to be interesting; an overgrown capital, . . . present variety, without producing interest."[38] As a nod to Anglo-American continuity, he complains that London is simply not exotic enough, in contrast to the locations Noah would shortly be visiting. In this sense, much of the rest of the narrative constitutes a descent into otherness that would provide a foil for Noah's own identity, beginning with his journey through Spain.

Once Noah is finally released by the British government, he sails for Cadiz, where in a number of ways his narrative begins to resemble that of an earlier fictional traveler, Mehemet of *The Algerine Spy* (1787). As I suggested earlier, Noah likely encountered Markoe's novel in his native Philadelphia, and so he would have been aware of the spy's criticisms of Spain, focused largely on the Reconquista and Inquisition. In the *Travels*, Noah spends pages upon pages musing about the former prosperity of southern Spain and comparing it to its current degraded and backward state and dependence on its American colonies. Like Mehemet, Noah speculates about how the country could have prospered if it had not expelled its Muslim and Jewish inhabitants. In a fit of posturing that reflects Noah's understanding of the natural superiority of American civilization, he advances an appeal: "Spain, Spain! if misfortunes brought on by ignorance and fanaticism, by indolence and tyranny, have not deadened your sensibilities, . . . the recollection of what you were a *thousand years ago*, in *barbarous* ages, must drive you mad! . . . Call back the Moors and the Jews, who gave you character and wealth; declare your provinces in South America, Sovereign and Independent . . . and, you may yet obtain a distinguished rank among the governments of the earth!"[39] As in *The Algerine Spy*, Spain functions as a test case for a western nation that has rejected forms of enlightenment and inclusion that, according to the protagonist, are perfected in the American experiment. Gifra-Adroher argues that Noah's impressions of Spain are clearly influenced by pervasive Anglo-American anti-Catholic bias.[40] However, in the context of the larger narrative arc of the *Travels*, Spain takes on added importance as a warning for the American republic if it were to embrace forms of religious bigotry; the example of Spain and the Inquisition hangs over the narrative as a threat of what the United States could become if it refuses to respect Jewish civil rights.[41]

From Spain Noah crosses the Pyrenees into France—a transition that Gifra-Adroher characterizes in temporal terms as a movement from past to present—and then finally embarks for North Africa. On entering Tunis, Noah writes, "I was examined through telescopes, in order to ascertain, what kind of an animal, had broke loose, from the aborigines in America, and had arrived among the descendants of Syphax and Masanissa."[42] This moment

136 **CHAPTER FOUR**

in the text recalls the work's own frontispiece, as Noah grounds his American "aboriginality" in *being seen*, this time by the eastern Other. A long-established trope of ethnographic writing, the "scene of arrival" plays the crucial role of legitimating the "intense and authority-giving experience of fieldwork," establishing the positions of "the ethnographer, the native, and the reader."[43] In the context of North Africa, this moment also recalls the conventional parade of American captives through the streets that appears in many of the period's captivity narratives.[44] However, Noah's scene of "reciprocal seeing" stands out for a number of reasons.[45] For one, it would seem strange that the inhabitants of Tunis, accustomed to the traffic of the Mediterranean and interactions with Europeans (and possibly also Americans), would be so fascinated with the entry of an American diplomat into the city. Noah perhaps exaggerates his status as an exotic figure, allowing him to perform Americanness for a non-western audience in a way that over-writes competing claims to his origin and identity as a Jew. He is, in the eyes of the Tunisians, first and foremost an American. Noah's description of his entry into the city that he will, in the narrative's future, leave under a cloud of controversy reflects an awareness that, from this point onward, he will be intensely scrutinized by both African natives and American readers.

In Tunis, Noah begins to focus specifically on his assessment of the Jewish community. Both Sarna and Ben Rejeb assert that the *Travels* is one of the best surviving accounts in English concerning nineteenth-century Jewish life in Tunis.[46] When approaching the state of the Tunisian Jewry in his narrative, Noah carefully prefaces his account with an acknowledgment of his own complicated positioning:

> On this subject, more will be expected from me than from casual observers. Professing the same religion, and representing a Christian nation in an important station, and in an interesting part of the world, it will be supposed that opportunity and inclination must have combined to afford the most correct information on the subject; while, on the other hand, an equality of rights, a reasonable participation of honours and office, together with the advantages of society and education, unite to banish those prejudices, insepa-rable from dark minds, and feelings wounded and irritated.

Noah insists on his authority and impartiality when dealing with the Jews of the Barbary while conceding his own position in relation to a "Christian" nation, acknowledging the extra burden placed on him both by the competing claims to his identity and by the rationale for his later dismissal.

He makes a fervent case for a nation held together not by religious or racial uniformity but by the right to political participation. He emphasizes too that the United States' overseas ambitions can benefit greatly from a close relationship with the Jews of the Barbary Coast. At one point he asserts, "I have reason to believe, that the number of Jews in the Barbary States exceeds 700,000, of which nearly 100,000 are capable of bearing arms." On the other hand, Noah notes that "the Jews in Barbary have suffered severely from the ignorance and prejudice of travelers, who have familiarized themselves with the dark shades of their character."[47] He specifically refers to first-hand observations of Jewish communities here, but he might as well have had in mind the Algerian Jewish villains of Royall Tyler's *The Algerine Captive* (1797) and Rowson's *Slaves in Algiers*. Noah takes on the task of confronting these unjust representations to defend not only the Jews of North Africa but also his own loyalty and effectiveness as an agent of the United States.

Noah's attempt to rehabilitate the image of Barbary Jews takes particular aim at Captain James Riley's recently published account of his captivity, *An Authentic Narrative of the Loss of the American Brig Commerce*. Published only two years before the *Travels* in 1817, Riley's narrative proved incredibly popular.[48] In contrast with many other traditional Barbary captivity narratives that involved an American protagonist captured by pirates, Riley was shipwrecked off the coast of Morocco in August 1815 and was captured by nomadic Arabs. After a long trek across the desert, the enslaved Riley and his crew arrived in Mogadore, Morocco, where they were redeemed by the British consul. In his *Narrative*, Riley sought to provide an authoritative account of the communities he encountered during his ordeal. Noah took particular issue with Riley's descriptions of emasculated Jewish men and immoral Jewish women, driven to desperation by Muslim domination. Describing affairs between Muslim men and Jewish women, Riley writes, "If a Jew happens to be in the house, the Moor either drives him out, or hires him to absent himself, or keep the door, which latter is commonly the case. The Moor compliments the woman, and no Barbary Jew thinks it a disgrace to wear antlers, provided they are gilded." In Safi, Morocco, Riley describes in great detail Jewish women adorning their "naked bosoms" with ornate jewelry while their husbands are away at synagogue on Saturday. He relates,

> Two of the most handsome and stylishly dressed damsels, with a number of the second-rate, came round to that side of the gallery where I sat quietly alone, writing down notes for my journal. . . . The two smartest looking girls,

138 **CHAPTER FOUR**

> who were about sixteen and eighteen years of age, with quite pretty faces, and richly dressed, invited me to go with them, and see their father's room: my curiosity prompted me to comply, and I suffered them to lead me along into their chamber, where their mother, . . . was sitting on a mattress. . . . The object of these sirens was to get money from me; but finding I was able to withstand their temptations, they at last permitted me to retire, but not before they had tried every indelicate art and enticement, of which they were complete mistresses, to effect their purpose.

Riley ends the passage with a hint of compassion, explaining that Safi itself is an impoverished town, and that the Jews there had no means of subsistence beyond begging and prostitution.[49] In an extended footnote in the *Travels*, Noah singles out Riley's account: "By none have [the Jews] been more severely handled, than in the Narrative written by Captain Riley. It was to have been expected that this man, who has the honour to be born in a free country, would have exhibited a spirit of liberality corresponding with the genius and disposition of his fellow-citizens." In Noah's eyes, Riley's criticisms of Moroccan Jews are not only unjust but also un-American. He quotes from Riley's encounter with the three Jewish women extensively, interjecting derisive comments. Referring to Riley as "chaste Neptune," Noah mocks the evils of the women "enticing a poor shipwrecked sailor, redeemed from slavery, and, *if he is to be believed*, squalid, wretched, and reduced to ninety pounds weight with misery, into a room to practice on his *virtue* and his *pocket*. O Monstrous!!" Without directly denying Riley's story, Noah simply suggests that, in any large community, "loose characters are to be found; they are the same in all countries and among all persuasions."[50] He effectively accuses Riley of confirmation bias, suggesting that the former captive's attempt to smear the Jewish population of North Africa (and perhaps America as well) is unworthy of the kind of American perspective that he calls for in the introduction to the *Travels*.

Noah's defense of Barbary Jews sets the stage for his own dismissal in the pages that follow. He relates the scene in detailed and dramatic fashion. Noah describes the arrival of Commodore Decatur's fleet and his journey out to the flagship. In a scene that mirrors his arrival in Tunis, he finds himself under the eager gaze of officers and crew, who "pressed forward to view their fellow citizen." Everyone always seems to want to view Noah. He then describes reading the letter in Decatur's cabin with the commodore present: "The receipt of this letter shocked me inexpressibly; . . . what was to be done? I had not a moment to determine. I cast my eye hastily on Commodore Decatur.

I was satisfied at a glance, that he knew not the contents of the letter. . . . I folded up the letter with apparent indifference, . . . and then proceeded to relate . . . the nature of our dispute with Tunis."[51] The highly charged moment in which Noah retains his facade of calm under the gaze of a national hero and symbol of the country's military power reads like a scene from one of the period's melodramas. The text's narrative of *being seen* climaxes in a moment of dramatic irony in which Noah must mask his response, rooted in his Jewish identity, for the good of his country.

Following this scene, much of the *Travels* centers on refuting the reasoning behind Noah's dismissal on account of his religion. He writes, "My religion an object of hostility? I thought I was a citizen of the United States protected by the constitution in my religious as well as in my civil rights." Rather than deny the disadvantaged position of Tunisian Jews at the hands of the Muslim majority, Noah uses the opportunity to proclaim the superiority of American values over eastern oppression: "Are we prepared to yield up the admirable and just institutions of our country at the shrine of foreign bigotry and superstition? Are we prepared to disfranchise one of our own citizens, to gratify the intolerant views of the Bey of Tunis?"[52] The incident offers a clarifying moment for Noah regarding what should be the essential difference between East and West. Inverting the idea of a Muslim-Jewish conspiracy, Noah points out that it is the Monroe administration that aligns itself with oriental despotism. While asserting that he was fully aware of representing "a Christian nation," Noah quotes at length from article 11 of the 1797 Treaty of Tripoli, signed by John Adams, which states that "the Government of the United States is not, in any sense, founded on the Christian religion."[53] In its final pages, the book becomes itself a kind of archive, as Noah interpolates numerous letters and reports defending his conduct. The many appendices include a series of letters collected by Noah and addressed to him from Adams, Jefferson, and Madison, each reaffirming the importance of religious liberty. Taking on the role of editor and compiler, Noah's final performance in the work dramatizes his disappearance into the texts of American identity.

Representing the final years of the Barbary crises period, the importance of the *Travels* lies in how, with his careful balancing of diasporic ties to Barbary Jews and his claims to American identity, Noah anticipates the emergence of what we now call minority or ethnic literature. Its performance of (white) authorship against an eastern backdrop contextualizes its argument for Jewish inclusion within America's imperial ambitions. At the same time, its defense of Tunisian Jewry and argument for Jewish American rights on the basis of national contribution parallel arguments advanced by African American activists such as Samuel Cornish and Williams Watkins in the same period, albeit with very different stakes.[54] Noah makes the case that the diaspora has the power to aid the republic abroad, but it remains too weak to manipulate or conspire against it. Jews in America comprise a distinct community to the extent that they serve as a litmus test for national inclusion, but they are not so different that they cannot effectively represent their fellow citizens. It is not coincidental that the Barbary crises provide the occasion and North Africa the space for these experiments with Jewish American symbiosis. As we have seen, Noah engages with an already decades-old discourse of revising and renegotiating the boundaries of American identity in relation to the Barbary. The *Travels* epitomizes the Barbary as a field of experimentation with representation and inclusion, a role it will continue to play in the antebellum era.

BESIEGING THE STAGE

Noah's *Travels* proved quite successful in the United States and was even published in Britain, although there is little evidence that it made any impact there.[55] There is evidence, however, that the book circulated among circum-Atlantic Jewish communities. In 1823, as part of a heated debate over Jewish enfranchisement in Jamaica, Jewish leaders published a pamphlet entitled *Narratives of the Proceedings of the Jews, in Their Attempt to Establish Their Right to the Elective Franchise in Jamaica* in which they quoted from Noah's *Travels* and repeatedly referenced the author's service to the United States.[56] Of course, they conveniently omit the fact of Noah's dismissal and the allegations of antisemitism the writer levels against the Monroe administration. Nevertheless, the text represented for that community proof of Noah's argument that open and liberal policies toward the Jewish diaspora would ultimately reap benefits for the nation.

In the final pages of this chapter, I want to briefly note the theatrical resonances of Noah's performances in the *Travels*. The same year Noah published the *Travels* he established a reputation as one of the country's foremost writers of melodramas with the success of *She Would Be a Soldier*.[57] Only a year later Noah would attempt to directly capitalize on his experience

FIGURE 5. Playbill for *Yusef Caramalli; or, The Siege of Tripoli* (1822). —Courtesy UPENN Colenda Digital Repository

---

THEATRE.

Second Night of Yusef Caramalli.

Wednesday Evening, January 30, 1822,

Will be presented a new Patriotic Melo-Drama, (for the 2d time here) called

Yusef Caramalli;

Or, the Siege of Tripoli.

Written by M. M. Noah, Esq. Author of She Would be a Soldier, Marion, &c. and performed in New York with most distinguished applause.

With new Scenery, Dresses and Decorations.

The new Scenes designed by Mr. H. Warren, and executed by him, Messrs. Robert Anners, J. Jefferson, and I. C. Darley.

Yusef Caramalli, Bashaw of Tripoli,	Mr. WOOD.
Hassan Ben Ali, Ben Musef, Ben Onous,	Mr. JEFFERSON.
Hamet, a Tripolitan Officer,	Mr. GREENE.
American Commodore,	Mr. HATHWELL.
Harry Mountfort, an American Captive,	Mr. H. WALLACK.
Mandeville, an American Officer,	Mr. NICHOLS.
Gonzalez, Mr. DARLEY. } Spanish { Vasco,	Mr. J. JEFFERSON.
Pedrigo, Mr. BURKE. } Prisoners. { Ricardo,	Mr. SCRIVENER.
Turkish Officer,	Mr. PARKER.
Boatswain,	Mr. MARTIN.
Hassan,	Mr. JOHNSTON.

Guards, Janissaries, Captives, MARINES, SAILORS, &c.

Rosabel, a Spanish Captive,	Mrs. DARLEY.
Inis, her Attendant,	Mrs. GREENE.

Female Slaves, &c. Mrs. Murray, Mrs. Bloxton, Miss Murray, Miss Hathwell, &c.

Sketch of the principal Scenery:

ACT FIRST,

A Magnificent Garden of the Bashaw.

Splendid Pavilions on each side—*Vases of Flowers,* and *Fountains*—Rosabel discovered reposing on a Couch, decorated with Flowers, &c.

A VIEW NEAR TRIPOLI.

The Harbour and part of the Town of Tripoli.

(Copied from an accurate Drawing)

The Ramparts, with Guns mounted—at a distance is seen

The Philadelphia Frigate at Anchor.

ACT SECOND,

The Harbour of Tripoli.

The *Frigate at Anchor—a small Zebeque approaches her—*Guns fir'd—the Tripolitans *alarmed, rouse the Guards—*an attack from the Batteries, when the

Frigate is Burnt by the Americans, &c.

*Scene 4th. The SEA SHORE, with a LARGE SHIP READY FOR SEA—*As the released Spanish Prisoners embark, Gonzales seizes Rosabel and throws her from the Dock into the Sea—Harry Mountfort plunges from a Rock to her rescue.

Act 3d, A Street in Tripoli. The American Embassy to the Bashaw, &c.

Scene 3d, The Sea Shore and Batteries—

The American Squadron seen at Anchor,

The Commodore lands, with Band of Music, and

A Procession of United States' Officers,

Marines and Seamen,

(With Badges of their different Vessels) they march round the stage, under a SALUTE, &c.

The Treaty of Peace is Signed

Between the United States and Tripoli.

Sixth and last scene—An Arched Fortress and View of the Sea. In this scene,

A NAVAL BALLET.

Two Pillars rise, on which are inscribed the Names of *Distinguished Officers* serving in the Tripolitan War.

A SCROLL DANCE:

The Turs of Columbia and a Nation's Gratitude.

A Double Hornpipe,

By Mrs. H. Wallack, and Miss H. Hathwell, And a General Dance by Misses, Hathwell, Mrs. Greene, Mrs. Murray, &c.

After which, (not acted these 5 years) a Farce, in 2 acts, called

St. Patrick's Day;

Or, the Scheming Lieutenant.

Written by R. B. Sheridan, Esq.

Lieutenant O'Connor,	Mr. BURKE.	First Soldier,	Mr. MURRAY.
Justice Credulous,	Mr. JEFFERSON.	Second do.	Mr. GREENE.
Doctor Rosy,	Mr. FRANCIS.	Third do.	Mr. PARKER.
Sergeant Trounce,	Mr. HATHWELL.	Fourth do.	Mr. MARTIN.
Corporal Flint,	Mr. SCRIVENER.	Drummer,	Mr. JONES.
First Countryman,	Mr. J. JEFFERSON.	Mrs. Bridget Credulous, Mrs. FRANCIS.	
2d do.	Mr. JOHNSTON.	Lauretta, (with a Song) Mrs. BURKE.	

The Managers respectfully announce the Engagement of Mr. PHI-LIPPS for 6 nights—due notice will be given of his first appearance as Count Belino, in the Devil's Bridge.

On FRIDAY, a favorite play and farce—And on Saturday will be revived the celebrated Tragedy of MAHOMET, the Imposter—Zaphna by Master FOREST, his first appearance this season. The Melo-drama of the WANDERING BOYS is in rehearsal.

142 **CHAPTER FOUR**

in the Barbary with the melodrama *Yusef Caramalli; or, The Siege of Tripoli* (1820). Like Ellison's similarly named *American Captive; or, The Siege of Tripoli* (1812), Noah's play focuses on the country's victory in the Tripolitan War in 1805. In its review of the play, the *New-York Literary Journal* proclaims, "Tripoli never fails to revive recollections dear to every American."[58] In their announcements, several newspapers reminded readers about the circumstances surrounding Noah's knowledge of the Barbary; for example, Philadelphia's *Saturday Evening Post* comments that Noah "was for several years a Consul at one of the Barbary ports, whence, however, he was recalled by his government on the score of his religion."[59] While the play seems to have had little to do with Tunis, like the *Travels*, the piece was framed by Noah's grievances against the government and by charges of antisemitism. The play itself does not survive, but Heather Nathans has pieced together a general idea of the plot from the *New-York Literary Journal's* summary and from disparate references to it from 1820 to 1841. She suggests that, based on the evidence available, although it appears to be a post–Tripolitan War triumphalist narrative, the plot bears a suspicious resemblance to Rowson's *Slaves in Algiers*. Nathans points in particular to the character of Hassan Ben Ali, who resembles Ben Hassan, although there is no evidence from the surviving materials that Ben Ali is Jewish or even a Jewish renegado.[60]

Despite the *Journal's* assertion that the play's setting during the Tripolitan War is "well calculated . . . to awaken the national spirit," one can easily get the impression from the account that Yusef Caramalli is not the villain. Of course, this might be a deliberate choice on the part of Noah, given that the Tripolitan War ended after successful negotiations with Caramalli that left Tripoli's leader in power, ultimately betraying the United States' ally, Yusef's brother Hamet.[61] From the summary and a surviving playbill for an 1822 performance, we know that the celebrated burning of the *Philadelphia* by Stephen Decatur was a central historical referent in the work, but much of the plot's conflict comes from the violent jealousy of Gonzales, a Spanish slave. According to the *Journal*, the play begins with Gonzales and his betrothed, Rosabel, captured by Yusef. Both Yusef and a captive American officer, formerly of the *Philadelphia*, named Harry Mountfort fall in love with Rosabel. Yusef pursues Rosabel, but when he learns that she is already engaged to Gonzales, he decides to "act nobly" and free the two Spaniards. Gonzales, however, in a fit of jealousy, throws Rosabel into the sea and sails from Tripoli. Mountfort rescues Rosabel, and when the unrepentant Gonzales returns, she entreats Yusef to allow her to pass sentence against him. Against the backdrop of Caramalli's peace negotiations with the Americans, Rosabel sentences Gonzales to exile on the nearest island and then marries Mountfort.

While Nathans points to *Slaves in Algiers* as an obvious inspiration for Noah's play, it is easy to see how *The Siege of Tripoli* offers a very different vision, not only for Jewish identity but also for America's place in the Atlantic world. As I discussed in chapter 3, Elizabeth Maddock Dillon's reading of Rowson's play emphasizes the work's resolution, in which the American and British captives join together to oppose their Muslim and Jewish oppressors. This staged reunion of British and American identities affirms American liberty as the offspring of British parents.[62] In Noah's play, by contrast, despite the formal battlelines of the Tripolitan War, it is the non-Europeans who achieve detente against the European aggressor. Seen through the lens of Noah's critique of Spain in the *Travels*, Gonzales becomes the regressive, oppressive bigotry of the Old World that America must reject. In this sense, despite the apparent absence of any obvious Jewish characters, with the aid of the writer's earlier work we can see how the specter of antisemitism haunts Noah's play.

The Siege of Tripoli seems to be lost to history, but a more radical performance related to the attempted founding of his new Jewish colony of Ararat, influenced by Noah's time in North Africa, has left more significant traces. To officially establish the colony in 1825, Noah held an elaborate ceremony in Buffalo, New York. Dressed in a theatrical red robe with a golden medal around his neck, Noah led a procession through the streets that featured government officials, local craftspeople, freemasons, and other dignitaries. He then delivered an address, reprinted in newspapers throughout the United States and Europe, officially opening the colony to Jewish immigrants from around the globe. His invitation specifically referenced the communities Noah encountered in North Africa and the "numerous population of Jews now under the oppressive dominion of the Ottoman Porte."[63] While the Ararat colony failed to attract even a single colonist, twenty-first-century scholars have focused extensively on the project's impact on notions of Jewish American identity in the period. Julian Levinson calls Noah's Ararat speech a "foundational text in the history of American Jewish optimism."[64] Despite a significant upsurge in critical attention to Noah's failed venture, few critics have connected Ararat with the writer's previous works, yet I would argue that this unique event was an extension of his earlier performances in the "Oriental Correspondence" and the *Travels*.[65] It is in these earlier texts that we see the ways in which Noah's attempts to define a Jewish American identity took shape on a global scale, in relation to both East and West.

As I hope to have demonstrated in these last two chapters, the texts of the Barbary archive can greatly expand our understanding of the origins of minority discourse in the United States through debates over Barbary Jewish identity. The Barbary crises framed discussions of Jewish assimilation and inclusion in terms distinct from earlier Anglo-American Shylock stereotypes by placing circum-Atlantic Jewish figures in between America and Africa, Christian and Muslim. Such fraught and tenuous positionings, I argue, gave rise to Noah's experimentation with new forms of hybrid identity and with attempts to reconcile the national and the diasporic in ways that anticipated the future development of ethnic and minority literature in the nineteenth century. In the final section of this book, I expand on this long-term legacy of the Barbary crises by looking at how the cultural memory of North African piracy and the suffering of white slaves contributed both to abolitionist discourse and, improbably, to the development of children's literature.

PART THREE

THE LONG SHADOW OF THE BARBARY

CHAPTER FIVE

"THE ADVANTAGE OF A WHIP-LECTURE"

"Where is Connecticut?" asked a young urchin the other day—"isn't it one of the *Barbary* States?" Poor fellow—he had probably heard of the new Blue Law, and the imprisonment of a young lady for teaching blacks.

—*The Liberator*, 1833

What *right* have Algerines my son to take,
  And force him from his home, a slave to make?
And doom his children every one a slave,
  Till life and strength are wasted in the grave?

—"Liberty," *The Liberator*, 1837

Fifty-five years after Mehemet of *The Algerine Spy* proposed his daring plan to capture Rhode Island for the dey of Algiers, the Algerines finally gained control of the state. Just as Mehemet had predicted, the state fell as a result of internal division; after the Revolution, Rhode Island continued to function under its colonial charter, which restricted voting rights to those with significant property holdings, leaving many Rhode Islanders disenfranchised. The state legislature repeatedly declined to revise the charter, and so in 1841 angry citizens banded together to hold a "People's Convention" to write a new state constitution. Soon after, this People's Legislature elected its own state governor, Thomas William Dorr, who led a band of armed followers against the Charterist governor Samuel Ward King. After a brief skirmish in Providence, Dorr fled to New York and the Charterist legislature began cracking down on the Dorrites. The law they passed, the "Act in Relation to Offenses against the Sovereign Power of the

State," punished anyone involved with the People's Constitution with fines and imprisonment. This draconian act was immediately attacked by the Dorrites in the press and labeled "The Algerine Law." The Charterists in turn became known as the Algerines of Rhode Island.[1] Of course, this domestic skirmish over voting rights, later known as the Algerine War, was not what Mehemet had in mind in 1787 when he proposed that the dey of Algiers employ Daniel Shays to conquer the recalcitrant state for the Ottoman Porte. Nevertheless, the fact that the "Algerine" label caught on so quickly and became so widespread speaks to the enduring cultural force of Algiers in the American imagination. That the term "Algerine" continued to circulate in American print culture as a byword for tyranny and oppression as late as 1841 is particularly noteworthy, as more than a decade earlier French forces had invaded Algiers and reduced the one-time Mediterranean power to the colony of French Algeria.

The immediate popularity of the Algerine label may too have been driven by the fears of white victimization and African barbarity that surrounded Rhode Island's Algerine War. Although Dorr himself was known for his abolitionist sympathies, by a significant margin the Dorrite "suffragists" voted to restrict the franchise to "white" residents in the People's Constitution.[2] While some Black residents of the state remained hopeful of expanding their rights, many actively supported the Charterist cause, likely due to fears of anti-Black demagoguery on Dorr's side.[3] William Brown, a descendent of enslaved men and women owned by the prominent Brown family, opposed Dorr's attempted insurrection by organizing two companies of Black Rhode Islanders "to assist in carrying out Law and Order." Many of the Dorrites blamed the Black volunteers for their failure, with one declaring, "If it were not for the colored people, they would have whipped the Algerines. . . . 'Who do you suppose was going to stay there when the Algerines were coming up with four hundred bull n——rs?'"[4] When the failed insurrectionists were not calling the Charterists Algerines, they often referred to them as the "n——r party."[5] In this context, we can see why the Algerine label came into such widespread use. As I have argued throughout this book, the Barbary in American culture long signified the intersection of political oppression and racial otherness.

Despite the fact that the Barbary crises have received increasing critical attention over the last two decades, the legacy of these conflicts in the antebellum era remains largely unexplored. As mentioned in this book's introduction, Paul Baepler speculated almost two decades ago concerning the possible connections between the Barbary captivity narratives of the late eighteenth and early nineteenth centuries and later American slave narratives, but little has been done to articulate more direct lines of influence.[6] In this chapter and the next, I seek to recover this connection and explore how writers repeatedly returned to and revised their understanding of the Barbary crises in the context of intensifying sectional and ideological tensions. As we shall see, anachronistic Algerine, Tripolitan, and other North African villains continued to haunt the margins of debates over slavery and state power long after the last American captives on the Barbary Coast were liberated. After 1830, Algerines, as opposed to French Algerians, persisted as anachronisms, convenient fictions acting as agents of the alternate temporalities of modernity at the gates of a national homogenous time, ready to contest and undermine antebellum racial hierarchies.

In her book *Abolitionist Geographies* (2014), Martha Schoolman argues for "geography as a key discourse of abolitionist political intervention," prompting us to expand our understanding of "abolitionist spatial practice" beyond the traditional "triadic map" of American North, South, and West.[7] Below I explore how the Barbary served antebellum-era writers as an alternative space of enslavement and liberation. While in most cases the Algerine was deployed in abolitionist works, I start below with an exception: the 1818 pro-slavery play *The Young Carolinians*. From there, I examine how the abolitionist press, and especially William Lloyd Garrison, consistently utilized the Algerine as a kind of shorthand for slave power, particularly during the international crises surrounding the slave ship revolts on *La Amistad* and the *Creole*.[8] From there, I explore a collection of evocative references to Algiers from African American writers such as Frederick Douglass, James McCune Smith, and Lewis Clarke, and I end the chapter with how abolitionists repeatedly referenced the Barbary Wars in the decades leading up to the Civil War as a precedent for militant opposition to slavery.

At the outset of this survey, I want to identify two threads running through the disparate references to the Barbary in the antebellum era that function as theories for why these crises survived in the public imagination for so long. The first, as I have touched on in previous chapters, is the United States' growing imperial ambitions in the Atlantic world. Both the site of the country's first invasion of an overseas territory and later the target for new European colonial conquest, the Barbary represents a space for Americans

150 CHAPTER FIVE

to imagine empire beyond western expansion. Importantly, the abolitionist press's continued circulation of the Algerine figure signals its complicity in this cultural project. In many cases, piratical Algerines in print seem to coexist alongside and even overwrite the contemporary reality of French Algeria and the suffering of its colonial subjects, perpetuating the idea that Africa is an antagonistic space that must be opposed and conquered by the West in self-defense.[9] Second, we can see how, in debates over slavery and racialized violence, the Barbary crises could function in ways that upheavals closer to home like the Haitian Revolution could not by providing conveniently othered villains and displacing the effects of antislavery violence. If less radical abolitionists were uneasy about developments in the former French colony, invoking Algiers gestured toward a time when the movement and the country as a whole was united in arms against slavery. Unlike Caribbean revolutionaries, Algerines embodied a threat that was both immediate in cultural memory and yet comfortably in the past. Additionally, North Africans were often more convenient antagonists than French planters. Muslims slavers allowed writers on both sides of the slavery debate to thoroughly disavow the violent excesses of slavery and distance them from Christianity and whiteness. In other words, by projecting the question of domestic slavery onto North Africa, the deep ideological clashes between white Americans could be reimagined along multiple axes of difference: West versus East, Christianity versus Islam, America versus Africa. Meanwhile, African American writers utilized the history of Barbary captivity to contextualize their own struggles within recent national memory and therefore to cast themselves as representative Americans.

PRIVATIZING THE ALGERINES

In the years following the end of the Barbary Wars in 1815, Americans continued to argue over what the experience of white slavery in North Africa meant in relation to American slavery. While in most cases it was abolitionists who invoked the image of Algerines and Tripolitans to characterize the barbarity of southern slaveholders, the defenders of slavery also referenced the Barbary to emphasize the comparative civility and benevolence of American masters. Even those sailors who directly experienced enslavement in North Africa were not unanimous in their condemnation of American slavery. James Riley's 1817 *Authentic Narrative*, an influential later Barbary narrative I introduced in the previous chapter and discuss more extensively in the next, was particularly noteworthy for ending with the liberated captive dedicating himself to the cause of his "enslaved and oppressed fellow creatures" at home.[10] On the other hand, Riley's shipmate Archibald Robbins interpreted his enslavement on the Barbary Coast as undermining any sympathy he might have for African Americans: "These Africans . . . take delight in enslaving each other. . . . It can hardly be expected that an American, who has for months and years been enslaved by them, can feel so much compassion towards a slave *here* as those do who have always enjoyed the blessings of humanity and liberty."[11] Those who have never personally experienced slavery in Africa, Robbins seems to suggest, could never appreciate the comparatively benevolent treatment of slaves in America.

A similar defense of slavery appears in Sarah Pogson's 1818 play *The Young Carolinians; or, Americans in Algiers*, which theatre historian Charles S. Watson cites as the "first defense of slavery in a southern play."[12] That play, like many abolitionist works, stages a direct comparison between the African and American slave systems. The first act opens on an idyllic southern plantation, where the master, States Woodberry, discusses with his sister Ellinor her fiancé, St. Julien, who is currently abroad. Present also is the house slave, Cudjo, who briefly interrupts the discussion to announce a visitor. This mild domestic scene then abruptly shifts to "The vicinity of the city of Algiers," where St. Julien toils among other slaves breaking rocks, with "Turks at different places standing over the slaves with goads and whips."[13] This quick scene change between the American South and Algiers recurs multiple times during the play, emphasizing a comparison common to the Barbary archive, but one that, in this case, works to the South's advantage.

Our first view of Algerian slavery emphasizes how irrational violence defines the system. An exhausted St. Julien momentarily stops working, only to be confronted by his "Turk" overseer:

> ST. JULIEN. Your cruelties have rendered me almost unable to work.
>   I paused from labor, or must have sank.
> TURK. Work then till thou dost sink—Dogs! Ye shall pay for your
>   feeding.

Excessive, inhumane, and purely exploitative, Algerian slavery lacks any of the paternalistic virtues touted by southern slaveholders. Pogson contrasts St. Julien's travails with Cudjo's more comfortable position in the Woodberry household. Later in the play, after a character dismissively tells Cudjo to "walk to Guinea," the house slave muses, "Ah! Too much better for stay here, my massa. . . . I get plenty good ting for eat, and when I sick, ah! My deary missess give me too much nasty stuff for cure me—plenty sweet tea to wash em down;—bye and bye get well again, she look pon me with one kind eye, same like a dove—glad to see poor old Cudjo well."[14] As Douglas A. Jones Jr. argues, "This speech posits a romanticized relation of interracial complementarity as the nucleus of chattel slavery."[15] Pogson suggests that a hierarchical white-Black society can maintain safety and security, while the inversion of that hierarchy in the Turk-American dynamic of North Africa inevitably breeds conflict. More subtly, the play suggests that the relationship between the Woodberrys and Cudjo maintains its stability because of the latter's indelible otherness. Like Ben Hassan in Susanna Rowson's *Slaves in Algiers* (1794), Cudjo is the only character who speaks in heavy dialect; in contrast, the southerners and the Algerians appear to sound the same. Although Pogson presents us with African characters who have agency in the text, clearly Cudjo could never be one of them.

Even as Pogson advances a view of southern slavery as mutually beneficial to master and slave, she appropriates a common abolitionist trope. Following their conversation, Ellinor and States sail for England but are also captured by Algerian pirates, with the former eventually ending up a slave in the house of Mustapha, the aga of the janissaries. The aga's son, Achmet, who is about to marry an Algerian woman named Selima, confesses his love to Ellinor. She rejects him on the grounds that she is already engage to St. Julien, who she has yet to learn resides elsewhere in the city. Mustapha discovers Achmet's infatuation and contrives to sell Ellinor to the dey. Ellinor pleads with Achmet and Selima to retain her until her ransom arrives, but Mustapha secretly informs Selima of her new husband's lust. Selima soon realizes that her husband will never truly love her while the enslaved American woman remains in their household.

The resulting love triangle of master-mistress-slave reflects a narrative repeated again and again across abolitionist literature. Pogson seems to set Ellinor up as a white tragic mulatta figure, having her lament: "Would that I had been of all my sex the plainest; then Achmet's heart had not felt that preference which now condemns me to the most wretched fate."[16] More than forty years later, the formerly enslaved Harriet Jacobs would describe the same situation in *Incidents in the Life of a Slave Girl* (1861): "Even the little child, who is accustomed to wait on her mistress and her children, will learn, before she is twelve years old, why it is that her mistress hates such and such a one among the slaves. . . . If God has bestowed beauty upon her, it will prove her greatest curse. That which commands admiration in the white woman only hastens the degradation of the female slave."[17] Of course, Ellinor's fate in the play differs greatly from that of the enslaved women that Jacobs describes. Selima confronts Ellinor and, once satisfied that the American slave has no interest in Achmet, contrives to help her escape to get her out of the picture, foiling a plot by her husband to whisk Ellinor away to his country home. This subplot recalls themes of female solidarity seen in *Slaves in Algiers*, yet again, that cross-racial sympathy only emerges because the play recognizes few racial barriers between Carolinians and Algerians, both at the top of the hierarchies of their respective homelands. The women recognize in each other the burden of being the master within a slave society. Needless to say, no similar bond would seem possible with someone like Cudjo.

I dwell here on Pogson's Algerine play because it speaks to the ways in which Americans did not always naturally associate the struggle with the Barbary Coast with the antislavery cause. At the same time, this play in 1818 previews for us how Barbary figures evolved to represent state power in a way they typically did not during the crises themselves. Works written during the crises often focused on the need for public virtue and national unity to liberate those enslaved in North Africa. As I discussed in chapter 3, Susanna Rowson's earlier play was closely associated with public fundraisers for the captive Americans. She dedicated the play "to the citizens of the United States of North-America," and she describes one of its principal protagonists, Olivia, as "a daughter of Columbia."[18] For Pogson, in contrast, the crises are largely privatized. The wealth of the Woodberry plantation, ironically built and maintained by slavery, pays for the freedom of the not-so-subtly-named States and his fellow Carolinians.[19] For the Woodberrys, even Barbary slavery becomes an upper-class family affair.[20] In Pogson's revision of the Barbary crises, victory over the Algerines comes thanks to the superior moral foundations of American slavery and the initiative of private citizens. Algiers, then, represents the excesses of racial violence and government oppression that have been tamed by the southern aristocracy. In some ways Pogson's play sets the stage for the repurposing of the Barbary crises in the mid-nineteenth century; nevertheless, her pro-slavery argument

ABOLITION AND THE NEW BARBARY PIRATES

To restate my assertion above, Pogson's 1818 play heralds a significant post-crises shift toward the representation of Algerines and Tripolitans as symbols of the abuse of government power, as seen too in my opening anecdote concerning the Algerines of Rhode Island. For abolitionists, these representations often evoked both the barbarity of southern slaveholders and the tyranny of federal efforts to protect the system. A simple cursory search of the archives of *The Liberator* shows that Garrison and his followers were particularly fond of the phrase "worse than Algerine" slavery to denote the exceptional brutality of the American slave system and the hypocrisy of the politicians who defended it.[21] Timothy Marr argues that, in the wake of Ottoman reforms after 1830 which placed Islam in a more positive light and with reports of Russian oppression in eastern Europe, Americans and particularly abolitionists frequently engaged in a "comparative orientalism" that presented Barbary slavery as "a more benign alternative to the harsh racial bondage of the New World."[22] As we will see, such comparisons were frequently made, but more interesting than the locating of Islam in the progressive present is how abolitionists leveraged Barbary history to grapple with America's republican past. As Robert Fanuzzi influentially argues regarding Garrisonian abolitionism, Garrison and his contemporaries sought most of all to resurrect an "anachronistic public sphere" that included the "unlimited exercise of free speech, the disinterested consideration of the public good, and above all, the resistance of a liberty-loving people." Part of that project, I argue, included invoking the threatening and disruptive intervention of Barbary pirates and slavers, even though they no longer referenced a present threat to Americans. In the same way that anxieties surrounding Algerian invaders provided a common threat against which the deeply divided early republican public sphere could rally and define itself, the temporally and spatially distant location of Algiers was utilized to represent American slavery as a relic of the past that had already been defeated. Fanuzzi writes of the "belatedness" of Garrison's public sphere: "He seemed to understand that belatedness could be an epistemologically privileged position that put abolition on the side of progress, revolution, and popular democracy."[23] By resurrecting the Algerines, Garrison and others could reframe the fight against slavery as already won—the United States just needed to catch up to its own history.

Circulating within the rational public sphere that Garrison and others hoped to foster, Barbary figures often represented the ways the slave power conspiracy was essentially foreign, oppressive, and irrational. When pro-slavery leaders called for law and order in response to the growing threat of violent resistance, Garrisonians invoked the Algerines to characterize the fundamental corruption of the power structure, from domestic laws to international treaties. They were a particularly useful symbol for Garrison's strategy of nonresistance through which he urged antislavery activists to withdraw from political and legal engagement entirely, including from military service. For example, in response to an earlier article opposing nonresistance that argued against the withdrawal from one's civic responsibilities, noted pacifist Henry Clarke Wright answered in the pages of the *Liberator*:

> So when you identify yourself with a military government, formed for military protection—'to establish justice, insure domestic tranquility, provide for the common defence, and promote the general welfare.' by military power— ... what is the difference between a warrior and an *Algerine* corsair? In your own language I ask—'IN WHAT RESPECTS DOES THE MILITARY COMMANDER (or the warrior, or commander-in-chief of the army and navy) DIFFER FROM THE AUTHORIZED COMMANDER OF A LETTER OF MARQUE AND REPRISAL, OR THE PIRATE COMMISSIONED BY THE GOVERNMENT OF ALGIERS?' NONE, as respects the nature of his commission and his office. You might as well say that God made those, born under the *Algerine* government, *pirates*; those, born in China, *idolaters*; and those, born in Constantinople, *Mahometans*, and justify them on this account, as to say that God made you a member of this government, and on that account excuse yourself for being a warrior.[24]

For Wright, militarized governments are all the same in their effective defense of slavery. If one's role is defined by the country one is born into, then an American soldier is morally no different from an Algerian following the orders of the dey of Algiers.

Along with frequent references to North African slavery, several papers printed updated versions of the republican-era Barbary satires discussed in chapter 2. In 1839, the Vermont abolitionist paper *Voice of Freedom* printed a letter allegedly from Hamet, the king of Morocco, praising Henry Clay's recent anti-abolition speech. Addressing Clay as "My Dear Cousin," Hamet

156 CHAPTER FIVE

lauds Clay's defense of the legal recognition of Black slaves as property but admits that he held reservations, "for even Moores have a conscience." Clay's argument seems to have allayed Hamet's concerns, however, as he suggests that the senator has proven that, "if Jews or Christians come into our dominions, laws and custom will justify us in confiscating their goods, and enslaving their persons. . . . What a golden rule! It works both ways, on whites as well as blacks, in republican America as in the States of Barbary." In conclusion, the monarch writes, "It is pleasing to find, that sentiments and practices, which have long prevailed among the Barbary Powers are sanctioned by honorable Senators in America. And we cannot but hope, that in your country the abstract notions that *all men are born equal and have certain inalienable rights*, will soon be exploded, and that the good old institutions of Morocco will be established under your auspices in every part of your Republic."[25] The formula here is familiar, as the African Muslim ruler's approval of the cruelty of American slavery was a common trope of eighteenth-century abolitionist satires. Hamet's letter bears more than a passing resemblance to Benjamin Franklin's "On the Slave Trade" (1790), with some key differences. Here the focus is no longer on the suffering of white and Black bodies but on the legal-territorial regimes that Hamet and Clay represent. The conceit is no longer of a text from the past translated into the present but rather of the direct address from one tyrant to another. The satire does not target the terms of the debate as much as it posits the kinship of slavocratic rule across America and Africa.

In the months following the publication of the Hamet letter, Algerines would play a particularly conspicuous role in the debate surrounding a wayward two-masted schooner recovered off the coast of Long Island. The ship, a Spanish vessel named *La Amistad*, had been taken over by its enslaved Black cargo led by a man named Sengbe Pieh, also known as Joseph Cinqué. Of course, the *Amistad* case is too well known to need extensive summary here but suffice it to say that the resulting Supreme Court deliberations rested on the question of whether the Black captives had been kidnapped from Africa, and were thus victims of the long-illegal trans-Atlantic trade, or whether they were lawful Spanish property, originating from Cuba, and had rebelled against their rightful masters. Within the American press debate raged over whether Pieh and the other captives were heroes or insurrectionaries. Former consul to Tunis Mordecai Manuel Noah, for his part, labeled them "pirates" in the pages of his newspaper the *New York Evening*

Star and expressed horror over the violence of the rebellion. In response, a writer for the *Boston Courier* asked, "Did Major Noah ever know any white men in the circumstances of these negroes? I presume not!" It seems obvious that this question was meant to be humorous, as it was well known from the *Travels* that Noah participated in the ransoming of white captives in Algiers during his tenure in Tunis. On this point the writer, identified as "G.B.," goes further into detail:

> Suppose, that an **Algerine** corsair had visited Boston, and fifty worthy Metropolitans had been kidnapped, hurried on board, taken to Algiers, and there sold to a Turkish dealer in Christian slaves; that they were shipped thence by the "owner" to Constantinople; that on the passage they killed the captain and several others, took command of the vessel, and, in striving to reach the "city of notions," were driven upon the shores of old England; that their surrender was demanded by the Ottoman Porte; and that English editors, on hearing these facts pronounced these Bostonians to be a set of "*mutineers*" and "*pirates*," and urged their government to give them up, to be tried as such by the Sublime Porte. What, in such a case, would we Americans say of those editors? Let the same be said, if we would maintain consistency of the editor of the Advertiser, and of all those, who adopt his course, relative to the Amistad affair; for *their* "case *is* exactly analogous" to the supposed one of the British editors.[26]

This piece is particularly noteworthy for the way it deploys its Algerine scenario to justify violence against slaveholders. The year before in the African American newspaper the *Colored American*, an article had used the example of Barbary slavery to justify the risk of abolition compelling the enslaved to rebel: "Let any reader suppose himself, with his friends and relatives, to be captured and carried into slavery in Barbary; let him ask himself the questions—should I, in that case, be more likely to resort to violence and insurrection to obtain my freedom, if I saw that a large portion of the people . . . opposed slavery and [made] great exertions for its abolition?"[27] Abolition does not directly incite rebellion; it merely creates an environment of sympathy for rebellious causes. We can see how both articles are concerned with media narratives surrounding antislavery violence. In G.B.'s argument, the Algerian pirates play an intermediary role as a mechanism to imagine the British press's vilification of American captives, recalling both the threat of white slavery and the early republic's vulnerability within the late eighteenth-century international community. That G.B.'s article involves a fairly complex and unlikely scenario speaks to the way that their analogy and many others engage with a form of probabilistic fictionality. Readers must imagine themselves as fictionalized versions of both the *Amistad* captives and white Barbary slaves.

The *Boston Courier's* writer was not by any means alone in relating the *Amistad* case to Barbary piracy. The *Daily National Intelligencer* asked whether an escaped Englishman "cast upon our shores" would be restored to his Algerian master, while the *Hampshire Gazette* went further to justify the violence against the *Amistad's* Spanish crew: "But suppose the prisoners had been Americans, and the masters of the *Amistad* had been Algerines, would any one have charged the former with *murder* or *piracy* for putting their Algerine *masters* to death?"[28] In another *Hampshire Gazette* article, the writer questions, if the insurgents had been American, whether any commentators would have "talked of the amiableness and 'respectability' of the Algerine who owned them."[29] The comparison was popular and influential enough to make its way into the Supreme Court arguments surrounding the case. In a piece that would be circulated in abolitionist papers as "Mr. Baldwin's Plea," Roger Sherman Baldwin, lawyer for the Africans, pointed out:

> The subject of the delivery of fugitives was under consideration before and during the negotiation of the Treaty of San Lorenzo; and was purposely omitted in the treaty. Sec. 10 Waite's State Papers, 151. 433. Our treaties with Tunis and Algiers contain similar expressions, in which both parties stipulate for the protection of the property of the subjects of each within the jurisdiction of the other. The Algerine regarded his Spanish captive as property; but was it ever supposed, that if an Algerine corsair should be seized by the captive slaves on board of her, it would be the duty of our naval officers, or our Courts of Admiralty, to recapture and restore them?[30]

This rather unusual plea cites legal precedent and treaties yet points out the ways in which sentiments of national (and racial) solidarity would necessarily take precent over international law. More than this, the invocation of Barbary slavery serves to make whiteness visible—the white bodies not only of the hypothetical prisoners but also of the court itself, debating abstract concepts to determine the fate of the very real Black bodies that are the objects of their deliberation. The Algerines and Tunisians in this case remind the court that white bodies too suffer, and they too rely on sympathetic allies for protection, even when that sympathy must override international agreements.

In most cases, it was the predatory Spanish who were compared to Algerian pirates. However, in one text sympathetic to the *Amistad* captives,

"THE ADVANTAGE OF A WHIP-LECTURE" 159

A True History of the African Chief Jingua, the Africans are mistakenly described as Muslims, and in an illustration, Pieh himself becomes a Barbary corsair, sailing toward the sun. In his reading of the illustration, Marcus Rediker identifies Pieh as wearing "a *keffiyah* (headdress), a *shemagh* (a traditional Muslim scarf), and a *kaif* (a curved Arabian sword)."[31] Despite the fact that the portrayal seems to play directly on the common charges of piracy against the Africans, the image is unquestionably heroic, in some ways legitimating Pieh's command of the vessel. Furthermore, in a rather indirect way, the depiction serves to confirm Pieh's origins, marking him clearly as an *African* pirate.

Significantly, the final sentences of *A True History* invert this depiction once again with a reference to the French subjugation of Algeria: "As long as Cuba continues in its present state, the *refugium peccatorum* and the receptacle of buccaneers, it is hopeless to attempt the reduction of the slave trade. Like the piractical state of Barbary, it is the opprobrium of the civilized

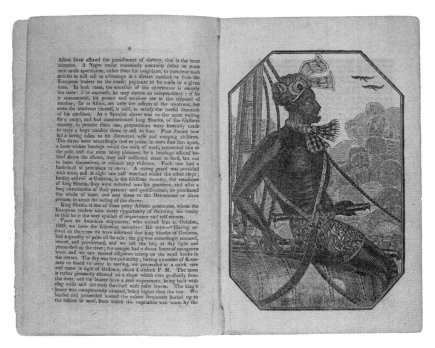

FIGURE 6. Sengbe Pieh as depicted in *A True History of the African Chief Jingua and His Comrades* (New York: The Booksellers, 1839), 9. —Courtesy Beinecke Rare Book and Manuscript Library, Yale University, New Haven, CT

160   CHAPTER FIVE

world, a nest of pirates and a den of thieves. We see no reason why it should not be taken possession of like Algiers, if its own weak and wicked government is not able or willing to uphold the common and established right of nations."[32] The author's image of Cuba as another Barbary Coast and their call to capture the island just as Algiers was invaded by the French represent a shift in the understanding of the American Barbary crises not just as a struggle for national security or a proto-imperial projection of power but as one series of conflicts within a larger global struggle against slavery itself. Yet, the author moves the focus from the suffering of the Africans to the "right of nations" and specifically the international consensus banning the slave trade, only indirectly dealing with the question of slavery itself in favor of articulating justice at a global scale. From our twenty-first-century perspective, we can see how the targeting of Spanish Cuba here bears an eerie resemblance to the calls for the United States to intervene in the Cuban War for Independence in the months leading up to the Spanish-American War more than half a century later, pointing again toward the ways in which antislavery rhetoric helped lay the foundations for narratives of trans-Atlantic and hemispheric American imperialism.

As a symbol for racial violence on the lawless seas, anachronistic Algerines were invoked again two years after the *Amistad* affair following the revolt on the American slave ship *Creole* led by Virginian Madison Washington. Washington and his compatriots rose up against their captors and gained control of the *Creole*, redirecting it from its destination of New Orleans to the Bahamas, where the enslaved were freed under British colonial law. In this incident, the United States found itself much in the same position as the Spanish government in the *Amistad* case, demanding the return of American property. During what became known as the *Creole* affair, Daniel Webster, then serving as the secretary of state under President John Tyler, despite his abolitionist sympathies, accused Washington and his followers of being "mutineers and murderers" and demanded their return. In response, the *New York American* published a long letter, later republished in *The Liberator*, purporting to "throw some light upon the principals involved in the present controversy." Very much in line with similar defenses of Sengbe Pieh, the anonymous commentator cites a long history of the United States paying ransom to North African pirates for the freedom of American captives, including in the letter the specific sums. During the Algerine crisis, the dey of Algiers demanded "$2833 a head, for our countrymen." President George Washington requested $40,000 from Congress to free thirteen Americans, but the crisis was only finally resolved with the payment of $525,000 for more than a hundred captives. After recounting this history of ransom, the writer acknowledges, "It seems strange to us, at the present day, to hear *white* men spoken of as *slaves.*" Nevertheless, the large sums paid to free the Americans spoke to how highly they were valued under the "Constitution of Algiers," just as Madison Washington and his compatriots were valued by their American owners. From here the writer develops a thought experiment in which American captives rebel against their Algerian masters and manage to escape in a ship to Gibraltar. Would not, according to the logic of Webster and others, the British authorities be required to turn over the slaves to their "rightful" owners, given their value? The writer concludes, somewhat acerbically, "I am inclined to believe that, with certain statesmen, a man's *complexion* makes a wonderful difference in the application of moral and political principles."[33] The conclusion itself seems the exact opposite of that reached by Benjamin Franklin in "On the Slave Trade." In that case, Franklin asserted the remarkable similarity in pro-slavery arguments across Algiers and the United States. This later writer, reflecting on the Barbary crises, can assume the uneven, hypocritical treatment of white slaves and North African slavery. Nevertheless, the similarity in phrasing suggests a line of influence that underlies the transhistorical reference to Algiers as a space of enslavement.

Rather than focusing on how the white enslaved bodies suffered, as so many republican-era narratives did, the writer in this case shifts the focus to how those bodies were *commodified* and assigned an exchange value. In other words, the writer points to the reduction of the American sailors' bodies to property—not private property, in this case, but *national* property—to be bought and sold through diplomacy. The implication is that the republic, which would certainly prefer to see itself as a liberator for paying the ransom of the American captives, was instead purchasing those citizens much in the way of a planter negotiating with a slave trader. In this sense, viewing the *Creole* affair through the lens of Barbary piracy allowed commentators to raise the precedent of white bodies reduced to their base value and haggled over as they reproduce the disagreements over exactly what a white American body is worth to the nation.

162 CHAPTER FIVE

DOUGLASS AMONG THE ALGERINES

Given how often Barbary pirates appeared in debates surrounding both the *Amistad* and *Creole* controversies, it is not particularly surprising that Algiers itself would appear briefly in Frederick Douglass's fictionalized narrative of the *Creole* revolt, *The Heroic Slave* (1852), which attempts to reconstruct the story of the incident from the perspective of Madison Washington. The novel, while once largely neglected by modern critics, has become what William Boelhower calls "a central Atlantic-world *exemplum*" for new paradigms of oceanic and Atlanticist study.[34] Boelhower points specifically to the climactic moment at the end of the novel, related in a Richmond coffeehouse by the white first mate of the *Creole*, Tom Grant. Grant describes Washington taking the helm of the *Creole* after the successful rebellion and declaring, "Mr. mate, you cannot write the bloody laws of slavery on those restless billows. The ocean, if not the land, is free." Grant expands on this sharp distinction between territorial and oceanic orders when challenged by a fellow patron who boasts that he would have suppressed the rebellion easily:

> Mr. Williams, all that you've now said sounds very well *here* on shore, where, perhaps, you have studied negro character. I do not profess to understand the subject as well as yourself; but it strikes me, you apply the same rule in dissimilar cases. . . . It is one thing to manage a company of slaves on a Virginia plantation, and quite another thing to quell an insurrection on the lonely billows of the Atlantic, where every breeze speaks of courage and liberty. For the negro to act cowardly on shore, may be to act wisely; and I've some doubts whether *you*, Mr. Williams, would find it very convenient were you a slave in Algiers, to raise your hand against the bayonets of a whole government.[35]

The mate emphasizes the Atlantic space as disconnected from the territorial power that maintains racial hierarchy. That power works the same in Africa as it does in the Americas, albeit through a different racial hierarchy. Grant casually connects Algiers to Virginia as analogous and fundamentally distinct from the oceanic order, which, according to him, tends toward freedom rather than oppression. In his reading of this moment in the text, Ivy Wilson argues that this reference to Algiers suggests an attempt to "[superimpose] French imperialism onto the question of slavery in the United States," an interpretation that would make sense chronologically in the early 1840s, when the scene supposedly takes place, but does not convey the implication of white victimization.[36] This misreading is telling, as it suggests how Algiers as a referent meant something very different to readers as late as 1852 than it does to us. Carrie Hyde, on the other hand, argues that the example of Algiers shows how the slave system could only be maintained in "the artificial environs of a plantation," thus, in such an unnatural structure, the roles of master and slave are arbitrary and subject to reversal.[37] The implication of this reading, of course, is that Algiers as a historical referent stands in for the plantation, for an "unnatural" site of endemic violence. Yet, we can take this much further to point to an Algiers effectively located outside of time and space, as a symbol for white slavery and territorialized state power. To the extent that the novel offers the unruly sea as a refuge from oppressive slave regimes and their legal strictures, Algiers suggests that the geography of enslavement can as easily affect, contain, and victimize white bodies as it does Black ones.

While comparably minor, this brief invocation of an anachronistic Algiers offers just one instance in which Douglass's career was surrounded and contextualized by allusions to the Barbary. In my reading of the poem "The American Algiers" (1797) in chapter 1 I discussed how the pleas of white slaves in Algiers, real and fictional, provided a framework through which white readers could interpret and limit the radical potential of the voices of the enslaved. In the case of Douglass, his own narrative (as well as legal) transition from slavery to freedom was repeatedly compared to the liberatory narrative of the Barbary slaves of the previous era. Take, for example, the controversy surrounding Douglass's legal manumission by his former master Thomas Auld. While many in Garrison's circle wanted Douglass to attain safety from recapture, some argued that accepting formal manumission would mean effectively legitimizing the slave system contrary to the strategy of nonresistance. In this debate Henry Clarke Wright, in a letter in *The Liberator* entitled "The Ransom" and addressed directly to Douglass, who at the time was in Britain, invokes the precedent of Barbary slaves: "The nation must and shall be humbled before its victims. . . . The plea, that [Douglass's manumission] is the same as a ransom paid for a capture of some Algerine pirate, or Bedouin Arab, is naught. You have already, by your own energy, escaped the grasp of the pirate Auld."[38] Wright makes a crucial distinction here, as an American captive in North Africa could theoretically escape captivity and be then freed. Only American slavery was seen as extending beyond its geographical boundaries, in accordance with the Fugitive Slave Act.

164 **CHAPTER FIVE**

The Barbary context for Douglass's career extends further beyond the pages of *The Liberator* to include his autobiographies. In his preface to *The Narrative of the Life of Frederick Douglass* (1845), Garrison quotes an anecdote from a speech given by Irish antislavery activist Daniel O'Connell: "An American sailor, who was cast away on the shore of Africa, where he was kept in slavery for three years, was, at the expiration of that period, found to be imbruted and stultified—he had lost all reasoning power; and having forgotten his native language, could only utter some savage gibberish between Arabic and English, which nobody could understand, and which even he himself found difficulty in pronouncing. So much for the humanizing influence of THE DOMESTIC INSTITUTION!" Garrison draws from this anecdote the lesson that "the white slave can sink as low in the scale of humanity as the black one."[39] It might have been easy for American readers to misread this particular reference as being to James Riley and his popular 1817 narrative of shipwreck and enslavement, yet neither the duration nor the phenomenon of language loss matched his story. Rather, O'Connell's allusion was more fully explained in an earlier speech given in 1840 and reprinted in *The Liberator* in 1842: "Why, some of you may recollect the case of the American ADAMS, who having been lost in Africa, the dark swarthy natives said was only fit for a slave; he was evidently inferior to their race; the whites were good for nothing but slavery."[40] O'Connell most likely references Robert Adams, the mixed-race American sailor whose narrative, which I discussed briefly in chapter 1, caused a sensation in Britain but was largely dismissed in the United States.[41] There are several reasons why Garrison might have chosen to include a less specific reference in the preface. For one, he might have wanted to remind readers of Riley's narrative while sidestepping those allegations that Adams had fabricated his entire narrative. Given that those charges were more prevalent in the United States than in Great Britain, where the narrative was first published and where O'Connell delivered his speech, Garrison's avoidance of Adams makes more sense. Of course, it is also worth noting that Adams himself would not have been considered white to Garrison's audience, and so he would have served as a poor example for the degradation of the white man in slavery. For Garrison, the crucial outcome of the narrative is that the victim effectively lost his voice and therefore could serve as an object of analysis to prove the degrading effects of slavery on civilized people, something he also highlights in the famous section of the autobiography in which the enslaved Douglass (then Bailey) gazes longingly out onto the water of the Chesapeake. Garrison's decision not to name Adams, and instead to utilize him as an anonymous, unspeaking exemplum of the regressive effects of slavery, anticipates Douglass's later frustrations with the Garrisonians' denying him narrative agency.[42] Recognizing this subtle resurfacing of the Barbary in this well-known text allows us to see in stark contrast how midcentury abolitionist print culture continued to privilege white empiricism over Black testimony.[43]

A less direct reference to Barbary slavery can be read into the text that effectively replaces Garrison's preface: James McCune Smith's introduction to Douglass's second autobiography, *My Bondage and My Freedom* (1855). In that text, Smith famously declares Douglass to be "a Representative American man," due to the fact that he had "passed through every gradation of rank comprised in our national make-up."[44] Although Smith does not mention Barbary captivity here, he does elsewhere in his work, most notably in his essay "The Destiny of the People of Color" (1843), in which he explores historical precedents for the condition of African Americans in slavery in the United States and their possible future after liberation. In that essay, he compares African American slavery with the biblical enslavement of the Jews, the conditions of slaves in Greek antiquity, and the much more recent examples of North African slavery. He notes that, as in the case of America, "on the coast of Barbary the masters are the majority and slaves (white) of a different complexion." However, he quickly concludes that the Barbary precedent has little to teach African Americans, as "the white slaves on the coast of Barbary have as yet wrought out no general fact in history: as if slavery was natural to them, they have tamely remained in bondage, occasionally escaping by flight or ransom."[45] Smith's tongue-in-cheek dismissal of this white slavery example both reverses racist claims that African Americans were genetically predisposed to obedience and counters allegations that those who had escaped plantations necessarily suffered from a disorder such as drapetomania. It is through the lens of this earlier essay that I suggest we can read Smith's later description of Douglass's representative Americanness. If the white slaves in Barbary have failed to truly enter history, Douglass's narrative of the movement from slavery to liberation and full manhood through his own "active toil" represents the true foundation for revolutionary American identity, a comparison that was made frequently in American Barbary narratives. In some ways, Smith's claim functions as the reverse of Garrison's earlier use of O'Connell's example—while Garrison focuses on the deleterious effects of enslavement on the mind and particularly the capacity for self-expression, Smith emphasizes the ways in which that experience authorizes Douglass to speak for the nation that itself has been enslaved, whether figuratively by the British Empire or more literally by Barbary slave masters.

Barbary figures occupy the margins of Douglass's autobiography in other ways as well. In fact, Douglass's first encounter with a voice explicitly framed as an African American slave in print was likely David Everett's play *Slaves in Barbary* (1797). In his autobiography, Douglass, then living in Baltimore, relates purchasing a copy of Caleb Bingham's *The Columbian Orator* shortly after teaching himself to read. Originally published in 1797, the anthology's subtitle offers "a Variety of Original and Selected Pieces; Together with Rules, Calculated to Improve Youth and Others in the Ornamental and Useful Art of Eloquence." This collection of readings includes short stories, plays, and speeches by Roman generals, Indian chiefs, American presidents, and, on the other end of the scale, small boys and dissipated students. Along with these passages are helpful guidelines for pronunciation, posture, tone, and gesture. Douglass credits the book with teaching him that he was not, in fact, a "slave for life," and that he could someday be free. In particular, he singles out a short piece, John Aikin's "Dialogue between a Master and a Slave," taken from the eighteenth-century British children's collection *Evenings at Home* (1792–1796). In the piece, an unnamed slave, being upbraided by his master for repeatedly attempting to escape from bondage, meekly yet eloquently submits to his fate. The slave's pathetic appeal so touches the master that the speaker earns emancipation.[46] Douglass, inspired by the power of the slave's argument, writes, "I could not help feeling that the day might come, when the well-directed answers made by the slave to the master, in this instance, would find their counterpart in myself."[47] While Douglass is clearly inspired by the ability of the slave to bring about his emancipation through rhetoric, the slave's submission offers a very different model than Douglass himself, who famously battles his overseer and later escapes to the North. Douglass mentions this dialogue, along with Richard Brinsley Sheridan's speech on Irish emancipation and a handful of other texts, as having a profound effect on him. Ironically, he does not mention Everett's play, which is the anthology's most explicit piece of American abolitionist literature and is also significant for offering one of the first speaking African American roles on the American stage.[48]

Everett's play, set in Tunis presumedly in the 1790s, presents a view of slavery perhaps more accurate to Baltimore and the antebellum South than the rhetoric presented in Aikin's master-slave dialogue. The plot features rebellious white slaves and duplicitous African masters, making the point that the status of slave is not racially determined but contingent on local circumstances and norms. The play opens on a note of defiance, as the formerly enslaved Venetian Ozro arrives to liberate his brother Amandar from his enslavement to his Muslim owner, Oran. The master immediately confronts Ozro, leading the latter to declare, "Talk not of chains! But rather learn to dread the hand, on which they have been bound!" In response, Oran immediately doubles the price for Amandar's liberation. Nevertheless, Ozro pays the ransom, although it is revealed later that the brothers are now the property of Hamet, the bashaw of Tunis. As Oran laments later, "He who frees a slave, arms an assassin."[49] This opening scene sets the tone for much of the rest of the work, which portrays the slave system of Tunis as violent and irrational, paranoid against the pervasive threat of defiance and vengeance.

Everett's play focuses almost entirely on questions of purchase, ransom, and freedom, with much of the work centering on a slave auction. During that auction we are introduced to the captives Kidnap, a white slave master from the American South, and Sharp, his Black former slave. As his new masters bring Kidnap up for auction, potential buyers mock him, with one declaring, "He has been a wholesale dealer in slaves himself; and is just beginning the hard lesson of repentance." Hamet, who asks Kidnap whether he comes from the "the boasted land of liberty," asks Sharp whether his former master had been humane. Sharp responds, "No, masser planter! He get drunk! He whip me! He knock a me down! He stamp on a me! He will kill a me dead! No! No! Let a poor negur live wid a you, masser planter . . . fore I go back to America again."[50] Hamet, disgusted by Kidnap's brutality, declares, "Deliver this man to the highest bidder. Let misery teach him, what he could never learn in affluence, the lesson of humanity." Kidnap is swiftly sold, and his purchaser then insists on also acquiring Sharp at an inflated price, announcing, "I intend to put [Sharp's] old master under his instruction, that he may occasionally have the advantage of a whip-lecture from his former slave, whom he has treated so kindly."[51] Once the episode with Kidnap and Sharp concludes, another captive, Francisco, comes up for auction. Francisco angrily declares that he had only come to Tunis to ransom his brothers, Ozro and Amandar. Hamet recognizes Francisco as the man

168 CHAPTER FIVE

who had previously freed him from slavery in Venice, and he then liberates all three brothers at the end of the play as an act of gratitude. Contrasting with many of the other Barbary works of the 1790s, Everett's play generally portrays the bashaw of Tunis as a merciful, just ruler; he depicts only the very minor characters of Oran and the American slaveholder Kidnap as beyond redemption, and both end the work threatened by impending violence. Most importantly, while Sharp remains enslaved at the end of the play, his elevation over Kidnap by his purchaser is framed not only as justice but as an act of African solidarity against the hypocrisy of America's rhetoric of freedom.

There are reasons why Douglass may not have mentioned reading this play in his autobiographies.[52] For one, the characters in the play are not particularly eloquent, with Sharp speaking in thick dialect. For another, the karmic moral of the work does not rely on the liberating power of rhetoric. However, as I have suggested, the play does offer an important message regarding the racial dimensions of slavery, particularly to mid-nineteenth-century readers, as it depicts white Americans and Europeans as just as vulnerable to being enslaved as northern and sub-Saharan Africans. Additionally, the enslavement of both Kidnap and Sharp by a new Arab master demonstrates a more complicated view of racial divisions and racialized violence than the simple opposition of Blackness and whiteness. Nevertheless, we can briefly speculate about how the Barbary trope of reversal, rather than the eloquence and resignation in Aikin's text, provides a productive lens through which we can read Douglass's own framing of his liberation in his autobiographies, particularly in his iconic struggle with the slave breaker Covey. In *The Black Atlantic* (1993), Paul Gilroy reads Douglass's struggle with Covey as "an alternative to Hegel," who notoriously dismissed the importance of Africa to universal history. The conflict functions as "a supplement if not exactly a trans-coding of [Hegel's] account of the struggle between lord and bondsman."[53] Inverting Hegel's allegory, Douglass emerges from his fight with the slave breaker to announce, "I was a changed being after that fight. I was *nothing* before; I WAS A MAN NOW. It recalled to life my crushed self-respect and my self-confidence, and inspired me with a renewed determination to be a FREEMAN."[54] Gilroy argues that there is a "suggestive connection" between Douglass's liberation from the western master-slave dynamic and the writer's later interest in the greatness of pre-slavery African civilizations such as Egypt.[55] Looking outside the Hegelian West allows us to understand the global and diasporic dimensions of Douglass's narrative and his embrace of physical resistance at this point in his narrative.

As Margaret Kohn has discussed, Douglass's account of the "liberatory effects of violence" in this pivotal scene, which runs across all three of his autobiographies, seems particularly at odds with his embrace of pacifism and Garrisonian nonresistance in 1845.[56] At the very least, it contrasts sharply with the model for liberation through resignation that Douglass remarks on in Aikin's "Dialogue." However, I would suggest that we can read this episode more effectively not in connection to Douglass's much later interest in Egypt but in Everett's Tunis. As Gilroy notes, Douglass's emergence into de facto if not de jure freedom through physical struggle "underscored the complicity of civilisation and brutality while emphasising that the order of authority on which the slave plantation relied cannot be undone without recourse to the counter-violence of the oppressed."[57] As I discussed above, Tunis in the play is a site of both endemic violence and retributive justice. The Tunisians of the play provide, ultimately, the reverse of the southern slave plantation. Yet, while Douglass's characterization of Covey throughout the narrative as brutal and hypocritical fits the model of Everett's Kidnap, Sharp's continued enslavement provides a poor precedent for the writer's own self-construction. In this sense, Douglass may have found more inspiration in the figure of Hamet, whose pirates plunder slaveholding westerners to expose them to the "whip lecture," but who also acts justly to those who deserve their freedom. In other words, Tunis may have provided a more immediate example for Douglass of the African voice in world history, and the seeming contradiction in his aggressive pacifism maps well onto the contradictions of Everett's noble bashaw as a figure for the reversal of the master-slave dynamic within the Black Atlantic. While we necessarily have to rely on speculation, as several biographers of Douglass before have, about the extent to which he was influenced by Everett's play, at the very least *Slaves in Barbary*, which we know Douglass had read before 1845, provides more immediate context for the writer's struggle than Hegel's work, which he had not.[58] Noting this connection to Barbary narratives allows us to better understand how, even in this early phase of his career, Douglass worked to revise and embed himself within a national history of liberation, one he invokes much later in *The Heroic Slave* when he celebrates Madison Washington's revolutionary Virginian heritage.[59]

Douglass and McCune Smith were not the only African American writers to take up the symbols of Algiers, Tunis, and the Barbary corsairs. Published the same year as Douglass's first biography, Lewis Clarke's *Narrative of the Sufferings of Lewis Clarke during a Captivity of More Than Twenty-Five Years. Among the Algerines of Kentucky* applies the Algerine label to southern slave society in what might be a reference to one of the most prominent early Algerine works.[60] Clarke's title closely resembles the subtitle of Royall Tyler's novel *The Algerine Captive; or, The Life and Adventures of Doctor Updike Underhill: Six Years a Prisoner among the Algerines* (1797).[61] Not only does Clarke repeat the phrase "among the Algerines" but he effectively labels himself an Algerine "captive." In the narrative, Clarke only refers to Kentuckian slaveholders as Algerines twice, with both references appearing in the context of local customs. For example, describing a feud within his master's family, Clarke observes, "These wars are very common among the Algerines in Kentucky; indeed, slave-holders have not arrived at that degree of civilization that enables them to live in tolerable peace, though united by the nearest family ties."[62] Clarke's reference here accomplishes several things at once. Observing Algerine society, he adopts the stance of ethnographic authority that characterized so many earlier Barbary texts, while simultaneously *othering* the violence inherent in the American slave system. The global scope of his remark on slaveholders suggests that Algerines in Kentucky are no different than Algerines in Algiers (even as the latter are now French colonial subjects). Although again a fleeting mention, Clarke's use of the "Algerine" label reinforces the way the Barbary archive continued to be a potent cultural touchstone for white and Black abolitionists well into the mid-nineteenth century.

FREEDOM IN "THE GREAT WOMB OF SLAVERY"

So far I have focused on how allusions to Barbary slavery functioned to remind white readers of the threat of violence against white bodies within shared national memory. Many of the references in abolitionist works, particularly those that name Algiers specifically, utilized the Barbary as a metonym for a global geography of slave territories, but not all discussions of North Africa were negative. At the same time that debate raged in America over the *Creole* affair, Ahmad Bey, the ruler of Tunis, outlawed all slavery in that state. From 1841 to 1847, the American abolitionist press reported extensively on the progress of emancipation in Tunis, with many pieces quoting a statement made by Ahmad Bey to the British consul, justifying abolition "for the glory of mankind, to distinguish them from the brute creation."[63] Outside the abolitionist press, however, fewer newspapers commented on the event. For many abolitionists, the general lack of attention paid to Ahmad Bey's efforts offered a clear example of how the successes of global abolitionism had been suppressed in the American press. In an article entitled "Barbary not Barbarian," *The Emancipator* took the mainstream press to task for not following closely enough the progress of abolition in Tunis, noting that the expected violence from the formerly enslaved had not manifested:

> Had a single African slave killed his master on the coast of Barbary, in ungrateful return for kind treatment (so called) in his chains, the newspapers of republican America would have rung with the horrid recital, dressed up in all the exaggerations of language. But when steps are taken by these Mohammedan barbarians, (as they are generally deemed,) to *lead* our Christian nation in the career of humanity, by decreeing universal emancipation, a black silence is observed. How many general newspapers have given an intelligible account of the glorious proceedings of the Bey of Tunis? We have looked in vain among them for even an allusion to the progress of the work, and to its exceedingly promising commencement in Tripoli.—With a single exception of a Philadelphia paper, we do not recollect to have seen the slightest notice of it, although it came in the last steamer but one.[64]

Given the enduring association of the Barbary States with piracy and slavery, the peaceful abolition of slavery in Tunis provided definitive proof that slavery could be eliminated from any society, no matter how deeply it was engrained in the economic and social fabric. As much as abolitionists sought to attract public attention to current events in Tunis, the focus on the Barbary Coast also gave them the opportunity to recast slavery itself as a specter of the past. Such was the tone struck by James Richardson, the British consul in Tunis and prominent antislavery correspondent, as he toured the aftermath of Ahmad Bey's decree: "I went, whilst in Tunis, to see the demolished slave-market. I felt deeply when I saw the ruin of this crying iniquity. Hundreds of years human beings had been exposed for sale in that place, like cattle! How strange that a Mussulman state should tear down that den of traffic for the bodies and souls of men, while in Christian America this foul system still flourishes in such vigor!! How dreadful the responsibility of the Americans!"[65] Certainly abolitionists invoked Tunis as a way of shaming their pro-slavery compatriots and offering a comparative critique of the brutality and hypocrisy of American slavery, but we can see even greater stakes when reading the tone of these reports through Gilroy's framework of the reversal of the master-slave dialectic and the defiance of Hegel's western progressive history. In this scheme, the United States risks not just falling behind but of falling outside of whiggish history entirely. In the ruins of the Tunisian slave markets we can read the sense of "belatedness" and temporal displacement that Dana Luciano characterizes as the "countermonumentalism" of Frederick Douglass's later speech "What to a Slave Is the Fourth of July." The counter-monumental perspective, Luciano writes, seeks to "transform the chronobiopolitical structures encoded within liberal-sentimental responses to slavery." Rejecting the appeal to "redemptionist teleology," the Tunisian ruins challenge "the naturalized structures" through which Americans "understand freedom, synonymous with Americanness, as their inheritance."[66]

As Schoolman has explored, British emancipation of the West Indies in the mid-1830s highlighted for abolitionists the "mixed status of abolition as a single development spanning oceans and continents."[67] The perceived failures of the emancipation process, evident in the economic decline of the once-prosperous planter class, seemed a warning to the United States. Tunis, on the other hand, offered no such complications for the narrative of global abolition. Situated comfortably outside of the white Christian world, Tunis could exist in the emancipatory present that was leaving the United States behind while abolitionists need not worry over its future or the well-being of Tunisian elites. This lack of concern speaks again for the convenience of the Barbary over the Caribbean: Muslim slaveholders could be directly compared to southern planters at one moment and then entirely distanced from them at the next.

One abolitionist who made good use of the occasion of Tunis's outlawing of slavery was lawyer and later senator from Massachusetts Charles Sumner. In 1847, he first delivered his popular lecture, later reprinted and widely circulated, entitled *White Slavery in the Barbary States*. At the outset, Sumner announces the novelty of his subject, saying that no person "has ever before attempted to combine in a connected essay the scattered materials" regarding white slavery in North Africa. Of course, there were many histories and travel narratives describing the present and past of Algiers during the Barbary crises decades earlier, including Mathew Carey's *Short Account of Algiers* (1794), but Sumner's claim to originality comes from his focus not on a geopolitical narrative of North Africa—although his lecture does provide that—but a transnational history of the institution of slavery with its foundations in Africa itself, which Sumner describes as the "great womb of slavery."[68] Unlike those earlier histories, fascinated by the cultures and peoples of the Muslim world and offering only short digressions into slavery itself, Sumner keeps his primary focus throughout on the enslaved and, in a broader sense, the place of slavery in the history of global civilization.

Despite the specificity of his title, Sumner leaves no question that when he is talking about slavery, he is also gesturing toward the American South. Early in the lecture he notes in particular "a singular and instructive comparison," remarking that the territory of the Barbary "is placed between the twenty-ninth and thirty eighth degrees of north latitude, occupying nearly the same parallels with what are called the Slave States of our Union." Taking this point further, Sumner writes, "Algiers, which has been the most obnoxious place in the Barbary States of Africa, which was branded by an indignant writer as 'the wall of the barbarian world,' and which was the chief seat of Christian slavery, is situated on the parallel of 36° 30' north latitude, being the line of what is termed the Missouri Compromise, marking the 'wall' of Christian slavery in our country west of the Mississippi." Expounding on this geographic "resemblance," he suggests that "perhaps the common peculiarities of climate, breeding indolence, lassitude, and selfishness, may account for the insensibility to the claims of justice and humanity which seem to have characterized both regions."[69] In Sumner's interpretation, the Missouri Compromise did not just formalize the boundary between slave and free states. In a transnational context, it shifted the chief distinction from that of East and West to that of global North and South. In doing so, he sets up the crucial ways in which midcentury abolitionists would recast the Barbary conflicts from their historical grounding in the centuries-long battles between Christianity and Islam to a series of struggles against international slave power.

Another prominent New England abolitionist to react to the news from Tunis was poet John Greenleaf Whittier, who compared the decisive action by which Ahmad Bey had "immortalized his name" to the obstruction of the Tyler administration and Congress: "It is a very mortifying reflection, that while a Mohammedan Prince has been thus engaged, . . . our Republican and Christian Government has become assiduously employed in strengthening the slave-system. . . . is the Crescent to be the symbol of freedom, and the Cross of slavery?" Whittier concludes with a clearly provocative question to his readers, "SHALL THE BIBLE ENSLAVE THE WORLD?"[70] Whittier clearly thought that the abolition of slavery in Tunis was an epochal event, referencing it in a number of his antislavery poems. In one of his most famous abolitionist poems, "The Crisis," written as a commentary on the extension of slavery with the territorial gains resulting from the Mexican-American War, Whittier directly contrasts the westward movement of racial oppression with events in North Africa:

> The day is breaking in the East of which the prophets told,
> And brightens up the sky of Time the Christian Age of Gold:
> Old Might to Right is yielding, battle blade to clerkly pen,
> Earth's monarchs are her peoples, and her serfs stand up as men;
> The isles rejoice together, in a day are nations born,
> And the slave walks free in Tunis, and by Stamboul's Golden Horn![71]

Similarly, in "The Christian Slave," a reaction to the cry from a New Orleans slave auction describing one enslaved woman praised as "a good Christian," he compares Christian hypocrisy directly with the liberatory power of Islam:

> Oh, shame! The Moslem thrall,
> Who, with his master, to the Prophet kneels,
> While turning to the sacred Kebla feels
> His Fetters break and fall.
>
> Cheers for the turbaned Bey
> Of robber-peopled Tunis! He hath torn
> The dark slave-dungeons open, and hath borne
> Their inmates into day:
>
> But our poor slave in vain
> Turns to the Christian shrine his aching eyes;
> Its rites will only swell his market price,
> And rivet on his chain.[72]

In his reading of the poem, Timothy Marr argues that Whittier highlights "the paradox of Muslim emancipation" to shame American Christians.[73] More subtly, the poet emphasizes American race-based slavery as a historical aberration. His almost supernatural image of the fetters falling from the praying thrall alludes to the history of the *renegado*, the captured European on the Barbary Coast who converts to be freed. Traditionally, these figures were seen as villains, yet Whittier deploys the converted slave to demonstrate the Muslim refusal to enslave other Muslims, in contrast to the ways American slaveholders seek out Christian slaves because they are more easily exploitable. He bitterly concludes that Islam has the power to free you, while Christianity only makes you more marketable.

Whittier's most extensive engagement with Barbary slavery in verse, however, came not in his celebrations of freedom in Tunis but in his narrative poem "Derne," an account of William Eaton's capture of the city during the Tripolitan War. First published in the *National Era* in 1850, this poem eschews comparative orientalism to present a straightforward account of liberation by force of arms. Rather than a peaceful emancipation, Whittier describes a surprise attack on the Tripolitan city and Eaton's rescuing the enslaved Christians within:

> Vain, Moslem, vain thy lifeblood poured
> So freely on thy foeman's sword!
> Not to the swift nor to the strong
> The battles of the right belong;
> For he who strikes for Freedom wears
> The armor of the captive's prayers,
> And Nature proffers to his cause
> The strength of her eternal laws;
> While he whose arm essays to bind
> And herd with common brutes his kind
> Strives evermore at fearful odds
> With Nature and the jealous gods,
> And dares the dread recoil which late
> Or soon their right shall vindicate.
>
> 'T is done, the hornëd crescent falls
> The star-flag flouts the broken walls
> Joy to the captive husband! joy
> To thy sick heart, O brown-locked boy!
> In sullen wrath the conquered Moor
> Wide open flings your dungeon-door,
> And leaves ye free from cell and chain,

The owners of yourselves again.
Dark as his allies desert-born,
Soiled with the battle's stain, and worn
With the long marches of his band
Through hottest wastes of rock and sand,
Scorched by the sun and furnace-breath
Of the red desert's wind of death,
With welcome words and grasping hands,
The victor and deliverer stands![74]

Whittier revels in the violent deaths of Muslim slaveholders at the hands of Christians protected by the righteousness of the antislavery cause. Of course, the simple opposition overlooks the fact that Eaton's force was made up almost entirely of Muslim mercenaries and supporters of the bashaw of Tripoli's pro-American brother. The scene of liberation repeats the image from "The Christian Slave" a few years earlier of the dungeon door being torn open, yet this time freedom comes after a bloody struggle in which the symbol of Muslim rule, the "horned crescent," is replaced by the "star-flag." Again, Whittier ignores the more complicated details of Eaton's expedition by reframing it as a Christian conquest of eastern oppression, sidestepping the fact that the general was capturing the city on behalf of the new bashaw he hoped to install.[75] Nevertheless, Whittier's poem joins several similar works in the 1850s attempting to reframe the Tripolitan War of a half-century earlier as part of a global crusade against slavery. Eaton comes to symbolize the power of the midcentury abolitionist movement, a connection the poet makes explicit in the final stanza:

Men speak the praise of him who gave
Deliverance to the Moorman's slave,
Yet dare to brand with shame and crime
The heroes of our land and time—
The self-forgetful ones, who stake
Home, name, and life for Freedom's sake.[76]

Whittier seems to draw here from the memory of the Tripolitan War as a victory that could unite the country—a moment in which North and South together opposed slavery, albeit in North Africa rather than America. Only the basest hypocrite, the poet suggests, would celebrate Eaton's victory while condemning the abolitionists who continue to carry out his work at home.

The reinterpretation of the Tripolitan War, and to a lesser extent the 1815 Algerine War, suggests a growing sense that the slave question would come down to violence. In his 1850 "Letter to the American Slaves," Douglass asserts that "the colored American, for the sake of relieving his colored brethren, would no more hesitate to shoot an American slaveholder, than would a white American, for the sake of delivering his white brother, hesitate to shoot an Algerine slaveholder."[77] In 1854, Horace Greeley cited another hero of that conflict to oppose the piecemeal purchasing of individual slaves' freedom when he wrote, "You may have heard, perhaps, of the sentiment proclaimed by Decatur to the slaveholders of the Barbary Coast: 'Millions for defense, not a cent for tribute!'"[78] In this context, it is not surprising that later defenders of John Brown compared him to both Eaton and Decatur after the raid on Harper's Ferry. Expressing disgust at Brown's sentencing, one commentator noted, "I remember well that a handful of men were sent out from this country to right the wrongs done to some of our countrymen by one of those Barbary States. . . . The faith of this country is, that a man—at least one of Brown's race—has a right to kill for his freedom; has a right to wade for this liberty through seas of blood, or climb to it over mountains of the slain."[79] Wendell Phillips invoked Algiers in the month preceding Brown's execution, condemning Virginia as "only a larger and blacker Algiers. The only prayer of a true man for such is, 'Gracious Heaven! Unless they repent, send soon their Exmouth and Decatur.'"[80] At one "meeting of sympathy" in Albany, the attendees resolved that, "while patriots may not all approve the course of John Brown, yet so long as the remembrance of the effort of Decatur's men to liberate the American captives from the Algerines . . . remains, we must accord to John Brown honor and glory equally with those brave heroes."[81] Douglass too made this connection, declaring that white men "captured by an Algerine pirate, carried to Algiers, put in chains, and forced to work from morning to night" would "thank any John Brown" who came to save them.[82] While these references might not have been as pervasive in the lead-up to the Civil War as they had been in decades prior, they demonstrate that abolitionists were well aware of the Barbary crises as setting a precedent for (white) militant opposition to slavery in American history. In the eyes of some, the Tripolitan War would provide the model for the upcoming conflict along the lines of the threat that the anonymous author of *The True History* directed toward Cuba during the *Amistad* crisis: intervention, pacification, regime change.

As I have demonstrated, the Algerines would continue to navigate the rough waters of American print culture even as their contemporary counterparts, the Algerians, suffered under colonial French rule. Their survival in publications like *The Liberator* and the *Anti-Slavery Standard* constitutes only part of their long afterlife as symbols for the intersection of political oppression and racial otherness. That said, as I have suggested, the continued focus on white victimization and African barbarity, even in service of cross-racial sympathy, recasts European-American imperialism as a project of liberation. As we know, this way of thinking about imperialism as a tool of national self-defense and "spreading freedom" would prove useful for the United States throughout the nineteenth and twentieth centuries and would drive the twenty-first-century War on Terror.

CHAPTER SIX

PETER PARLEY IN TRIPOLI

Q. What do you think about property in slaves?
A. Let me reply to that question by asking others. If you were taken by an Algerine
pirate, and an Arab bought you, and paid honestly for you, should you consider
yourself the *property* of the Arab?

—Lydia Maria Child, *Anti-Slavery Catechism* (1836)

As we saw in the previous chapter, the inclusion of David Everett's *Slaves in Barbary* in Caleb Bingham's popular rhetoric textbook *The Columbian Orator* (1797) meant that generations of young Americans continued to encounter Barbary narratives long after the end of the crises period.[1] The dynamic between the American slaveowner Kidnap and his African American slave Sharp in that play might well have helped shape young people's views of slavery and abolition as well as their understanding of Africa itself. Algiers and its association with white slavery survived as a cultural reference point for American children, even those coming of age long after the city was reduced to a French possession. In fact, as I demonstrate, Barbary pirates would (and in some ways, still do) have a long afterlife in children's literature, sometimes appearing quite unexpectedly.

Take, for example, Samuel Griswold Goodrich's "The Story of Robert Seaboy" (1833). At first glance, this short story seems a straightforward morality tale about the kind treatment of animals and the importance of family— the type of story that still fills children's bookshelves today. It begins with the titular Seaboy as an old man encountering a group of mischievous young boys shooting birds for fun. Seaboy scolds the boys and implores them to be "the friends, not the enemies, of birds." To reinforce this lesson, he tells them about how, as a boy, he once stole a nest full of baby robins. Despite his attempts to care for the stolen chicks, they died the next day. Any reader today would recognize this conventional story as one told countless times before and since 1833. However, in this case, the story does not end with the chicks' deaths. Not content to leave the boys with the specter of his own regret, Seaboy punctuates his lesson in dramatic fashion:

> When I was fourteen years old, my father took me to sea. [The Mediterranean] was frequented at that time by sea-robbers, called corsairs. One day, we were met by a corsair vessel, and a sharp battle followed. I was on the deck of our vessel, when some of the pirates sprang from their own ship and entered ours. . . . One of the pirates laid his strong arm around my waist, and sprang back into his vessel. . . . The robbers escaped, and I was carried into captivity. For nearly two years, I remained at Algiers, suffering great cruelty and hardship.
> At length, I was released, and returned to my parents. I was now happy; but during my captivity, I frequently dwelt upon my cruelty to the little birds; and I suffered the more keenly from remembering, that I had as little mercy upon these helpless creatures, as the Algerines had upon me.[2]

For many modern readers, this sudden escalation of violence may seem out of place within what had, at first, appeared to be a simple didactic short story. Why, of all possible villains, did Goodrich choose Algerian pirates to punish Seaboy for his animal cruelty and disregard for family bonds?

Previously I discussed how references to white slavery in North Africa circulated widely in antebellum abolitionist print. As Goodrich's "Robert Seaboy" demonstrates, the Algerines also made their way into the nascent field of children's literature. In fact, Barbary pirates and slave masters would continue to appear in Anglo-American children's works throughout the nineteenth century and well into the twentieth.[3] In this final chapter, I explore a set of questions raised by these Barbary figures that provide an entry point into the complex and growing critical discourse surrounding children's literature in the antebellum period. Would Goodrich's young readers in the 1830s have recognized the reference to a series of national crises that had ended almost two decades earlier? Why do these North African figures remain so prevalent in children's literature for so long, and what lessons were children asked to draw from narratives of white slavery? Such questions point to larger concerns that can bridge the critical gap between the fields of children's and adult literature in the period: how do the genres and tropes of eighteenth- and nineteenth-century literature circulate within the still largely unexplored archive of works for juvenile readers, and how do these excerpts, fragments, and echoes articulate reading skills and modes of engagement carried forward by their audiences to future texts for children and adults? To put it simply, what can adaptations of Barbary captivity narratives tell us about how young audiences were trained to read about slavery as adults?

In the following, I examine Goodrich's adaptations of the Barbary captivity genre through two longer works. The first is the *Tales of Peter Parley about Africa* (1830), an educational travel narrative told from the perspective of the author's alter ego, Peter Parley, that includes the beloved character's capture and imprisonment by Tripolitan pirates during the first Barbary War. In the second, *The Story of Captain Riley, and His Adventures in Africa* (1832), Parley re-narrates James Riley's popular account of his shipwreck and enslavement on the coast of North Africa in 1815. In these works, Goodrich leads his readers through the conventional structure of the Barbary narrative, from capture and enslavement to redemption and freedom, offering lessons on the brutality of slavery and the racial geography of North Africa along the way. My analysis first explores how this genre provides the perfect narrative vehicle for Goodrich's own views on race and slavery in relation to what Courtney Weikle-Mills calls children's imaginary citizenship. Then, in my reading of Peter Parley's African travel narrative, I examine the crucial distinctions that Goodrich draws between "captivity" and "slavery" and how those terms structure the encounter with the African Other. Finally, I demonstrate how he adapts Riley's account to model the literacy skills necessary to properly read and interpret the genre of the slave narrative.

To date, representations of Barbary piracy and slavery in children's literature have received little more than passing reference in the critical literature on North African captivity and in the emergent field of childhood studies; however, Goodrich's often heavy-handed adaptations can provide valuable insights into the "afterlife" of popular Barbary narratives. On one level, these works demonstrate how the genre was used to instill in children the complexities of antebellum racial epistemology by training them to identify and categorize the many peoples of North Africa in relation to whiteness. Going further, the deeper significance of Goodrich's adaptions lies in the way they teach their young audiences not just to read race but to read firsthand accounts of slavery in a global context. Adaptations of Barbary narratives for children provide us with a unique opportunity to establish more significant linkages between this early national genre and the antebellum audiences of later African American slave narratives because, to state the obvious, child readers grow up. The audience that read *The Story of Captain Riley* in 1832 would encounter *The Narrative of the Life of Frederick Douglass* (1845) almost fifteen years later or Harriet Jacobs's *Incidents in the Life of a Slave Girl* (1861) thirty years later. How might their earlier training as readers of white slavery texts have influenced their engagement with these accounts? Goodrich's texts offer an ideal entry point into this line of inquiry because the blunt didacticism of children's literature makes visible underlying literacy skills and cultural assumptions that readers might have brought to later antislavery narratives and to midcentury abolitionist works in general. We might ask, how did early American children's literature prepare readers to encounter both the textual and paratextual features of the slave narrative— not just the suffering bodies of enslaved Africans that demand their sympathy but also the paternalistic framing offered by the white editor that authorizes the voice of the formerly enslaved within a white power structure?[4] In my readings of Goodrich's treatment of Barbary texts I emphasize how the fictional Peter Parley models discursive structures of authority through which the white slave in North Africa becomes the locus for modes of sympathy and identification that underlie liberal citizenship and Goodrich's own moderate abolitionist beliefs. In short, children learn the skills to read the slave's suffering and derive social lessons of fortitude and compassion without fundamentally challenging racial hierarchies immanent to the politics of sentiment.[5]

In some respects a departure from my preceding chapters, this final chapter nevertheless effectively concludes the arc of this book in several ways. First, it points to how further work in the Barbary archive can help us address other longstanding divisions and omissions within mainstream literary studies beyond the gap between the early republican and antebellum periods I have discussed thus far—for one, the often-institutionalized divide between studies of adult literature and children's literature.[6] Second, my focus on pedagogy gives us an opportunity to look back on the works of the Barbary archive and recognize the ways in which they have always been involved in a project of educating and in some cases disciplining a new American citizenry in advance of the upheavals of modernity and the racial politics of the antebellum era. The framework of imaginary citizenship, which I outline in the section to follow, can usefully be applied to many Barbary texts for adults to excavate the various dimensions of white slavery foundational to narratives of national emergence and the subsequent reconceptualization in the nineteenth century of a vulnerable republic into an aspiring empire.

REAL SUFFERING, IMAGINARY CITIZENS

As the proliferation of questions above would indicate, the following study provides only one starting point for the exploration of representations of the Barbary crises, white slavery, and Muslim North Africa in early children's literature. To that end, I focus narrowly on Goodrich due to his prominence in the period. It would be difficult to overstate Goodrich's influence on the development of American children's literature and on pedagogical practices in general. His career spanned from the late 1820s to his death in 1860 and included the publication of more than 130 books and several literary magazines. Daniel Roselle notes that as late as 1902, 28 of Goodrich's books were still in print, and by 1912 total sales of his works amounted to approximately 12 million volumes.[7] But Goodrich's influence extended well beyond his long-lasting popularity and healthy sales numbers. Gillian Avery argues in her foundational study of American children's literature, *Behold the Child* (1994), that Goodrich was the founder of the "American style" of children's literature, which focused on educational and moral lessons over British preferences for whimsy and fantasy.[8] Across his works, Goodrich emphasized a scientific approach to learning through empirical observation, promoting "a democracy of learners, rather than an aristocracy of intellect."[9] Such an approach explains in part his attraction to Barbary captivity narratives written by common sailors and working captains and based on direct experience.

By reading Goodrich's adaptations of adult Barbary texts as tools to educate readers in the generic features of the slave narrative, I hope to offer a productive intervention into the critical conversation exploring race and abolitionism in children's literature. As Deborah C. De Rosa's landmark 2003 study has shown, abolitionist sentiment in popular children's literature was far more prevalent than earlier critics have acknowledged. These messages were often expressed explicitly through "the voices of victimized slave children, resistant slave mothers, rebellious white women, and abolitionist children."[10] Building on De Rosa's work, Paula T. Connolly observes that one of the central tropes of children's abolitionist literature was the "white abduction story," which "precariously treads the boundaries of empathy and essentialism"; this variety of narrative centers white "enslavement and recovery, . . . to the general exclusion of black characters."[11] While Connolly and Caroline Levander have read Goodrich's works in the context of captivity and abolitionism, they have not explored how the writer's appropriation of the Barbary narrative genre complicates the racial landscape of juvenile antislavery discourse with its shifting descriptions of the opposition of white American and Black African and of free and enslaved.[12]

As we have seen, William Lloyd Garrison and his fellow radical abolitionists frequently invoked Algiers and Tripoli as shorthand for the racialized violence and political corruption that supported the slave system. For the more moderate Goodrich, Barbary narratives allowed him to embed potentially polarizing references to slavery within engaging adventure narratives. Although the Connecticut-born Goodrich was undoubtedly himself an abolitionist, unlike those of his contemporary Lydia Maria Child, his writings for children generally avoided any explicit association with the abolitionist movement, thus he evaded the kind of outcry that ended Child's career as a children's writer.[13] Goodrich's widespread popularity in the antebellum era meant that his books addressed a national audience which was deeply divided on the question of slavery. As a consequence, many of his messages were carefully crafted to avoid offending his readers, North and South. Connolly has argued that Goodrich's cautious approach to this controversial issue exemplifies a strain of moderate abolitionism common in early children's literature; even as they express sympathy for African Americans, his works are "firmly rooted in assertions of the ideological, cultural, moral, and even genetic superiority of white Protestant Americans, [providing] glimpses of a larger world while offering young white readers a ptolemaic assurance of their preeminent cultural, racial, and religious place within it."[14] Yet, despite Goodrich's caution and moderation, Connolly notes that Goodrich was still sharply criticized by some southern commentators, who complained that he "insulted[ed] and misrepresented[ed] the institutions of the South" in his "Anti-Slavery School Books."[15] These accusations, however, never seemed to damage Goodrich's career as they had Child's. Within his Barbary works we can account for his uninterrupted popularity in the ways Goodrich thoroughly encodes the encounter with slavery within structures of racial dominance that, inevitably, show the ascendance of the white subject over the wide variety of racial and ethnic groups that inhabited the Barbary Coast.

As I have argued throughout this book, Barbary narratives, particularly those produced in the early nineteenth century, were often *about* slavery as an institution—in North Africa and in the American South—in a way that was not true of the Indian captivity narratives written before and after this period.[16] The whiteness of the protagonists gave audiences a safe opportunity to sympathize and identify with the slave without undermining racial hierarchies, while African Muslim slave masters could be effectively distanced from their American counterparts as objects for study and criticism. To see these racial categories working within Goodrich's adaptations of Barbary works, we need only to return briefly to "Robert Seaboy." In that short story, the author departs from the conventions of the Barbary narrative by only referring to his protagonist as a "captive" and never as a "slave," allowing Seaboy to draw lessons from two years of "great cruelty and hardship" while avoiding the social death of enslavement. Certainly the stakes of the term must have been high; Patricia Crain has recently noted that Jacob Abbott, Goodrich's contemporary and rival for status as the country's preeminent children's author, was a lifelong abolitionist who frequently dealt with issues of racial prejudice in his books yet never once mentioned the word "slave" in any of them.[17] Despite Goodrich's careful avoidance of the term, Seaboy's time in Algiers is unmistakably a reference to slavery, encoded further in his abduction of the birds from their parents. As Lesley Ginsberg points out, the capture and forced domestication of animals, and birds particularly, was common in abolitionist children's literature as "an explicit metaphor for the master/slave relationship."[18] Nevertheless, Seaboy's analogy draws a connection not only with the chicks but also between the narrator's own past behavior and that of the African rovers who abduct him from his family. Goodrich manages to subtly condemn slave masters by punishing Seaboy for enslaving the chicks like a Barbary pirate—for, in a manner of speaking, being barbarous. At the same time, the moral of "Robert Seaboy" rests on the narrator's ability to invoke the necessary sympathetic identification with those who are enslaved and apply that reading to his own situation.

"Robert Seaboy" draws parallels between North African slavery and the subordinate position of the child while also emphasizing the social and political imperatives that follow liberation. In other works such as *The Young American* (1840), Goodrich associates the child explicitly with the (white) slave: "If we take no account of slaves, still the children of white persons are not born free; they are under the control of their parents till they are twenty-one years old."[19] However, as Goodrich suggests in Seaboy's own conversion from thoughtless youth to wise adult, for children to become free and autonomous citizens they must draw the correct lessons from their previous lack of rights. In her book *Imaginary Citizens* (2013), Weikle-Mills argues that childhood in the nineteenth century came to be understood as a form of "imaginary citizenship" in which children were technically entitled to the privileges afforded by the Constitution but were not actually able to exercise those rights. This category, Weikle-Mills argues, shaped thinking regarding other groups, particularly women and the enslaved, whose rights were either sharply circumscribed or nonexistent, in a period when the definition of citizenship itself remained in flux.[20] The conditions of childhood offered a way of conceptualizing racial otherness and gender difference in relation to citizenship and political enfranchisement, or the lack thereof. As Seaboy's case demonstrates, the Barbary captivity genre and its figuring of the movement from slavery, powerlessness, and suffering to a recovery of the rights of citizenship parallels childhood as a deferral rather than a categorical denial of civic rights.

Seaboy's moral message further exemplifies Weikle-Mills's argument that forms of "affection and identification" were fundamental to children's understanding of themselves as individual citizens in relation to the nation.[21] However, if she describes children's citizenship as anchored in what Michael Warner calls the "privatizing discourse of sentiment" rather than public reason, that does not necessarily make it entirely introspective or passive in practice.[22] She notes that critics such as Warner and Lauren Berlant have used the figure of the child to characterize liberal citizenship, in which "personal acts and values" become the individual's "primary activities," as an abdication of the right to political participation—what the latter derides as "infantile citizenship."[23] In contrast, Weikle-Mills argues that it is precisely children's capacity as imaginary citizens to represent an emotional attachment to the nation that "helped to reconcile the notion of citizenship as public and active with the ways that it also had to be private and imaginary," in the sense that individuals could "consent imaginatively" to the social contract. Enacting this form of consent—at least for the white child—entailed actively assuming the role of reader: "Reading often allowed individuals not just to pretend that they were citizens but to understand themselves as citizens: to see the social contract as an expression of their own consent even when it could not be given." In the absence of actual political power, reading allowed children to practice forms of civic participation such as voting and holding office in anticipation of their eventual enfranchisement.[24]

This tension between active and passive, real and imaginary citizenship runs throughout Goodrich's Barbary narratives, which often model reading as a mechanism to personalize—or in Warner's terms "privatize"—the suffering of others. As Connolly notes, moderate abolitionist writers were far less likely than their more radical contemporaries to endorse abolitionist activism, and Goodrich certainly had an economic incentive to avoid any explicit statements along these lines.[25] Nevertheless, his texts include participatory elements that hint at how model citizen-readers should embed literacy practices within larger structures of social and political behavior. Through direct address and instructions to act out scenes, his Barbary narratives repeatedly ask readers to engage beyond the books in ways that prefigure the transition from imaginary to real citizenship. In this way, these stories of Barbary slavery encourage children to imagine themselves not only as participants in representational government but also as actors within narratives of liberation and emancipation while providing an understanding of the social and racial limitations of those processes. Overseeing this project as a figure of benevolent authority, Goodrich's faithful narrator Parley performs the ideological role of white editor by framing and mediating the child's encounter with slavery and racial difference on the Barbary Coast.

"A BARBAROUS AND CRUEL RACE"

In "Robert Seaboy," Algerian pirates disrupt what otherwise might be considered a rather straightforward warning to be kind to animals. This same form of generic eruption manifests on a larger scale in the *Tales of Peter Parley about Africa*, the second in a long-running series of educational texts that include volumes about North America, Europe, Asia, and Australia. While most of the other works in the series follow generic travel narrative conventions, Parley's *Tales about Africa* instead takes the form of a fictional captivity narrative. The volume begins with Peter Parley, the narrator, serving as the second mate on an American merchant vessel in the Mediterranean around the year 1805. Suddenly, corsairs attack his ship; after a brief fight the pirates shoot the captain and stun Parley with a blow. The pirates then carry the captured crew to Tripoli, about which Parley comments,

"Tripoli is a considerable country in the northern part of Africa. The principal town is also called Tripoli. The people are a barbarous and cruel race." Parley offers the first physical description of his captors when he arrives ashore escorted by soldiers "with dark skins, and strange dresses."[26] This initial fleeting mention of the racial characteristics of the Tripolitans sets up a more extensive association of barbarity and violence with Blackness that runs through the remainder of the work.

By shifting from the familiar travelogue genre to the Barbary captivity narrative, Goodrich invites his readers to associate Africa with slavery, domination, and a lack of freedom; rather than an exotic location to explore and observe, Africa captures you. Yet, as we shall see, this (temporary) reversal of the racial power dynamic serves in the end to justify a teleological narrative of white subjugation of the continent. Goodrich portrays Parley as an innocent victim of Tripolitan aggression in the context of the First Barbary War. Compared to Algiers, where some American sailors were enslaved for a decade or more, Tripoli only held American captives for a very brief period. During this crisis, only a single merchant vessel, the brig *Franklin*, was captured, and its small crew was almost immediately ransomed by American officials. As a result, no significant accounts were written by civilian merchant captives in Tripoli in this period. What Tripolitan narratives do exist were written by crew members of the USS *Philadelphia*, captured by Tripolitans when the ship ran aground during the 1803 naval blockade of the city.[27] Goodrich's portrayal of Parley as an innocent civilian captive retrospectively magnifies what in reality was a small-scale conflict and reinforces the justification for the military action to come, specifically the United States' first invasion of an overseas territory with William Eaton's attack on the city of Derne. The work sets the stage for a somewhat different understanding of that conflict in the context of the country's growing imperial ambitions.

Parley's narrative reproduces some of the most common tropes of the Tripolitan narrative, including his forced march through the city under the gaze of its residents and the prisoner's diet of bread and water. Yet, as in the case of Seaboy, Goodrich carefully avoids referring to Parley as a slave. In a clear departure from his source material, Goodrich portrays Parley as confined to a dungeon in a castle rather than subject to hard labor like so many of his real-life counterparts. For former captives such as William Ray, a crew member from the *Philadelphia* who entitled his own account *The Horrors of*

Slavery (1808), the brutality of North African slavery offered an opportunity to expose various forms of economic oppression that beset supposedly free American laborers.[28] Even Jonathan Cowdery, the former doctor of the *Philadelphia* who served out his captivity in relative ease as the personal physician to the bashaw of Tripoli, explicitly refers to himself as a slave.[29] Goodrich instead saves his young readers from having to imagine the beloved Parley enslaved by adapting his Tripolitan setting into a more mundane scene of sympathy. During Parley's weeks of confinement, he domesticates a spider and feeds it flies. When the spider disappears one day, Parley mourns the loss of his only friend. This scene echoes the story of Robert Seaboy and the birds; the dependent relationship between the spider and Parley demonstrates acceptable bonds of sympathy extending from the white child to the object of paternalistic care, naturalizing rather than challenging hierarchies of power. Such moments, as I have suggested, take on an added layer of significance when interpolated into generic structures that are, like the Tripolitan narrative, often deeply invested in exploring the dialectical opposition of slavery and freedom. Just as in Robert Seaboy's relationship with the birds in his narrative, the protagonist's treatment of animals potentially reflects the ways in which he would treat those marginalized or disenfranchised within his own society, according to the convention of children's literature of the period. In this case, by proving his benevolence, Parley sets the stage for the reclamation of his own rights and citizenship.

Fortunately, Parley is not in the dungeon too long before he is rescued by his old friend Leo, an Italian bandit now spying for William Eaton's expedition. Parley and Leo then join Eaton and participate in the capture of Derne, winning the Tripolitan War. Within a few pages, Parley redeems his captive status and reclaims the privileges of American citizenship through his active participation in a new imperial venture. This final reversal manifests too in the resumption of Parley's ethnographic gaze as he once again asserts empirical authority over the racial makeup of Africa. Parley notes, "[Africa's] inhabitants consist chiefly of two races of men, Arabs and negroes. These races have mixed, and produced others, partly Arab and partly Negro. . . . The inhabitants of Barbary are chiefly Moors, who are nearly the same as Arabs. Their skin is dark, like that of our Indians."[30] Parley's North Africa is a place of racial confluence and mixture, suggesting a kind of transgressive space that complicates the racial order he hopes to teach his readers. At the same time, by focusing on "Arabs" and "negroes," he sharpens the distinction between slaver and enslaved as racial types, and the division between North Africa as a site of enslavement and the rest of the continent more associated with the trans-Atlantic slave trade.

Goodrich's comparative approach, in particular his use of Native American characteristics as a basis for approximating racial descriptions and his attention to racial mixing, follows the conventions established by earlier firsthand accounts while simplifying more complex distinctions. Take, for example, the descriptions included in John Foss's narrative of captivity in Algiers, which I already cited briefly in chapter 3. In a longer passage, he describes Turks as "a well built robust people, their complexions not unlike Americans," although with beards that make them appear "more like monsters than human beings." Moors are "generally a tall thin, spare set of people, . . . and of a very dark complexion, much like the Indians of North America." Arabs, on the other hand, "are of a much darker complexion than the Moors, being darker than Mulattoes." Between these gradations are "Cologlies," the children of Moorish mothers and Turkish fathers, who are "of a more tawney complexion" than the almost-white Turks.[31] Jacob Rama Berman has argued that in Foss's narrative, these cross-racial and cross-cultural comparisons, filling in the gaps among recognizable American types—white, "Indian," "Negro," "Mulatto"—served to destabilize the consolidation of whiteness and American citizenship by invoking the complexities of identity within the American public sphere.[32] Goodrich's simplification of this racial narrative seeks to do just the opposite, to reinforce the stability of race and, by extension, whiteness as monolithic and undiluted.

Parley's journey from powerless captive to armed ethnographer offers a somewhat extreme model for the child reader's own progression from imaginary to real citizenship. Going further, the narrative reinforces children's identification with the newly liberated Parley by encouraging them to join him in interpreting Africa and the bodies that inhabit the continent. At the foot of each page Goodrich includes questions about the content, inviting readers to rehearse the information presented. Under his descriptions of African peoples, he requests that the reader "describe the Moors of Barbary," thus asking children to participate in the ideological process of comparative racialization that, in turn, consolidates whiteness as the basis for authority.[33] This and other ethnographic questions over the course of the work provoke an active engagement in the encounter with racial difference. In this case, acting out one's imaginary citizenship involves not just reading texts but also reading people and positioning them within the complex pseudoscientific discourse of race in the antebellum period.

While Parley describes the racial characteristics of North Africans in, for the most part, a morally neutral fashion, his discussions of Islam are more partisan: "The people are Mahometans. As I have said before, they hate Christians. Their religion teaches those who believe in it, to despise all that do not hold the same faith. It teaches, that no Mahometan is bound to be kind, just, or true, to those who believe in any other religion." Goodrich suggests a subtle but potent lesson on religious tolerance at the expense of the Muslims he examines. Parley's condemnation of Islam in general, and Arabs specifically, continues as he shifts his focus toward West and Central Africa and toward the enslavement of Black Africans:

> The negroes who are very numerous in the middle parts of Africa, are constantly hunted by these pirates of the land, and many thousands of them are every year, torn from their homes, separated from their friends and families, and carried away into distant countries. There, deprived of their liberty, they labor for the luxury and enjoyments of rich persons who buy them. They die in a land of exile, and never know what becomes of their children or their friends, whether they are living or dead, happy or unhappy.

The reader can be forgiven for mistaking this description for one of North American slavery, particularly in its emphasis on the "land of exile" and the impossibility of return. Goodrich does remark on and condemn the American slave trade in the *Tales about Africa*, but he does so in markedly different terms. In a later section on West Africa, Parley observes that "the number of slaves that have been taken from this coast and sold in the United States, the West Indies, and South America, must be many hundreds of thousands." While acknowledging efforts by Britain and the United States to the stop the trade, he condemns the continued presence of slavery in "several Christian countries." Parley reflects that it is "painful" to think of "how many people have been dragged from their homes, from all that was dear to them, and carried into foreign countries, to labor, suffer, and to die!" As vehemently as Parley condemns the devastation of West Africa, his language becomes far more measured as he shifts his attention to North America:

> In various parts of North and South America, there are many slaves; in some places, all the hard labor is performed by them. They are owned by white men, who buy and sell them in the same manner, as they do other property. There are, no doubt, many good people who have slaves. But slavery is a bad system, and brings great evils with it. Instead, therefore, of defending slavery,

every good person should condemn it, and use his efforts on all proper occasions, to hasten the time, when there shall be no slavery in any land.[34]

Recalling the captivity of Robert Seaboy that opened this chapter, Goodrich locates the primary tragedy of slavery not in the brutal labor itself—in the site of enslavement—but in the breakup and destruction of families in West Africa. By extension, this representation erases and devalues the family structures that continue to be denied, undermined, and destroyed on the plantations of the American South. Notably, Goodrich's sharpest words are reserved for the Atlantic slave trade, which Congress had outlawed in 1808. As Connolly writes, the focus on the slave trade allowed children's writers like Goodrich to locate the worst aspects of the slave system outside the United States.[35] On the other hand, when discussing American slavery, Goodrich is careful to distinguish the "system" from the actual white people operating within in. Although he directly expresses his own abolitionist beliefs, he carefully distances the crimes of slavery from anywhere his readers might actually live.

Even when directly referencing American slavery, Parley makes clear that the practice is an aberration, a blight on what should be true Christian values. His refusal to categorically condemn white slaveholders—who might otherwise be considered "good people"—stands in contrast to his descriptions of Arab slave traders, who are labeled as "pirates" and thus, by definition, inhabit an extranational space that is beyond the moral foundation of a people or a country. Later in the work, Goodrich implores his readers to treat both free and enslaved Africans with kindness, remarking that "the color of the skin makes no difference. The obligation is universal, to do to another, as you would have another do to you."[36] Goodrich's assertion of moral equivalence throws into stark relief his uneven treatment of African and American slavery, an idea evidenced too by Goodrich's avoidance of the language of enslavement for Parley. In chapter 1 I discussed how the authorial and editorial power of the Barbary captives—the power to encode and decode their experience, as Paul Baepler puts it—was key in enabling them to transcend their former slave status.[37] In this context Goodrich instructs his young readers in the consumption and understanding of that coding to solidify racial differences even as he explicitly condemns racial subjugation. In other words, rather than condemning American slavery by aligning it with Barbary slavery, Goodrich's triangulation promotes sympathy for Black Africans—who in the narrative exist only as silent, passive victims—at the expense of North African Muslims. Barbary slavery is worse precisely because its perpetrators refuse to abide by the proper racial order and therefore disrupt the potential for acceptable bonds of sympathy.

The dependence of this critique of slavery on the racial identity of the bodies involved frames Goodrich's later interpolation of Captain James Riley's widely circulated captivity narrative, *An Authentic Narrative of the Loss of the American Brig Commerce* (1817). Shortly after Parley participates in the siege of Derne and the end of the Tripolitan War, he begins to relate the story of Riley's shipwreck, enslavement, and eventual redemption. As discussed in earlier chapters, Riley's *Authentic Narrative* proved immensely popular, particularly among those, such as Abraham Lincoln, who embraced its antislavery message. Despite, or perhaps because of, the popularity of Riley's account, Goodrich's retelling includes a preface that first cautions his reader and recommends a skeptical approach to the text:

> It was on the coast near this Cape, that Captain Riley and his crew were wrecked, about ten years afterwards, that is, in 1815.
> Captain Riley has written a book, giving an account of his shipwreck, and his sufferings in Africa. This account is very interesting, but it has one fault, he is too fond of telling large stories.
> He tells of a great many things, that are perhaps nearly all true, but yet his descriptions are so extravagant, that many people disbelieve his whole book.

Notably, these allegations come from a fictional character who has just escaped captivity to take part in the capture of Derne and the winning of the Tripolitan War. It would be tempting to read Goodrich's admonishments with a note of irony, yet they advance the writer's oft-stated goal of developing educational materials based on fact rather than fancy. He performs the skeptical and responsible approach to the text for his readers while noting the social cost of fantasy: "Nothing is more unfortunate, than to get a habit of telling great stories. A person who has this habit, is very soon laughed at, and despised. Good people will place no confidence in, nor have any esteem for a person who tells great stories."[38] Goodrich's interpolation of Riley's text then seems as much about interrogating the truth and defining the value of this popular account of white slavery as it is about relating an exciting and engaging story to his readers.

After cautioning his readers, Parley encourages them to witness and even participate in a series of encounters with racial difference, further

Riley and his men seized by the Arabs.

FIGURE 7. "Riley and His Men Seized by Arabs," in Samuel Griswold Goodrich, *The Tales of Peter Parley about Africa: With Engravings* (Boston: Gray and Bowen, and Carter and Hendee, 1830). —Courtesy American Antiquarian Society, Worcester, MA

naturalizing operative hierarchies that they must properly navigate within a global context. To give one example, early in the narrative Parley describes the wreck of the *Commerce* and Riley's subsequent encounter on the beach with "an old man, with a hideous face, and long hair standing out in all directions, two frightful old women, and several children." Parley comments that "these creatures were almost naked, and had a wild and savage look." His descriptions provide a mix of signifiers: he identifies family units but notes again and again the beastly and animal-like qualities of the individuals. After Riley and his crew encounter another group of Arabs and flee in a leaky boat, Parley notes that their "inhuman enemies were waiting on land, to take their lives if they came ashore." These encounters culminate in Riley and his crew captured and "reduced . . . to a state of slavery."[39] This declension of class and racial status contrasts sharply with Parley's own imprisonment, which ultimately fails to challenge his racial superiority over his captors. More importantly, Goodrich makes explicit here what he thoroughly encodes elsewhere—that the white figure is not just taken captive but enslaved.

Once again in this section Goodrich calls on the reader to actively participate in the narrative. In the march over the desert to Mogadore, Riley and his crew "endured the greatest misery, from hunger, thirst, and fatigue. They had a great variety of adventures, and were once attacked by robbers." At the bottom of the page, an engagement question asks the child: "Will you relate some of Captain Riley's adventures and sufferings, in crossing the desert?"[40] This passage precedes the condemnations of the North African and North American slave systems described above, inviting white children to imagine themselves as the victims of Barbary slavery precisely to emphasize a racially stratified view of slavery as a global phenomenon. This broader perspective allows Goodrich to depict American slavery as comparatively humane, perpetrated by southern slaveholders with otherwise good intentions. If Goodrich's treatment of American slavery seems evasive, we can see how the narrative establishes the child reader's vicarious experience of North African slavery through Riley as the impetus for future action to, as he phrases it above, "hasten the time, when there shall be no slavery in any land."

Parley's relation of Riley's *Narrative* comes to a swift close as the narrator continues his voyage around the continent. The brevity of this reference to a famous text suggests that Parley offers not a substantive summary but rather a *reading* of Riley. This reading prioritizes making visible the interpretive practices necessary to translate the slave's questionable firsthand account into a guidebook for good citizenship and a potential platform for future civic participation. The key to such a reading lies in the counterintuitive logic that distinguishes between Parley and Riley as a fictional ex-captive and a real ex-slave. As Riley, unlike Seaboy or Parley, is explicitly enslaved, the captain becomes the object rather than the subject of his own narrative, allowing Goodrich to effectively model reading skills that encourage sympathy with the suffering victim while simultaneously distancing the enslaved body from any means of narrative agency.[41] Within this context, we might read Riley's relationship with Parley (and thus Goodrich) as the reverse of what Russ Castronovo calls "discursive passing": the "intervention in the cultural authority of language" that allowed formerly enslaved African Americans such as Frederick Douglass to participate in the authorized discourse of revolutionary patriarchy.[42] Riley, in contrast, is subject to a kind of discursive racialization that reproduces the power dynamics of the slave narrative while still serving, in the words of Brigitte Fielder, to "universalize and prioritize whiteness and white life experience as normative positions of readerly identification."[43] To put it another way, through Parley's editorial authority, Riley's narrative is made to pass as a less subversive iteration of the African American slave narrative in order to teach children the social and political dimensions of slavery and emancipation. That the suffering slave's account must be authorized by a fictional framework here highlights the contradictions inherent in a paternalistic abolitionist ideology that requires white editors to validate Black experiences.

"THE INTEREST OF FICTION AND THE AUTHORITY OF TRUTH"

While retelling Riley's *Narrative* in the *Tales about Africa*, Parley notes that he cannot dwell on all of the details of the original, suggesting, in direct address, that "perhaps you will sometime read the whole story in Captain Riley's book."[44] Although he recommends further reading for his audience, Goodrich ultimately does not leave children to their own devices as discerning consumers. Not long after the publication of *Tales of Peter Parley about Africa*, Goodrich published a book-length adaptation of Riley's account, *The Story of Captain Riley, and His Adventures in Africa* (1834). This new adaptation was the first in what would be a series of true adventures stories under the title "Peter Parley's Little Library," which sought to curate and adapt popular adult texts for children's consumption. Goodrich announces in the first volume's advertisement for the series his belief that "real biography may be made as attractive as fictitious tales" and his desire to "do something, by the publication of these books, towards rendering truth a substitute in education, for the too common use of romance." As the voice shifts to Parley's for the series' preface, he further articulates his selection criteria:

> I have been requested to make a selection of true stories for children, and suggest the manner of preparing them, with a view to furnish a Little Library, which may at once possess the interest of fiction and *the authority of truth*.
>
> In consenting thus far to superintend the publication, I have chosen, as the first of the series, the Narrative of our countryman, Captain James Riley. It is certainly a detail of most extraordinary adventures, and not only affords a display of great sufferings and great energy of character, but also *furnishes much information respecting a part of the globe and a race of people but little known.*[45]

Goodrich emphasizes both the educational possibilities of Riley's account and the necessity for a true and independently verified text to replace the tendency toward fiction and romance. A brief look at the other proposed works in the Little Library series suggests just what Goodrich identifies as educational: John Jewett's Indian captivity narrative, explorer Jean-Françoise de Lapérouse's doomed expedition into the Pacific, and an account of Alexander Selkirk's stranding on the Juan Fernández archipelago. The common thread in these adaptations is that the suffering of the protagonist serves a pedagogical purpose, but only when it can be validated by some other authority. By this logic it makes perfect sense that Goodrich chose to begin his series with a North African slave narrative. Decades earlier, Royall Tyler's Updike Underhill proposed the circulation of his own captivity narrative to combat the profusion of foreign-authored fanciful novels within early republican print networks.[46] That both Tyler and Goodrich point to the Barbary narrative says quite a lot about the role of that genre across the history of post-independence American print in promoting truth, virtue, and edification through bodily suffering.

This second adaptation again shifts Riley's *Narrative* from first-person to Peter Parley's authoritative third-person narration of events. At times, Parley's interpretations of Riley's encounters with Barbary figures are even more intrusive as the work of reading racial difference becomes more complex. Take, for example, Riley's first encounter with Arabs on the shore after a brief tangent on the crew's despair: "But I will return to my story; and after reminding you, that Captain Riley and his men were now on the border of Zahara, . . . we will introduce you to the first living thing that met their sight; and what do you think it was?" Goodrich draws from the same episode in the *Tales about Africa*, but here the process of recognition of the Other plays out over multiple stages. He asks his audience to openly speculate about the "thing" the crew encounters on shore, which he goes on to describe in the next paragraph as a "strange looking object in human form," before finally stating in a third paragraph: "It was an old man, of a color between an American Indian and negro."[47] The process of identification and final racial approximation occurs in a drawn-out, step-by-step process from speculation to visual confirmation and finally to a tenuous conclusion. Riley's original text is far more abrupt, simply noting that "we saw a human figure approach our stuff, such as clothing, which lay scattered along the beach for a mile westward of us. It was a man!"[48] Goodrich does not just draw out the description; he also changes the order of the details in Riley's text to foreground the racial characteristics of the figure while preserving

Riley's own description in relation to the "American Indian" and "Negro," two reference points that would likely be as familiar to a child as to an adult. Goodrich's deconstruction and reconstruction of the Other offers the child a guide for reading the racial dimensions of any encounter and for approximating the appearance of the unknown body.

As with so many other children's works then and now, illustrations accompany many of the scenes of Riley's journey, some approximating the engravings included in the original printing of the *Narrative*. In the case of Riley's first encounter with the North Africans on the beach, the image in Goodrich's adaptation further emphasizes the racial differences between the two groups while potentially reinforcing the child reader's identification with the captive. Riley's original text includes a wide, panoramic image of the beach, with two armed men chasing another man, presumedly Riley himself, in the foreground, and the remainder of the crew and Arabs huddled to the right side of the image. The emphasis seems to be on the landscape itself, desolate and dangerous, a point emphasized by the appearance of the wrecked brig near the top-left corner. None of the figures in the foreground are portrayed with any fine detail, and more importantly for our purposes, their skin is all shaded similarly. Goodrich's version provides a very different emphasis. At the center are just two figures, with Riley again fleeing to the sea and an Arab behind, menacing him with a spear. The latter figure is shaded much darker than Riley, who remains unshaded. The same is true of the figures huddled at the right side of the image. The figures offer a clear distinction of white and Black, with the Arab appearing much more like a Black West African than a North African. Additionally, Riley's proportions—a large head and comparatively short arms and legs—are unmistakably childlike. The image makes clear who the child should identify with.

As Goodrich proceeds through Riley's narrative, he observes moments in which the racial expectations of Riley's crew are both confirmed and troubled. After his initial enslavement, Riley finds himself bought and sold several times. Of one new master, Parley relates, "Hamet was not so dark in his color, and his captives hoped, not so hard in his heart, as the other Arabs, but they were mistaken."[49] Interestingly, Riley's original language describes Hamet as "of a much lighter colour"; Goodrich's revision shifts the comparison to that of Blackness rather than whiteness, clearly distancing the figure from Riley and his white crew.[50] In either formulation, the failure of Riley to predict Hamet's moral character by his complexion demonstrates again how the

FIGURE 8. "Wreck of the Brig Commerce on the Coast of Africa," in James Riley, *An Authentic Narrative of the Loss of the Brig Commerce* (New York: T. and W. Mercein, 1817), 36. —Courtesy American Antiquarian Society, Worcester, MA

FIGURE 9. "Riley Attempting to Escape," in Samuel Griswold Goodrich, *The Story of Captain Riley, and His Adventures in Africa* (Boston: Carter, Hendee, 1834), 36. — Courtesy American Antiquarian Society, Worcester, MA

Barbary space complicates the establishment of consistent racial taxonomies. More often than not, the racial descriptions approximate in relation to fixed, identifiable characteristics. Another figure, Sheikh Ali, has a complexion "between a negro and an Arab," while one soldier, "though half negro, had all the lofty deportment of a genuine Moor or Arab."[51] As in Riley's original, descriptions deploy a variety of visual and cultural factors to approximate identity.

The child's participation in scientific processes of comparative racialization parallels the active identification with Riley's enslaved status through a more developed articulation of specific reading practices that reach beyond the bounds of the text itself. At one particularly noteworthy moment in the narrative, when Riley and his crew spend the night by the shore, the narrator directs his readers to consider their own situations:

> Now, my children, you may also go to rest; and I dare say, that when you lay your little heads on the soft pillows, and think of all the comforts that surround you, you will feel very grateful to Him who has given them all, and saved you from a rocky bed as your only place of repose.
>
> When you reflect on the difference between your happy condition, and the wretched state of the poor mariners whom we now leave for the night, you will, no doubt, feel resolved never again to be vexed or ruffled by any little denial, or disappointment that may thwart your wishes, amid all the blessings which it falls to your lot to enjoy.

Goodrich guides the child reader through an interpretation of suffering that channels sympathy into an understanding of the social restraint that responsible citizenship requires; here, that process means articulating the relationship between the imaginary outcomes of reading and the real and necessary practices that lie outside the book. The narrative imposes voluntary limits on the text, portioning it out as a way of teaching children the ritual of the bedtime story. This ritualization of reading appears in small interventions throughout the text, such as near the end of the story when the narrator declines to provide further descriptions of Morocco because he wishes to "finish our narrative to-night." While depicting siege equipment outside the walls of Mogadore, Parley even instructs his young reader on how to build a working toy model.[52] Through these narrative interventions, Goodrich directs his audience not only to read the text but to perform it within the context of their lived experiences, providing a tactile corollary to the abstraction of literature and, by extension, the imaginary national and racial ties that connect the child to Riley's suffering body in the same way that Weikle-Mills describes children practicing civic activities like voting and holding office.

This persistent framing of the text almost entirely defines the narrative progression of the story, to the exclusion of the more explicit abolitionist message of the original. Goodrich's narrative control manifests again the tension between active and passive forms of social belonging central to the concept of imaginary citizenship. That tension comes to a head at the very end of the story as the enslaved Riley regains his freedom. One of the most influential aspects of Riley's original narrative is its abolitionist message, which develops over the course of the slave's trials in the desert and culminates in his statement as the narrative nears its conclusion: "Adversity has taught me some noble lessons: I have now learned to look with compassion on my enslaved and oppressed fellow creatures, and my future life shall be devoted to their cause;—I will exert my remaining faculties to redeem the enslaved, and to shiver in pieces the rod of oppression; and I trust I shall be aided in that holy work by every good and every pious, free, and high-minded citizen in the community, and by the friends of mankind throughout the civilized world."[53] Even in a genre known for professions of abolitionist sentiment, Riley's declaration, which continues over the book's final paragraphs with a call for immediate rather than gradual emancipation, stands out as forceful and unequivocal. By saving this declaration for the final pages, Riley presents this lesson as gradually accrued through the suffering presented in his account, a narrative that the reader too has just passed through.

The Story of Captain Riley ends very differently, and very abruptly. When Riley and his crew finally return to the United States, Parley simply comments, "Home, is a sweet word to place at the end of such a long relation of sufferings and wandering; so I will now say no more. But if you like this way of hearing stories, perhaps I may hereafter pursue the same course and tell you another."[54] Goodrich emphasizes the restoration of a domestic, national space as the telos of Riley's—and the child's—long journey into freedom. Parley, whose authority as storyteller is, to this point, uninterrupted, specifically requests the child's consent, anticipating the reader's transition from imaginary to real citizenship alongside Riley's liberation.

Goodrich's omission of Riley's statement certainly fits his more moderate brand of abolition, and it undoubtedly saved him from alienating his national audience. Rather than prescribing activism, his final lines emphasize reading as "self-ownership."[55] This mode of juvenile empowerment, like Riley's more literal emancipation, functions as the necessary antecedent to action. Without necessarily advocating for the abolitionist movement, Goodrich provides children with the reading skills to translate the often tacit, but occasionally more explicit, condemnations of slavery that characterize the Barbary captivity genre into some form of future civic engagement. Of course, this lesson requires privileging the white child's imaginary citizenship and agency over the formerly enslaved person's voice—in this case, the moral lesson that Riley derives from his own experiences.

In closing, I would like to draw at least tentative connections between this final silencing of Riley and a key moment in Frederick Douglass's second autobiography, when, in the first months of his antislavery advocacy, the orator was told, "Give us the facts, . . . we will take care of the philosophy."[56] For Douglass, this moment was emblematic of the racial paternalism that he sought to overcome through his own work. In the case of Goodrich's depictions of white slavery, his audience's emergence from dependence into agency rests on the lessons interpreted from a suffering body assumed to be incapable of drawing its own reliable conclusions. That *The Story of Captain Riley* launched Goodrich's Little Library series, which simulates the larger library of works and genres that adult citizens were expected to navigate, suggests that he was particularly concerned with readying readers to encounter texts about slaves and slavery. He, through Parley and the Barbary archive, instilled in his young readers a model of active reading—of both texts and bodies—based on carefully moderated, sympathetic identification that would channel and limit the radical potential of the speaking slave in the antebellum era.

CODA

SELIM'S ARCHIVE FEVER

Across this project the Barbary archive has been at times expansive and exclusive. While I have endeavored to include multiple genres that engaged with North Africa, I have sidestepped some texts that would seem to have a natural home within this framework. Most obvious is my neglect of the actual captivity narratives, aside from some scattered references and my discussions of the narratives of John Foss and James Riley. As I noted in my introduction, excepting Mordecai Manuel Noah, none of the other writers I discuss actually set foot on the Barbary Coast. Their understanding of North Africa came primarily as an assemblage of fragments circulating in the public sphere. That is, I have explored, more than the actual experience of Americans in North Africa, the ways in which the Barbary was imaginatively constructed as a site onto which writers could project the parallel problematics of postcolonial nation formation and the disruptions of modernity. For that reason, I have been more interested in imagined white slaves of the Barbary as figures in print that point to the complex development of American fictionality. A more regrettable exclusion on my part comes, with the exception of Omar ibn Said (also known as Prince Moro) of the first chapter, in my neglecting to discuss the many, many enslaved Muslims in North America in the period. Those encounters and narratives undoubtedly deserve more extensive and sustained treatment following the work of Michael A. Gomez and Sylvaine A. Diouf, among others.[1] It is also worth noting that the Barbary endured in American culture long after the Civil War in surprising ways, such as in San Francisco's red-light district, named the Barbary Coast by sailors in the late nineteenth century for its associations with danger and transgression.[2] For the purposes of this book, however, the Civil War provides a convenient endpoint.[3]

Even with these carefully maintained, self-imposed limitations, there are always ruptures, gaps, and fragments in the archive. In the final pages of this project, I want to consider one such case: the story of Selim the Algerine. A figure of local Appalachian lore until accounts of his travels were published more widely in the years before the Civil War, Selim's crisscrossing of the revolutionary Atlantic world symbolizes the many lost Barbary narratives that Americans encountered at the local and national levels. Selim's story first appeared in an 1816 issue of *The Panoplist, and Missionary Magazine* as "The Converted Algerine" but was later rediscovered and reprinted in Episcopal bishop William Meade's *Old Churches, Ministers and Families of Virginia* (1857) and finally circulated more widely in *Graham's Illustrated Magazine* that same year under the title "Selim, or the Algerine in Virginia." The story begins when, in the wake of Edward Braddock's disastrous expedition during the Seven Years' War, a backwoods Virginia colonial discovers while out hunting "a man in a most wretched and pitiable condition, his person entirely naked (except a few rags tied about his feet) and almost covered over with scabs, quite emaciated and nearly famished to death."[4] Unable to understand anything the mysterious naked man was saying, the backwoodsman took him under his care and brought him to the home of a nearby military officer, identified as a Colonel Dickerson.

Over the next few months, Selim would learn English, making "surprising" progress: "He procured pen, ink, and paper, and spent much of his time in writing down remarkable and important words, pronouncing them, and getting whoever was present to correct his pronunciation." His immediate affinity for the technologies of writing suggests Selim was highly literate, an observation further confirmed by his backstory. Once sufficiently proficient in English, Selim related to the Virginians that he came from a "wealthy and respectable" family in Algiers but was captured as a small boy traveling to Constantinople for his education by a Spanish man-of-war. He was later transferred to an allied French ship, which carried him to New Orleans. From there, the French "sent him up the rivers Mississippi and Ohio to Shawnee towns, and left him a prisoner of war with the Indians." After learning of Anglo settlements to the East from a captured white woman taken on the Virginia frontier, Selim escaped into the wilderness, where he wandered lost until he was discovered by the backwoodsman.[5]

Selim's remarkable narrative has him circumnavigating a broad swath of the late eighteenth-century northern Atlantic, the victim of European colonials and Indigenous Americans alike. Yet, the narrative is oddly demur when describing Selim's actual status over this period. He "spends time" among the French and is repeatedly referred to as a prisoner of war rather than as a slave. On this point, the material appended to the original narrative offers some clarification. In a rare instance in which we are given the quoted words of Selim himself, a descendant of one of Selim's Virginian friends notes his odd habit "passing his hand over his face." When asked about it, Selim explains, "It is the blow—that disgrace to a gentleman—given me by that Louisiana planter; but—*thank God! Thank God!* but for the Saviour I could not bear it."[6] Although not further remarked upon, Selim emerged from his captivity psychologically scarred by slavery. It remains unclear why this is not made more explicit in the narrative. Either readers would have already read this in his description as a "prisoner" and no clarification was necessary, or perhaps, as in the case of Samuel Griswold Goodrich's Peter Parley, the label of "slave" would have necessarily constituted an obstacle to the audience's sympathies that the writers wanted to avoid.

During his time with Dickerson, Selim becomes friends with a Presbyterian minister named John Craig, who ultimately helps the Algerian convert to Christianity. The account of their first meeting includes the only direct quotation from Selim in the original piece published in *The Panoplist*:

> When I was in my distress, I once in my sleep dreamed that I was in my own country, and saw in my dream the largest assembly of men my eyes every beheld, collected in a wide plain, all dressed in uniform and drawn up in military order. At the farther side of the plain, and almost at an immense distance, I saw a person whom I understood to be one of great distinction; but, by reason of the vast distance he was from me, I could not discern what sort of person he was. I only knew him to be a person of great eminence. I saw every now and then one or two of this large assembly attempting to go across the plain to this distinguished personage; but when they had got about halfway over, they suddenly dropped into a hole in the earth, and I saw them no more. I also imagined that I saw an old man standing by himself, at a distance from this large assembly, and one or two of the multitude applied to him for direction how to cross the plain in safety; and all who received and followed it got safe across. As soon as I saw you, . . . I knew you to be the man who gave these directions.[7]

This detailed dream is noteworthy for a few reasons. First, it is the only account we have from Selim about the meaning of his narrative and his eminent conversion. Second, the figuring of distance, peril, and facilitation provides a more subtle commentary on the vast trans-Atlantic space he traversed and would traverse again. Not unlike the "swoon" discussed by Laura Doyle in *Freedom's Empire*, the journey across the plain and the specter of being swallowed up symbolize the trauma of passage, with Craig standing in for the white colonial power that would tame that perilous, featureless waste.[8]

Selim's time in Virginia seems to have been rather pleasant; at one point, he even had his portrait painted by Charles Willson Peale. His story, however, comes to a sad end. Against Craig's advice, Selim insists on returning to Algiers with the conviction that his wealthy father will accept his son's conversion. The local gentry take up a collection to fund Selim's passage, and the Algerian travels home. Years later, however, he appears again in Virginia, seeking out his friends and suffering from a "derangement of his mental powers" as a result of having been rejected by his family in North Africa. After wandering the area for some time, Selim's tale ends with him being taken to a "madhouse" in Williamsburg.[9] There is no other explanation offered for Selim's illness, nor for how he was able to return to Virginia. Sadly, even the Peale portrait has been lost.

Selim's journey crisscrossing the Atlantic and his wanderings in the American interior make a remarkable story, but very little of that tale will ever be recovered. Like the four suspected Algerian-Jewish spies who arrived in Norfolk, Virginia, in 1785 and the two Algerian gentlemen who made their way down the East Coast in 1794, Selim resurfaces only as fragments within early American print culture. It is, of course, impossible to know how these short reports, anecdotes, vignettes, and allusions were understood by readers who encountered them in the period. Fact or fiction, Selim's story represents many of the key narratives of the Barbary archive I have explored over the last six chapters: the global connections between backwoods Virginia and the trans-Atlantic, the racial and cultural otherness of Selim himself registered in print, and the frequency with which early republican tropes and figures were recirculated in the antebellum era, marking continuities that complicate common modes of periodization.

This book has its origins in my surprising encounter with Algerines in the pages of the *Colored American* newspaper in 1839, and it has been animated by the question of what these figures continued to mean for readers beyond the Barbary crises. My construction of the Barbary archive as a complex web of references to North Africa was an attempt to begin answering this perhaps unanswerable question. That task has become significantly more possible with the widespread digitization of materials over the last several decades, making immeasurably easier the kind of reading I have practiced across novels, novellas, plays, poems, pamphlets, newspapers, and magazines of the period. Yet, much more work needs to be done. My hope is that there are many Barbary materials out there to be found and made accessible that will give us a clearer understanding of how North Africa has endured in American public memory. On the other hand, reflecting on the rise of new digital archival technologies, a notable Algerine observed just a few decades ago that "the archive . . . will never be either memory or anamnesis as spontaneous, alive and internal experience. On the contrary: the archive takes place at the place of originary and structural breakdown of the said memory. . . . There would be no archive without the radical finitude, without the possibility of a forgetfulness."[10]

NOTES

INTRODUCTION: APPEALING TO THE NATION

1 Mathew Carey, "For the Columbian Magazine," *Columbian Magazine* (Philadelphia), September 1786, 5. Notably, the narrator never seems to meet any future Americans; the newspaper rather than the individual citizen serves to represent America in 1850, a remarkably prescient vision of urban modernity based on, in David M. Henkin's words, "the circulation of strangers through public space." Henkin, *City Reading: Written Words and Public Spaces in Antebellum New York* (New York: Columbia University Press, 1998), 2.

2 Notably Carey's prediction only misses the admission of Wisconsin as the thirtieth state by two years.

3 Carey, "For the Columbian," 5.

4 The prominence of Algerian piracy in the story contests Edward Said's assertion in *Orientalism* that the United States had little interaction with the Muslim world until after World War II. Said, *Orientalism* (New York: Vintage Books, 1994), 2–4.

5 In at least one reprinting of this article, in an 1815 edition of *Analectic Magazine*, news of the battle with Algiers was the only fictional report included. This selection seems particularly appropriate for 1815, given that the United States was at the time engaged in the Algerian War, also known as the Second Barbary War. Although the naval engagements of this actual war were nowhere near the scale of the battle imagined here, it is worth noting that Americans were interested in connecting Carey's prophecies with their real-life fulfillment.

6 For a discussion of the aftermath of the Compromise of 1850, see Robert S. Levine, *Dislocating Race and Nation: Episodes in Nineteenth-Century America Literary Nationalism* (Chapel Hill: University of North Carolina Press, 2009), 189.

7 Carey, "For the Columbian," 6.

8 Carey's choice to highlight the future success of African colonization is especially ironic given the inspiration for his musings, Louis-Sébastien Mercier's novel *Memoirs of the Year Two Thousand Five Hundred*. In that novel, the staunch abolitionist Mercier has his time-traveling narrator stumble across a statue memorializing "the figure of a negroe . . . noble and commanding" with the inscription: "To the Avenger of the New World." The traveler's companions explain that this unnamed hero led a successful slave revolt that "broke asunder the chains of all his countrymen" and "poured forth the blood of all their tyrants; French, Spanish, English, Dutch, and Portuguese." Mercier, *Memoirs of the Year Two Thousand Five Hundred*, transl. W. Hooper (Philadelphia: Thomas Dobson, 1795), 128–129. Not only does Carey deem it important to create an alternate solution to enslavement

209

210 **NOTES TO PAGES 3–5**

but he also begins his pseudo-historical narrative with the defeat of militant African (Algerian) forces.

9 Lloyd Pratt, *Archives of American Time: Literature and Modernity in the Nineteenth Century* (Philadelphia: University of Pennsylvania Press, 2010), 2.

10 Even before these two ships were captured by the Algerians, the American merchant ship *Betsy* was captured in 1784 by Moroccan pirates. However, the crew of the *Betsy* was soon released, and Morocco became the first country to recognize the independence of the United States.

11 My analysis is not particularly interested in developing strict boundaries to determine what texts do and do not belong in the Barbary archive as I have conceived of it. Rather, this concept is meant to signify connections between texts across time, space, and genre. Those texts set on the Barbary Coast are the most obvious candidates for inclusion in this formulation, but I am also interested in how themes and figures central to Barbary texts resurface frequently in works that otherwise have little to do with North Africa, such as the disruptive intervention of Barbary bodies in the early republican period, or the use of the term "Algerine" to represent pro-slavery state violence in later decades.

12 Paul Baepler's anthology could be considered the starting point for most modern literary studies of Barbary texts. Baepler, ed., *White Slaves, African Masters: An Anthology of American Barbary Captivity Narratives* (Chicago: University of Chicago Press, 1998). A few years earlier, Robert J. Allison's *The Crescent Obscured* (1995) brought renewed attention from historians to the Barbary crises period. Predictably, scholarship in this area grew significantly in the wake of the September 11 attacks and the beginning of the War on Terror. Some studies, like Joseph Wheelan's *Jefferson's War* (2004) and Frederick C. Leiner's *The End of Barbary Terror* (2006), explicitly connected Barbary piracy with terrorism, while Frank Lambert's *The Barbary Wars* (2005) emphasized the economic role of the corsairs. In this book I take the position that equating Barbary piracy with twenty-first-century terrorism is not only reductive and based on a problematic association of Islam with terrorism but also obscures the ways in which North African slavery was used as a lens through which so many early writers critiqued the brutality of American slavery, a comparison I explore at length in chapters 1 and 5. In other words, many nineteenth- and even eighteenth-century writers were keen to point out that there were no "innocent" American victims of Barbary captivity as long as America thrived on its own violent, inhumane system. See Allison, *The Crescent Obscured: The United States and the Muslim World, 1776–1815* (New York: Oxford University Press, 1995); Wheelan, *Jefferson's War: America's First War on Terror 1801–1805* (New York: PublicAffairs, 2004); Lambert, *The Barbary Wars: American Independence in the Atlantic World* (New York: Hill and Wang, 2005); and Leiner, *The End of Barbary Terror: America's 1815 War against the Pirates of North Africa* (New York: Oxford University Press, 2006).

13 Gordon Sayre, "Renegades from the Barbary: The Transnational Turn in Captivity Studies," *American Literary History* 22, no. 2 (Summer 2010): 349.

14 A second, related limitation of existing scholarship on Barbary texts has to do with the fact that, in almost every case, literary studies have used Barbary materials

as a kind of preamble for a broader arc with a focus elsewhere. Timothy Marr's important book *The Cultural Roots of American Islamicism* (2006), for example, broadly examines American representations of Islamic belief throughout the nineteenth century, beginning with Barbary texts but advancing to studies of Mormonism, Herman Melville, and the Zouave soldiers of the Civil War. Similarly, Jacob Rama Berman's *American Arabesque* (2012) traces American cultural constructions of the Arab from the Barbary crises through the romantic period and well into the twentieth century. Another study, Hester Blum's *The View from the Masthead* (2008), engages with North African captivity narratives as a jumping-off point for a longer and more complex discussion of maritime labor and sailors' rights. Marr, *The Cultural Roots of American Islamicism* (New York: Cambridge University Press, 2006); Berman, *American Arabesque: Arabs, Islam, and the 19th Century Imagination* (New York: New York University Press, 2012); Blum, *The View from the Masthead: Maritime Imagination and Antebellum American Sea Narratives* (Chapel Hill: University of North Carolina Press, 2008).

15 Jared Gardner, *Master Plots: Race and the Founding of American Literature, 1787–1845* (Baltimore: Johns Hopkins University Press, 1998), 27.

16 Bruce Dain, for example, points to how Thomas Jefferson, in *Notes on the State of Virginia* (1785), rejects Enlightenment notions of environmentalism in his discussions of Black writers such as Ignatius Sancho and Phillis Wheatley, presenting instead the growing understanding of Black racial identity as essential and unchanging. See Dain, *Hideous Monster of the Mind: American Race Theory in the Early Republic* (Cambridge, MA: Harvard University Press, 2002), esp. 26–36. Similarly, Ezra Tawil points to how early nineteenth-century frontier romances deploy sentiment, rather than potentially superficial physical properties, as the most important distinction between races. See Tawil, *The Making of Racial Sentiment: Slavery and the Birth of the Frontier Romance* (New York: Cambridge University Press, 2006).

17 Katy Chiles, *Transformable Race: Surprising Metamorphoses in the Literature of Early America* (New York: Oxford University Press, 2014), 2.

18 Royall Tyler, *The Algerine Captive; or, The Life and Adventures of Doctor Updike Underhill* (1797; reprint New York: Modern Library, 2002), 101.

19 Chiles, *Transformable Race*, 203.

20 Paul Baepler, "The Barbary Captivity Narrative in American Culture," *Early American Literature* 39, no. 2 (2004): 238.

21 Sarah Tindal Kareem, for example, builds on Gallagher's exploration of fictionality in study of "wonder" in the eighteenth-century novel as the way texts like *Robinson Crusoe* "[present] their contents as both strange and true." Kareem, *Eighteenth-Century Fiction and the Reinvention of Wonder* (New York: Oxford University Press, 2014), 10.

22 Catherine Gallagher, "The Rise of Fictionality," in *The Novel*, vol. 1, *History, Geography, and Culture*, ed. Franco Moretti (Princeton, NJ: Princeton University Press, 2006), 345.

23 Matthew Pethers and Thomas Koenigs, "Special Issue Introduction: Early American Fictionality," *Early American Literature* 56, no. 3 (2021): 682–683.

212   NOTES TO PAGES 8–13

24 As I discuss in the first section of chapter 1, the first of this period's immensely popular Barbary narratives, *A Journal, of the Captivity and Sufferings of John Foss*, was published the year after Tyler's novel in 1798.

25 Tyler, *The Algerine Captive*, 5–7.

26 In *Revolution and the Word* (1986), Cathy Davidson reads Tyler's preface as heralding the beginning of the dominance of the novel, although not all the texts that the writers sees proliferating in America are novels. Davidson, *Revolution and the Word: The Rise of the Novel in America, Expanded Edition* (New York: Oxford University Press, 2004), 101–102. Tyler/Underhill's points about fanciful fiction in 1797 bear a striking resemblance to Samuel Griswold Goodrich's criticism of the state of children's literature in the 1830s, which I explore in the final chapter of this book. It is telling that in both cases, the suffering and redemption of the white slave, even when fictionalized, provides the antidote for the novel's corrosive effect on public virtue.

27 Lindsay DiCuirci, "Found among the Papers: Fictions of Textual Discovery in Early America," *Early American Literature* 56, no. 3 (2021): 825.

28 Thomas Koenigs, *Founded in Fiction: The Uses of Fiction in the Early United States* (Princeton, NJ: Princeton University Press, 2021), 61–62, 64.

29 Tyler, *Algerine Captive*, 197–199.

30 See Gardner, *Master Plots*, 25, and Gesa Mackenthun, "The Transoceanic Emergence of American 'Postcolonial' Identities," in *A Companion to the Literatures of Colonial America*, ed. Susan Castillo and Ivy Schweitzer (Malden, MA: Blackwell, 2005), 343.

31 Lawrence A. Peskin, *Captives and Countrymen: Barbary Slavery and the American Public, 1785–1816* (Baltimore: Johns Hopkins University Press, 2009), 27.

32 "Philadelphia, November 19," *Philadelphia Evening Herald*, November 19, 1785.

33 "The Humble Petition of the American Captives," *Salem [MA] Gazette*, January 27, 1795.

34 "Algiers, April 9th, 1793, and 8th of Captivity," *Gazette of the United States and Evening Advertiser* (Philadelphia), December 16, 1793.

35 "Boston, May 20. From Algiers," *Courier of New Hampshire* (Concord), May 23, 1795.

36 *OED Online*, s.v. "suspense, n.," https://www.oed.com.

37 Lennard J. Davis, *Factual Fictions: The Origins of the English Novel* (New York: Columbia University Press, 1983), 70, 212.

38 Koenigs, *Founded in Fiction*, 61–62.

39 Peskin, *Captives and Countrymen*, 92–93.

40 Since 2016 there has been a growing consensus that "fake news" poses a major challenge to twenty-first-century news media and to the U.S. political system. At the same time, there seems little consensus over what exactly "fake news" is. What distinguishes it from, say, hoaxes, pranks, or simply bad reporting? Most commentators are careful to mark the difference between "fake news" and satire (fakenewswatch.com, for example, defines fake news sites as satire sites that are not funny), although those distinctions become blurred when articles from TheOnion. com and other sites are shared by outraged readers on social media as if they were true. Thus, the definition of "fake news" tends to depend on what one emphasizes:

the political and economic motivations of the author or the motivations of the reader/sharer, the context within which a piece is produced, the context a piece sheds as to goes viral, or the new context it accrues through comments, tweets, and status updates. There may be little consensus about what exactly fake news is, but historians have pointed out again and again that this is not a new concern for media. In the American context, many commentators point to the period of "yellow journalism" that led up to the Spanish-American War as the origins of this particular scourge so corrosive to the legitimacy of popular media. However, I would argue that this concept provides a potentially productive lens through which we might read the struggles of early American print to deal with the Barbary crises and thus to establish an authoritative voice independent from the British media that still in many ways dominated the journalistic and literary cultures of the former colonies.

41 "Extract of a Letter from Capt. Truxton," *Massachusetts Centinel* (Boston), November 16, 1785. All of the American captives held in Algiers during the Algerine Crisis were, like Truxton, themselves sailors. This parting image of the philosopher-in-chains more closely resembles Tyler's later Dr. Underhill than any contemporary victims of Algerian piracy.

42 Koenigs, *Founded in Fiction*, 169–170.

43 "The Following Letter," *Thomas's Massachusetts Spy; or, Worcester [MA] Gazette*, November 24, 1785.

44 "London, November 8," *Columbian Herald* (Columbia, SC), January 2, 1786.

45 "Lies Collected from British News-Papers," *State Gazette of South Carolina* (Charleston), December 22, 1785.

46 "London, Sept. 21," *Columbian Herald*, December 8, 1785. Franklin would later comment in a letter to Ferdinand Grand about how the "English Papers, not only send me gratis, as you observe, to Algiers, but they are sending all the United States to Destruction." Franklin, *The Letters of Benjamin Franklin: 1783–1788*, ed. Albert Henry Smith (New York: Macmillan, 1907), 9:493.

47 Together these questions add up to the broader, more consequential, and perhaps more evasive question: how did early Americans read their newspapers? While seemingly a fairly simple question, the answer, if we could ever arrive at one, is quite consequential to text-based narratives of American nation-building derived from the work of Benedict Anderson and Michael Warner. Anderson in particular sees the newspaper page as an essential stage for the conceptualization of national figures or characters imaginatively connected to one another. For Anderson, the acceptance, conscious or not, of the fictive nature of the newspaper page by the individual reader follows the same logic by which that reader accepts the imagined connection between them and the other Americans or Germans or Indonesians who are at that moment reading that same page. He describes this community as resulting from the newspaper's "novelistic format" in which we are able to imagine the subjects of reporting as "characters" moving in time and space. My intention here is not to suggest in any reductive way that the presence of a hoax disproves Anderson's concept. Instead, I want to ask what other forms of reading, what familiarity with genres and forms of address, and what knowledge *outside* of print was necessary for early republican readers to make sense of

the Truxton letter? What does it mean for the "character" of the early republic that readers frequently encountered not just hoaxes and false reports but also satirical works that fall far afield of our current understanding of what constitutes journalism or reportage? Can such diverse and multi-generic newspaper pages, not unlike present-day news feeds that place articles from the *New York Times* and *The Onion* side by side without editorial comment, really serve to imagine the nation as "a sociological organism moving calendrically through homogenous empty time?" Anderson, *Imagined Communities: Reflections on the Origin and Spread of Nationalism* (New York: Verso, 2006), 33, 26. See also Warner, *Letters of the Republic: Publication and the Public Sphere in Eighteenth-Century America* (Cambridge, MA: Harvard University Press, 1990).

48 British complicity in and even orchestration of Barbary piracy is a theme that runs throughout the Barbary archive. Malini Johar Schueller points out that Jefferson included a reference to Barbary piracy in an early draft of the Declaration of Independence: "He [King George III] has waged cruel war against human nature itself, violating its most sacred rights of life and liberty in the persons of a distant people who never offended him, captivating them and carrying them into slavery in another hemisphere, or to incur miserable death in their transportation thither. This piratical warfare, the opprobrium of INFIDEL powers, is the warfare of the CHRISTIAN king of Great Britain. Determined to keep open a market where MEN should be bought and sold, he has prostituted his negative for suppressing every legislative attempt to prohibit or to restrain this execrable commerce." *Journals of the Continental Congress, 1774–1789* (Washington, DC: Government Printing Office, 1906), 5:498. While the main point of the passage is to suggest that King George has imposed the slave trade on the colonies as part of his tyrannical rule, Schueller argues that Jefferson directs most of his invective against North Africa. King George's crime is to rule over the colonies like the dey of Algiers. Schueller, *U.S. Orientalisms: Race, Nation and Gender in Literature, 1790–1890* (Ann Arbor: University of Michigan Press, 1998), 47–48. Philip Gould argues that the United States' negotiations with Algiers in the period were "directly related" to its strained political relationship with Great Britain, and that many representations of Algerian brutality were influenced by public anger over the concessions made in the Jay Treaty, fueling political animus between Federalists and Republicans throughout the 1790s. Gould, *Barbaric Traffic: Commerce and Antislavery in the Eighteenth-Century Atlantic World* (Cambridge, MA: Harvard University Press, 2003), 89–90. Somewhat diverging from Gould, I would argue that we should see discussions based in the Barbary not simply as an expression of Anglo-American relations but as an opportunity to disrupt those linkages.

49 Daniel Walker Howe, *What Hath God Wrought: The Transformation of America, 1815–1848* (New York: Oxford University Press, 2007), 225. For more discussion of the logistical challenges faced by print networks in the period, see also Robert A. Gross, "Introduction: An Extensive Republic," in *An Extensive Republic: Print, Culture, and Society in the New Nation, 1790–1840,* ed. Robert A. Gross and Mary Kelley (Chapel Hill: University of North Carolina Press, 2010), 5–6.

50 Kariann Akemi Yokota, *Unbecoming British: How Revolutionary America Became a Postcolonial Nation* (New York: Oxford University Press, 2014), 9.

51 Koenigs, *Founded in Fiction*, 3.

52 Paul Gilroy, *The Black Atlantic: Modernity and Double Consciousness* (New York: Penguin Books, 1993), 3, 6.

53 William Q. Boelhower, "The Rise of the New Atlantic Studies Matrix," *American Literary History* 20, nos. 1–2 (Spring–Summer 2008): 92–93.

54 William Q. Boelhower, *Atlantic Studies: Prospects and Challenges* (Baton Rouge: Louisiana State University Press, 2019), 102, 107–108.

55 Also relevant to Boelhower's analysis, this book touches on the Barbary resonances of the *Creole* affair and Douglass's later novel in chapter 5.

56 Laura Doyle, *Freedom's Empire: Race and the Rise of the Novel in Atlantic Modernity, 1640–1940* (Durham, NC: Duke University Press, 2008), 4.

57 Marr, *The Cultural Roots of American Islamicism*, 31.

58 Paul Giles, *Transatlantic Insurrections: British Culture and the Formation of American Literature, 1730–1860* (Philadelphia: University of Pennsylvania Press, 2001), 1.

59 Notably, Hegel draws a sharp distinction between North and sub-Saharan Africa; the former he refers to as "European Africa." Describing the Barbary Coast in *Lectures on the Philosophy of History* (1840), Hegel writes, "The northern part of Africa, . . . lies on the Mediterranean and the Atlantic; a magnificent territory, on which Carthage once lay—the site of the modern Morocco, Algiers, Tunis, and Tripoli. This part was to be—must be attached to Europe: the French have lately made a successful effort in this direction. . . . Here in their turn have Carthaginians, Romans, and Byzantines, Mussulmans, Arabians, had their abode, and the interests of Europe have always striven to get a footing in it." Even as he spares North Africa from his broader dismissal of the continent, he does so by reducing the region to a site for capture and colonization. His interest, however, in the coast's Carthaginian history is shared by a number of American writers during the Barbary crises, a theme I explore further in chapter 2. Georg Wilhelm Friedrich Hegel, *The Philosophy of History*, transl. J. Sibree (New York: Colonial Press, 1899), 91–93.

60 This book focuses only on the United States' post-independence conflicts with the Barbary Coast. However, there were many earlier cases in which Americans, as subjects of the British Empire, had been captured by Barbary pirates. Several, including Joshua Gee and Abraham Browne, later wrote narratives of their captivity. The first American Barbary narrative is credited not to a captive but to Puritan minister Cotton Mather, who wrote of the plight of New Englanders then enslaved in "*Algiers, Salley, Barbary*, and other places on the Coast of *Africa*" in his sermon "The Glory of Goodness." See Mather, "The Glory of Goodness: The Goodness of God, Celebrated," in *White Slaves, African Masters: An Anthology of American Barbary Captivity Narratives*, ed. Paul Baepler (Chicago: University of Chicago Press, 1998), 61–69. For recent work on Gee and Browne, see Greta LaFleur, *The Natural History of Sexuality in Early America* (Baltimore: Johns Hopkins University Press, 2018), 63–102.

61 In his 2005 study of early American imperialism, Andy Doolen uses the term "fugitive empire" to describe the "hidden imperialism, reputedly antithetical to republican values, that shaped our culture and institutions in America's formative

NOTES TO PAGES 21–32

years," as well as "the histories of slaves and the institutions of slavery that make manifest precisely how U.S. imperialism has imprinted its racial geographies on our nation." Doolen, *Fugitive Empire: Locating Early American Imperialism* (Minneapolis: University of Minnesota Press, 2005), xiii. In this book I hope to offer further evidence through the Barbary archive that the forms of imperial projection ascendant in the late nineteenth century around the Spanish-American War and that found new life in the twenty-first century's War on Terror were, in fact, a part of the United States' self-conception from the founding era and have long structured the country's engagement with the Muslim world.

62 F. O. Matthiessen argues that the period 1850–1855 was a major turning point, seeing in it the "terminus to the agricultural era," the rise of industrialized (and organized) labor, the "last struggle of the liberal spirit of the eighteenth century," and the "full emergence of the acquisitive spirit." Matthiessen, *American Renaissance: Art and Expression in the Age of Emerson and Whitman* (New York: Oxford University Press, 1941), ix.

63 Sandra M. Gustafson, "Histories of Democracy and Empire," *American Quarterly* 59, no. 1 (March 2007): 107–108.

64 Sandra M. Gustafson, "What's in a Date? Temporalities of Early American Literature," *PMLA* 128, no. 4 (October 2013): 962, 969. As recently as 2017, the Society of Early Americanists voted to amend both its mission statement and its constitution to shift the upper limit of its temporal range from 1800 to 1830, a testament to the growing interest in the literature of the first decades of the nineteenth century.

65 See Trish Loughran, *Republic in Print: Print Culture in the Age of U.S. Nation Building, 1700–1870* (New York: Columbia University Press, 2009).

66 Loughran, *Republic in Print*, 4.

67 Christopher Apap, *The Genius of Place: The Geographic Imagination in the Early Republic* (Durham: University of New Hampshire Press, 2016), 10.

CHAPTER ONE: THE PATRIOT AND THE SABLE BARD

1 John Foss, *A Journal, of the Captivity and Sufferings of John Foss; Several Years a Prisoner in Algiers* (Newburyport, MA: A. March, 1798), 2–3. Hester Blum argues that such warnings, common to Barbary captivity narratives, demonstrate how the narratives were directed explicitly at other sailors, who might have use of the navigational data and ethnographic observations within the text. See Blum, *The View from the Masthead: Maritime Imagination and Antebellum American Sea Narratives* (Chapel Hill: University of North Carolina Press, 2008), 58.

2 Foss, *A Journal, of the Captivity*, 53, 55, 3.

3 Timothy Marr, *The Cultural Roots of American Islamicism* (New York: Cambridge University Press, 2006), 55, 53.

4 Paul Baepler, Introduction, in *White Slaves, African Masters: An Anthology of American Barbary Captivity Narratives*, ed. Paul Baepler (Chicago: University of Chicago Press, 1998), 27–28. Baepler draws heavily on James Clifford's assertion that ethnographers, through the "fiction" of ethnography, practice "cultural *poesis*": "the constant reconstitution of selves and others through specific exclusions, conventions, and discursive practices." Clifford, "Introduction: Partial Truths,"

NOTES TO PAGES 32–34   217

in *Writing Culture: The Poetics and Politics of Ethnography*, ed. James Clifford and George E. Marcus (Berkeley: University of California Press, 2010), 24. I explore this term further in chapter 5.

5 Significant portions of the first edition of Foss's *Journal* and much larger sections of his expanded second edition were plagiarized from other accounts of Algiers, most notably Mathew Carey's *Short Account of Algiers*, discussed later in this chapter. Lifted sections in the second edition include a graphic description of punishments inflicted on Christian slaves, leading Lawrence Peskin to suggest that perhaps Foss was not a direct witness to as much barbarity as he would suggest. Peskin, *Captives and Countrymen: Barbary Slavery and the American Public, 1785–1816* (Baltimore: Johns Hopkins University Press, 2006), 73.

6 Foss, *A Journal, of the Captivity*, 22.

7 John Foss, *A Journal, of the Captivity and Sufferings of John Foss; Several Years a Prisoner at Algiers*, 2nd edition (Newburyport, MA: Angier March, 1798), 52–54.

8 Peskin suggests that Foss deliberately evades any reference to American slavery to prevent invoking the stigma of slavery he now shares and to avoid offending "slave-owning benefactors." Peskin, *Captives and Countrymen*, 73.

9 Foss, *A Journal, of the Captivity*, 1st edition, 2. In *The Rise and Fall of Early American Magazine Culture* (2012), Jared Gardner outlines what he calls the "editorial function" in the early republic as an alternative to the identity of the individual author. The editor rises above factionalism to create a space for the "spectacularly contradictory" voices of the nation. Gardner, *The Rise and Fall of Early American Magazine Culture* (Urbana: University of Illinois Press, 2014), 15–16. Foss in some ways alternates between the paradigms of author and editor. While, as with any captivity narrative, the text centers on his individual journey from captivity to freedom, nonetheless large portions of the work are composed of anecdotes and even plagiarized portions of other texts, particularly Mathew Carey's *A Short Account of Algiers*.

10 Royall Tyler, *The Algerine Captive; or, The Life and Adventures of Doctor Updike Underhill* (1797; reprint New York: Modern Library, 2002), 105, 96. Sarah Sillin has persuasively argued that the unifying power of sympathy in the novel also surfaces the threat of national dissolution, as Tyler often portrays Underhill as a "captive to feeling" who is vulnerable to forms of "foreign" sympathy that threaten the coherence of the nation. Such risks are evident not only in the fact that Underhill's sympathy for the Africans prompts him to nurse them ashore and thus leads directly to his capture by the Algerians but also in his alienation from the *Sympathy*'s crew members, who scowl at his "yankee nonsense about humanity." Despite Underhill's continued willingness to participate in the slave trade, his predilection for sentiment threatens the resurfacing of cultural and sectional divisions that could tear the nation apart. See Sillin, "'Made to Feel Wretched': Royall Tyler and the Trouble with Global Sympathy," *Early American Literature* 51, no. 1 (2016): 104–105.

11 My argument throughout this chapter aims to build on recent scholarship focusing on questions of the body in early American literature. Sarah Schuetze observes that bodies were "intimately involved" in the production, circulation, and consumption of texts in early America, yet those bodies "have become largely

removed from our readings of historical texts." Schuetze, "Bodies," *Early American Studies: An Interdisciplinary Journal* 16, no. 4 (Fall 2018): 607. Scholars in the fields of gender and sexuality studies and the health humanities such as Greta LaFleur, Kyla Schuller, and Sari Altschuler, among a growing list of others, have sought to recover those bodies through early American models of biopolitics. See Greta LaFleur, *The Natural History of Sexuality in Early America* (Baltimore: Johns Hopkins University Press, 2019); Kyla Schuller, *The Biopolitics of Feeling: Race, Sex, and Science in the Nineteenth Century* (Durham, NC: Duke University Press, 2018); Sari Altschuler, *The Medical Imagination: Literature and Health in the Early United States* (Philadelphia: University of Pennsylvania Press, 2018); and the special issue of *American Quarterly* on "The Origins of Biopolitics in the Americas," edited by LaFleur and Schuller. As we shall see, work in the Barbary archive can contribute to such interventions because texts surrounding North African slavery were deeply interested not just in the circulation of texts and bodies across the Atlantic but also in the integrity of the suffering white body as a representation of the coherence of the national body, held together through forms of national sympathy and fellow feeling.

12 Laura Doyle, *Freedom's Empire: Race and the Rise of the Novel in Atlantic Modernity, 1640–1940* (Durham, NC: Duke University Press, 2008), 184. Here Doyle specifically examines the race-liberty plot in Daniel Defoe's *Robinson Crusoe* (1719), which itself includes a Barbary captivity narrative. Long before Crusoe's famous stranding, he embarked on a slave-trading expedition to West Africa that resulted in his capture and enslavement by Moroccan pirates. Royall Tyler repeats much of this early structure in *The Algerine Captive*, with the difference that Underhill repents his participation in the slave trade, while Crusoe, after his escape, notoriously sold a young Moroccan boy he kidnapped into slavery.

13 Mathew Carey, *A Short Account of Algiers and of Its Several Wars against Spain, France, England, Holland, Venice, and Other Powers of Europe, from the Usurpation of Barbarossa and the Invasion of the Emperor Charles V. to the Present Time* (Philadelphia: Mathew Carey, 1794), 16.

14 David Waldstreicher, "Reading the Runaways: Self-Fashioning, Print Culture, and the Confidence in Slavery in the Eighteenth-Century Mid-Atlantic," *William and Mary Quarterly* 3rd series, 56, no. 2 (April 1999): 247.

15 While Carey does not explicitly blame French immigrants for the epidemic, he notes that those "newly settled in Philadelphia, have been in a very remarkable degree exempt" from the illness. Mathew Carey, *A Short Account of the Malignant Fever, Lately Prevalent in Philadelphia* (Philadelphia: Mathew Carey, 1794), 62.

16 "Forty Zequins Reward," *Philadelphia Gazette and Universal Daily Advertiser*, December 8, 1794. In his brief mention of this satire, Peter P. Reed posits that it originated in the November 24, 1794, issue of the *Federal Orrery* in Boston. That printing included a short heading that called it "a most admirable satire on the *democratic professions*, and *despotic practices* of our ranting southern demagogues." Reed, *Rogue Performances: Staging the Underclass in Early American Theatre Culture* (New York: Palgrave Macmillan, 2009). Most reprintings of the piece, including the issue of the *Philadelphia Gazette* I quote from, drop the heading and allow the mock advertisement to speak for itself.

NOTES TO PAGES 37–41   219

17 Cotton Mather, "The Glory of Goodness: The Goodness of God, Celebrated," in Baepler, ed., *White Slaves, African Masters*, 64.

18 Reed, *Rogue Performances*, 66–67.

19 Shane White quotes a similar mock advertisement that ran in *Douglass' Monthly* in 1861, this one written by an enslaved man in South Carolina, Sambo Rhett, offering a reward for the return of his master, who ran away from his plantation after an enslaved woman fought back against his attempt to whip her. See White, "The Allure of Advertisement: Slave Runaways in and around New York City," *Journal of the Early Republic* 40, no. 4 (Winter 2020): 611–633.

20 David Waldstreicher, *Runaway America: Benjamin Franklin, Slavery, and the American Revolution* (New York: Hill and Wang, 2004), 9.

21 Frederick Douglass, *The Life and Times of Frederick Douglass, Written by Himself* (Boston, De Wolfe and Fiske, 1892), 246–247.

22 "Forty Zequins Reward."

23 Hortense J. Spillers, "Mama's Baby, Papa's Maybe: An American Grammar Book," *Diacritics* 17, no. 2 (Summer 1987): 67.

24 Donna Haraway, "The Persistence of Vision," in *Writing on the Body: Female Embodiment and Feminist Theory*, ed. Katie Conroy, Nadia Medina, and Sarah Stanbury (New York: Columbia University Press, 1993), 283.

25 Corey Capers, "Black Voices, White Print: Racial Practice, Print Publicity, and Order in the Early American Republic," in *Early African American Print Culture*, ed. Lara Langer Cohen and Jordan Alexander Stein (Philadelphia: University of Pennsylvania Press, 2012), 110.

26 "List of American Vessels," *The Diary* (New York), February 11, 1797.

27 *The American in Algiers; or, The Patriot of Seventy-Six in Captivity. A Poem, in Two Cantos* (New York: J. Buel, 1797), i.

28 James M. Greene, "Ethan Allen and Daniel Shays: Contrasting Models of Political Representation in the Early Republic," *Early American Literature* 48, no. 1 (2013): 138–139.

29 As Gordon Sayre puts it, traditional modes of reading captivity narratives focus on how they "direct their discourse to an audience made up of their compatriots, coreligionists, and comrades, to an 'us' who will share the grief of bondage of one of 'ours' at the hands of one of 'them.'" Sayre, "Renegades from the Barbary: The Transnational Turn in Captivity Studies," *American Literary History* 22, no. 2 (Summer 2010): 351.

30 Benjamin Cooper has recently argued that Allen's narrative should be considered within a distinct tradition of veteran and prisoner-of-war literature, which, unlike popular Native American captivity narratives such as Mary Rowlandson's *The Sovereignty and Goodness of God* (1682), sought specifically to embody American identity as an answer to public indifference to the plight of veterans. Cooper, *Veteran Americans: Literature and Citizenship from Revolution to Reconstruction* (Amherst: University of Massachusetts Press, 2018), 40–41. It is easy to see how the public's neglect of Revolutionary War veterans might have inspired the figure of the Patriot in this poem, since that lack of support leads to his ultimate (re) enslavement.

31 *American in Algiers*, 5; Carey, *A Short Account*, 36.

220 **NOTES TO PAGES 41–51**

32 *American in Algiers*, 6–8.

33 *American in Algiers*, 10, 13, 16.

34 Bruce Burgett, *Sentimental Bodies: Sex, Gender, and Citizenship in the Early Republic* (Princeton, NJ: Princeton University Press, 1998), 58–59.

35 *American in Algiers*, 21.

36 *American in Algiers*, 21.

37 Phillis Wheatley, "On Being Brought from Africa to America," in *Complete Writings*, ed. Vincent Carretta (New York: Penguin Books, 2001), 13.

38 Noah Webster, *American Dictionary of the English Language*, s.v. "translate," www.webstersdictionary1828.com, quoted in Colleen Glenney Boggs, *Transnationalism and American Literature: Literary Translation, 1773–1892* (New York: Routledge, 2007), 39.

39 Henry Louis Gates Jr., *The Signifying Monkey: A Theory of African-American Literary Criticism* (New York: Oxford University Press, 1988), 130.

40 *American in Algiers*, 22–23.

41 *American in Algiers*, 27, 25.

42 *American in Algiers*, 28.

43 Thomas Jefferson, *Notes on the State of Virginia* (1785; reprint Philadelphia: Prichard and Hall, 1988), 150.

44 *American in Algiers*, 29.

45 *American in Algiers*, 30.

46 Olaudah Equiano, *The Interesting Narrative and Other Writings*, ed. Vincent Carretta (New York: Penguin Books, 2003), 56.

47 *American in Algiers*, 31.

48 Philip Gould, *Barbaric Traffic: Commerce and Antislavery in the 18th Century Atlantic World* (Cambridge, MA: Harvard University Press, 2009), 95–96.

49 *American in Algiers*, 33.

50 Joseph Rezek, "Print, Writing and the Difference Media Make: Revisiting *The Signifying Monkey* after Book History," *Early American Literature* 50, no. 3 (2015): 898.

51 William Grimes, *Life of William Grimes, the Runaway Slave. Written by Himself* (New York: William Grimes, 1825), 68, quoted in Susanna Ashton, "Slavery, Imprinted: The Life and Narrative of William Grimes," in Cohen and Stein, eds., *Early African American Print Culture*, 127.

52 Ashton, "Slavery, Imprinted," 127.

53 *Humanity in Algiers; or, The Story of Azem*, ed. Duncan Faherty and Ed White, *Common-Place: The Journal of Early American Life* (Fall 2014): 3, http://jto.common-place.org. It is very possible that the similarity in language to Mathew Carey's earlier work is not entirely coincidental. Faherty and White have traced the quoted phrase "a vile, piratical set of unprincipled robbers" to a 1788 essay printed in the *American Museum*, edited by Carey. Faherty and White, Introduction to *Humanity in Algiers*, 3n4.

54 *Humanity in Algiers*, 2, 3.

55 *Humanity in Algiers*, 4, 3.

56 As Faherty and White note, no connection had been found between this novella and the surviving members of the *Dauphin*'s crew.

57 Faherty and White, Introduction.

NOTES TO PAGES 51–58   221

58 *Humanity in Algiers*, 1–2, 5.
59 *Humanity in Algiers*, 5, 28.
60 Ros Ballaster. "Narrative Transmigrations," in *A Companion to the Eighteenth-Century English Novel and Culture*, ed. Paula R. Backscheider and Catherine Ingrassia (Malden, MA: Blackwell, 2005), 76.
61 Teresa A. Goddu, *Selling Antislavery: Abolition and Mass Media in Antebellum America* (Philadelphia: University of Pennsylvania Press, 2020), 57.
62 "Prince Moro," *Columbian Star* (Washington, DC), August 6, 1825, 128.
63 "Art. IX. The Narrative of Robert Adams," *North American Review and Miscellaneous Journal*, July 1817, 204.
64 "Prince Moro," 128.
65 "Prince Moro," 128.
66 Omar ibn Said, *The Life of Omar ibn Said, Written by Himself*, transl. Ala Alryyes (Madison: University of Wisconsin Press, 2011), 77.

CHAPTER TWO: BARBARY(AN) INVASIONS

1 This chapter is reprinted from *Early American Literature* 50, no. 2 (2015): 331–358.
2 "Glorious News!!" *Impartial Herald* (Newburyport, MA), August 30, 1794.
3 John Foss, *A Journal, of the Captivity and Sufferings of John Foss; Several Years a Prisoner in Algiers*, in *White Slaves, African Masters: An Anthology of American Barbary Captivity Narratives*, ed. Paul Baepler (Chicago: University of Chicago Press, 1999), 73.
4 "Natives of Algiers," *Gazette of the United States* (Philadelphia), September 22, 1794.
5 "By the Day's Mail," *Gazette of the United States*, October 27, 1794.
6 Jacob Rama Berman, *American Arabesque: Arabs, Islam, and the 19th Century Imagination* (New York: New York University Press, 2012), 31.
7 Records of the two Algerian gentlemen appear to stop cold after an October 16 report from Providence that mentions them passing through the city the previous week. However, on December 19 in the *Massachusetts Mercury* there appears for the first time an advertisement for "Mr. Ibrahim Adam Ben Ali, from Constantinople, Practitioner in Medicine" in Boston. The advertisement offers, among other things, Ben Ali's "incomparable ALGERINE MEDICINE for the Scurvy." In the summer of 1795, Ben Ali apparently moved to New York and advertised his services there. By 1799, he had relocated to Philadelphia, and then in 1800 to Baltimore. While the advertisement looks like a hoax, someone calling himself Mr. Ibrahim Adam Ben Ali did peddle his medical services in cities up and down the East Coast. There are a few very short accounts of people seeking medical advice from the "doctor." An 1800 article about quack medicine from Walpole, New Hampshire's *Farmer's Museum* complains that "even Turkey is not ignorant of great encouragement which America extends to those who are solicitous for the health of her citizens. In Baltimore, Ibrahim Adam Ben Ali, physician from Constantinople, or more probably some crafty native, who has assumed a Turkish name, and 'culled a few simples,' and indiscriminately applies to them in various opposite cases, offers a variety of poison under specious and plausible names." Is it possible that this Ben Ali, with some accomplice, posed as Algerian

222 **NOTES TO PAGES 59–60**

gentlemen traveling to Philadelphia in 1794? Did they reach Providence only to double-back and return to Boston in order to set up a new con under an assumed name combining their previous aliases, Sieur Ibrahim and Mahomed Ben Ali? Or, perhaps previous reports had been confused, and the exiled Algerians gave up on their hopes of returning home and set themselves up for good in America. At this point, we can only speculate. "Mr. Ibrahim Adam Ben Ali, from Constantinople, Practitioner of Medicine," *Massachusetts Mercury* (Boston), December 19, 1794; "Incidents at Home," *Farmer's Museum, or Literary Gazette* (Walpole, NH), August 4, 1800.

8 Michael Warner, *Letters of the Republic: Publication and the Public Sphere in Eighteenth-Century America* (Cambridge, MA: Harvard University Press, 1990), 43. Warner argues that classical pseudonyms allowed political elites to claim to speak for the anonymous masses and for the nation itself, rather than just for their own interests. Over the last few decades, a number of critics have pushed back against Warner's privileging of print pseudonymity. Christopher Looby and Sandra M. Gustafson, for example, argue for the central role of embodied forms of public expression and authority such as oratory and performance in early republican culture. Gustafson has argued that Warner's overemphasis on print as the source of public authority has led to an "opposition of printed works and oral forms . . . [that ignores] the substantial overlap and integration of spoken and written or printed texts." These critics have questioned whether even Publius or Cato could truly leave the body behind. Looby, *Voicing America: Language, Literary Form and the Origins of the United States* (Chicago: University of Chicago Press, 1996); Gustafson, "American Literature and the Public Sphere," *American Literary History* 20, no. 3 (Fall 2008): 465. As Trish Loughran asks, "Does pseudonymous authorship—even when it includes more than one author—effectively amount to a sense that there is no author? And . . . do printed objects, when unsigned, really appear to 'emanate from no one?'" Loughran, *The Republic in Print: Print Culture in the Age of U.S. Nation Building, 1700–1870* (New York: Columbia University Press, 2009), 132. At stake is the question of whether Americans could imagine a national address that could transcend the local origins of both print and oratory.

9 Eran Shalev, *Rome Reborn on Western Shores: Historical Imagination and the Creation of the American Republic* (Charlottesville: University of Virginia Press, 2009), 152.

10 Paul Baepler, Introduction, in Baepler, ed., *White Slaves, African Masters*, 2–3.

11 The phenomenon of pseudo-translation has gained increasing attention in recent years, with most studies drawing from the definition formulated by Gideon Toury: "texts which have been presented as translations with no corresponding source texts in other languages ever having existed." Toury, *Descriptive Translation Studies and Beyond* (Amsterdam: John Benjamins, 2012), 40.

12 Over the last several years, researchers, particularly in the field of comparative literature, have begun to excavate the trope of pseudo-translation in the context of broader discussions of what constitutes "world literature." Brigitte Rath, for example, proposes reading pseudo-translation as "a mode of reading that oscillates between seeing the text as an original and as a translation pointing towards an imagined original, produced in a different language and culture for a different

NOTES TO PAGES 60–61   223

audience." As part of the American Comparative Literature Association's 2014 *State of the Discipline Report*, Rath remarks that, of the 154 scholarly sources that she has found using the term "pseudo-translation," two-thirds of them have been from the last decade. Rath, "Ideas of the Decade—Pseudotranslation," *State of the Discipline Report*, American Comparative Literature Association, April 1, 2014, https://stateofthediscipline.acla.org.

13 Lindsay DiCuirci, "Found among the Papers: Fictions of Textual Discovery in Early America," *Early American Literature* 56, no. 3 (2021): 809–843.

14 Emily Apter, *The Translation Zone: A New Comparative Literature* (Princeton, NJ: Princeton University Press, 2005), 212.

15 The stakes of translation took still another form in the early republic, as diplomatic treaties were routinely printed in newspapers, including treaties with North African states. That the works I study below make false claims to translation from Arabic seems to have direct relevance to treaties with Morocco and Tripoli (translated from Arabic) and with Algiers and Tunis (translated from Turkish). Because those documents constituted federal law, the public had to be confident that they meant the same thing in both languages. In at least one case, the 1797 Treaty of Tripoli, the American diplomat who drafted the treaty, Joel Barlow, appears to have included an article in the English version that was not in the Arabic copy signed by the bey of Tripoli. This is not a small omission, as it is the famous (or perhaps infamous) article that declares that "the United States is, in no sense, founded on the Christian religion." Hunter Miller, "Note Regarding the Barlow Translation," Avalon Project, Lillian Goldman Law Library, Yale Law School, 2008, http://avalon.law.yale.edu.

16 Loughran, *Republic in Print*, 20–21. Loughran's criticism of what she calls the "text-based model of U.S. nation-building" is aimed squarely at the theories of Benedict Anderson and Michael Warner that still very much structure the field of early American studies. For Anderson, the rise of print-capitalism and of newspaper cultures in the late eighteenth century allowed the emergence of forms of simultaneity that enabled the nation to emerge as an imagined community moving through "homogenous, empty time." Anderson, *Imagined Communities: Reflections on the Origin and Spread of Nationalism* (New York: Verso, 2006), 26. Writing more specifically in the context of early America, Warner argues that within republican ideology that valued abstract reasoning and disinterestedness, the circulation of print came to represent an ideal public within which documents such as the Constitution could claim authority over a national community. Warner, *Letters of the Republic*, 58–67. As Loughran points out, both of these models, to some extent, rely on the far-flung circulation of print artifacts across the great distances and uneven terrain of the early United States, circulation that she suggests would have been largely impossible from a practical and logistical standpoint. There is, of course, nothing particularly new about exposing the gaps within the models developed by Anderson and Warner; however, I would suggest that Loughran's most important contribution is the way she critiques what have become the calcified assumptions on which so many early American literary studies rest: that there is something called the "nation" in the early republic, and that writers looked to that formation, rather than to their local circumstances, when constructing their narratives.

224 **NOTES TO PAGES 61–66**

17 Warner, *Letters of the Republic*, 61.

18 Benjamin Franklin, quoted in Warner, *Letters of the Republic*, 73–74.

19 Warner, *Letters of the Republic*, 81.

20 Benjamin Franklin, "On the Slave Trade," in *The Complete Works, in Philosophy, Politics, and Morals, of the Late Dr. Benjamin Franklin* (London: J. Johnson, 1806), 2:459.

21 Franklin, "On the Slave Trade," 2:460.

22 Franklin, "On the Slave Trade," 2:459.

23 Malini Johar Schueller, *U.S. Orientalisms: Race, Nation and Gender in Literature, 1790–1890* (Ann Arbor: University of Michigan Press, 1998), 48.

24 This argument is consistent with Elizabeth Fenton's reading of Royall Tyler's criticism of deliberation in *The Algerine Captive*. Fenton focuses on the key chapter in which Tyler's Underhill debates the truth of Christianity and Islam with a mullah, himself a renegado convert. See Fenton, "Indeliberate Democracy: The Politics of Religious Conversion in Royall Tyler's *The Algerine Captive*," *Early American Literature* 51, no. 1 (2016): 71–100.

25 Charles Sumner, *White Slavery in the Barbary States: A Lecture before the Boston Mercantile Library Association, Feb. 17, 1847* (Boston: John P. Jewett, 1853), 89–90. I deal more extensively with the abolitionist Sumner's analysis of Barbary slavery in chapter 5.

26 "By Al Koraschi Ebnallad, Sovereign and Supreme Dey of Algiers, Lord of the Algerine Territories and the Atlantic Ocean," *Pennsylvania Packet or Daily Advertiser* (Philadelphia), May 3, 1785.

27 Robert J. Allison, *The Crescent Obscured: The United States and the Muslim World, 1776–1815* (New York: Oxford University Press, 1995), 3.

28 Duncan Faherty, "'The Mischief That Awaits Us': Revolution, Rumor, and Serial Unrest in the Early Republic," in *The Haitian Revolution and the Early United States*, ed. Elizabeth Maddock Dillon and Michael Drexler (Philadelphia: University of Pennsylvania Press, 2016), 77.

29 Lotfi Ben Rejeb asserts that in this genre, "The outsider was the rhetorical mask of an intellectual elite in a state of introspection." Rejeb, "Observing the Birth of a Nation: The Oriental Spy/Observer Genre and Nation Making in Early American Literature," in *The United States and the Middle East: Cultural Encounters*, ed. Abbas Amanat and Magnus Bernhardsson (New Haven, CT: Yale Center for International and Area Studies, 2002), 257. Other popular precursor texts in the oriental spy/observer genre include Montesquieu's *Persian Letters* (1721) and Oliver Goldsmith's *The Citizen of the World* (1760–1761). Goldsmith's text in particular has been mentioned as inspiring Markoe's novel, although elsewhere I have made the case that *The Algerine Spy in Pennsylvania* draws most extensively from *The Turkish Spy*. See also Jacob Crane, "The Long Transatlantic Career of the Turkish Spy," *Atlantic Studies* 10, no. 2 (2013): 228–246.

30 Sandra M. Gustafson, *Eloquence Is Power: Oratory and Performance in Early America* (Chapel Hill: University of North Carolina Press, 2000), 200.

31 Confusion over the authorship of *The Algerine Spy* continued well into the twentieth century. Recently, while looking in an original copy of *The Algerine Spy* held by the Historical Society of Pennsylvania, I found a note in pencil on the inside

cover: "Another John Tyler / See Oberholtzer Literary History of Penn." The corresponding page in Ellis Paxton Oberholtzer's 1906 book refers to Royall Tyler's novel *The Algerine Captive*. Oberholtzer, *The Literary History of Philadelphia* (Philadelphia: George W. Jacobs, 1906), 177. It appears that the twentieth-century reader of this copy confused Markoe's novel for Tyler's far more well-known work written a decade later, or at least assumed they were authored by the same person.

32 Timothy Marr, Introduction, in Peter Markoe, *The Algerine Spy in Pennsylvania*, ed. Timothy Marr (Yardley, PA: Westholme, 2008), xvi.

33 Srinivas Aravamudan, *Enlightened Orientalism: Resisting the Rise of the Novel* (Chicago: University of Chicago Press, 2012), 44.

34 To my knowledge, no scholar yet has assigned any significance to these initials. Most simply assume that Markoe was trying to mislead his readers as much as possible.

35 Markoe, *Algerine Spy*, 5.

36 Markoe, *Algerine Spy*, 1–3.

37 I discuss this early section further in chapter 3 when I analyze the role of Jewish characters in Barbary texts.

38 Markoe, *Algerine Spy*, 9. At the time that Markoe was writing, Philadelphia was home to a large French-speaking population. Many of these immigrants—like the Markoes themselves, who were descended from the French Huguenot Marcou family—came to the United States by way of the Caribbean. Marr, Introduction, xv.

39 Markoe, *Algerine Spy*, 20–21.

40 Joel Barlow, *The Visions of Columbus: A Poem in Nine Books* (Hartford, CT: Hudson and Godwin, 1787), 248.

41 Shalev points out that comparisons between America and Carthage began during the Seven Years' War, when French Canada was described as the "American Carthage" threatening Britain's empire. Shalev, *Rome Reborn*, 62, 182.

42 Timothy Marr, *The Cultural Roots of American Islamicism* (New York: Cambridge University Press, 2006), 35.

43 Markoe, *Algerine Spy*, 62. Very few of Peter Markoe's letters survive. However, one remarkable letter written by Markoe to his father in 1775 bears a striking similarity to this passage in *The Algerine Spy*. Arriving in London to study law on the eve of the American Revolution, Markoe noted how London society took no notice of the political crises erupting in the North American colonies: "The account from America causes less Alarm here than can be possibly imagined." Markoe observed that the lower classes were completely distracted in their own pursuits, and that the upper classes were preoccupied with staging regattas, which were just then becoming fashionable in the city. Markoe commented ominously that "a scene of splendid effeminacy, borrowed from Italy, will be displayed on the Thames in the midst of civil war. . . . How little they value the Efforts of America. Perish they may not be too woefully undeceived." Peter Markoe to Abraham Markoe, June 11, 1775, Markoe Family Papers, box 2, Historical Society of Pennsylvania, Philadelphia.

44 Markoe, *Algerine Spy*, 64.

45 Markoe, *Algerine Spy*, 84–85.

46 Schueller, *U.S. Orientalisms*, 71.

226 **NOTES TO PAGES 71–77**

47 Lauren Berlant, *The Female Complaint: The Unfinished Business of Sentimentality in American Culture* (Durham, NC: Duke University Press, 2008), 108.

48 Mehemet's arguments for a unicameral legislature, modeled on Pennsylvania's own governing body, resemble the arguments put forth in a letter signed by Centinel, author of several of the *Anti-Federalist Papers*, and published on October 5, 1787. In that letter Centinel criticizes the Federalist plan to include three branches of government restrained by checks and balances. He argues that "if, imitating the constitution of Philadelphia, you vest all the legislative power in one body of men, . . . elected for a short period, and necessarily excluded by rotation from permanency, . . . you will create the perfect responsibility for then, whenever the people feel a grievance they cannot mistake the author." Centinel, "Number I (Oct. 5, 1787)," in *The Anti-Federalist Papers and the Constitutional Convention Debates*, ed. Ralph Ketcham (New York: Signet Classics, 2003), 231. The *Algerine Spy* shares similar concerns about the power of the people and government accountability. Mehemet's letter does not target Adams specifically but rather criticizes more broadly the grandiose rhetoric used in the debate, deploying a set of three "proofs" in the form of "similes." These include the fact that a football game can only be played with one ball, that adding a second cook would complicate the cooking of beef on a spit, and that one cannot crush a single egg in one's hand but the addition of a second egg would make it easy to crack both. Notably, these similes are all related to the body in some way, introducing a sense of physicality and corporeality into the terms of the debate consistent with the function of the Barbary figure across the works I examine.

49 Markoe, *Algerine Spy*, 103, 104.

50 Markoe, *Algerine Spy*, 101–102.

51 Jeremy Engels, *Enemyship: Democracy and Counter-Revolution in the Early Republic* (East Lansing: Michigan State University Press, 2010), 92–93, 13.

52 Marr, *Cultural Roots of American Islamicism*, 41.

53 Markoe, *Algerine Spy*, 122, 125.

54 J. Hector St. John de Crèvecoeur, *Letters from an American Farmer and Sketches of Eighteenth-Century America* (1782; reprint New York: New American Library of World Literature, 1963), 64.

55 Markoe, *Algerine Spy*, 5.

56 Robert Battistini, "Glimpses of the Other before Orientalism: The Muslim World in Early American Periodicals, 1785–1800," *Early American Studies: An Interdisciplinary Journal* 8, no. 2 (Spring 2010): 448.

57 Edward Said, *Orientalism* (New York: Vintage Books, 1994), 7.

58 Joseph Hanson, *The Mussulmen Humbled; or, A Heroic Poem, in Celebration of the Bravery, Displayed by the American Tars, in the Contest with Tripoli* (New York: Southwick and Hardcastle, 1806), 4–5.

59 Joseph Rezek, "The Orations on Abolition of the Slave Trade and the Uses of Print in the Early Black Atlantic," *Early American Literature* 45, no. 3 (2010): 669.

60 "The Public Are Respectfully Informed," *Evening Post* (New York), March 6, 1805.

61 George Clinton Densmore Odell, *Annals of the New York Stage* (New York: AMS Press, 1970), 2:229.

NOTES TO PAGES 77–88   227

62 *Chronicle* (New York), March 5, 1805, quoted in Odell, *Annals of the New York Stage*, 2:229.
63 *Evening Post* (New York), March 11, 1805, quoted in Odell, *Annals of the New York Stage*, 2:229.
64 Odell, *Annals of the New York Stage*, 2:229.
65 "Theatre," *Evening Post* (New York), April 4, 1805.
66 Washington Irving, *Letters of Jonathan Oldstyle, Gent. / Salmagundi; or, The Whim-Whams and Opinions of Launcelot Langstaff, Esq. and Others*, ed. Bruce I Granger and Martha Hartzog (Boston: Twayne, 1977), 90.
67 Irving, *Letters of Jonathan Oldstyle*, 92, 142–143, 145.
68 Marr, *Cultural Roots of American Islamicism*, 68.
69 Christopher Looby, *Voicing America: Language, Literary Form and the Origins of the United States* (Chicago: University of Chicago Press, 1996), 82.
70 Irving, *Letters of Jonathan Oldstyle*, 241, 243.
71 Schueller, *U.S. Orientalisms*, 71.
72 Irving, *Letters of Jonathan Oldstyle*, 244.
73 Irving, *Letters of Jonathan Oldstyle*, 170, 173, 171.
74 "Theatre," *New-York Commercial Advertiser*, March 29, 1805.
75 Throughout the nineteenth century there have been many examples of literary analogies drawn between Turkish and Arabic peoples and Native Americans. In one particularly salient example, Irving begins his later short essay "Traits of Indian Character" by describing the Native American as "formed for the wilderness, as the Arab is for the desert." Irving, *History, Tales and Sketches*, ed. James W. Tuttleton (New York: Literary Classics of the United States, 1983), 1002. For a discussion of Irving's "Arabization" of Indians, see Wai Chee Dimock, "Hemispheric Islam: Continents and Centuries for American Literature," *American Literary History* 21, no. 1 (2009): 28–52, and Berman, *American Arabesque*, 70–108.
76 Michele de Montaigne, "On Cannibals," in Montaigne, *Essays*, transl. J. M. Cohen (New York: Penguin Books, 1958), 108, 119.

CHAPTER THREE: "A VAGUE RESEMBLANCE TO SOMETHING SEEN ELSEWHERE"

1 *Maryland Journal* (Baltimore), November 25, 1785.
2 William Foushee to Patrick Henry, December 6, 1785, in *Calendar of Virginia State Papers and Other Manuscripts*, ed. William P. Palmer (Richmond, VA: R. U. Derr, 1884), 4:71.
3 Robert J. Allison, *The Crescent Obscured: The United States and the Muslim World, 1776–1815* (New York: Oxford University Press, 1995), 5–6. An account from Charleston, South Carolina, seemingly confirms the theory that these mysterious visitors were North African Jews, while adding confusion to other aspects of the story. On March 16, 1786, a local paper reported that two (not three) suspicious persons dressed in "Moorish habit" and thought to be the same men arrested in Virginia "on suspicion of their being Algerines" were then residing in the city. On their arrival, the visitors were questioned by "a young gentleman of the law," with

one receiving "a little manual correction" for his "impertinence and vulgarity." In response to the scene, a mob gathered and carried the men to a local woman who "understood their language." The report concludes that the visitors "appeared to be two men of the Jewish nation . . . from Algiers" who had traveled to Charleston over land from Virginia. William L. King, *The Newspaper Press of Charleston, S.C.: A Chronological and Biographical History, Embracing a Period of One Hundred and Forty Years* (Charleston, SC: Edward Perry, 1872), 44. While aspects of this account sound plausible, the information does contradict a number of details reported in Virginia.

4 At the time of the Revolution there were only approximately 2,500 Jews in what would be the United States, although those communities were concentrated in the major political and economic centers of Charleston, Philadelphia, New York, and Newport, Rhode Island. Much of this population and a large majority of the community leaders were Sephardic "port Jews," with historical, cultural, and economic ties to Sephardic communities in North Africa, Iberia, and North Atlantic ports such as London and Amsterdam. See Edwin Wolf and Maxwell Whiteman, *The History of the Jews of Philadelphia from Colonial Times to the Age of Jackson* (Philadelphia: Jewish Publication Society, 1957), 81, and William Pencak, "Jews and Anti-Semitism in Early Pennsylvania," *Pennsylvania Magazine of History and Biography* 126, no. 3 (July 2002): 385.

5 Even before the outbreak of the Algerine Crisis, American political rhetoric often associated Jewish and Muslim identities as both anti-Christian and anti-American, particularly in debates over the rights to vote and own land. In 1776, for example, as Pennsylvania debated the requirement of a Christian oath in order to own land, one commentator in the *Pennsylvania Evening Post* fretted that, with the absence of such a test, "Jews, Turks, and Heathens" could become the principal landowners and political powers in the state, making it "unsafe for Christians." *Pennsylvania Evening Post* (Philadelphia), September 26, 1776.

6 Louis Harap, *The Image of the Jew in American Literature: From Early Republic to Mass Immigration* (Philadelphia: Jewish Publication Society of America, 1974), 34, 204.

7 See Lawrence A. Peskin, "American Exception? William Eaton and Early National Antisemitism," *American Jewish History* 100, no. 3 (July 2016): 299–317.

8 Lawrence Peskin comes closest to providing a thorough survey of representations of Jews in Barbary works. See Peskin, "From Shylocks to Unbelievers: Early National Views of 'Oriental' Jews," *Journal of the Early Republic* 39, no. 2 (Summer 2019): 267–298. In this chapter I hope to build on his work by going beyond the Shylock stereotype.

9 Throughout this chapter I use the term "Barbary Jews" broadly to encompass not only Jewish communities in Algiers, Tunis, and Tripoli but also Iberian Jews with ties both to the United States and North Africa.

10 See Christopher James Bonner, *Remaking the Republic: Black Politics and the Creation of American Citizenship* (Philadelphia: University of Pennsylvania Press, 2020), and Derrick R. Spires, *The Practice of Citizenship: Black Politics and Print Culture in the Early United States* (Philadelphia: University of Pennsylvania Press, 2019). Jews in the early republic, of course, faced far fewer restrictions than free

African Americans, yet their liminal positioning—their persistent "foreignness"—made them a vital testing ground for citizenship's limits.

11 Spires, *Practice of Citizenship*, 35.

12 The 1790 Naturalization Act was replaced only a few years later by the 1795 act, which retained the "free white" clause but increased the residency requirement. The strengthening of restrictions on naturalization was primarily a response to the surge of European and European-Caribbean immigration brought about by the Haitian and French Revolutions. See Douglas Bradburn, *The Citizenship Revolution: Politics and the Creation of the American Union, 1744–1804* (Charlottesville: University of Virginia Press, 2009), 130–137.

13 Ambiguity over the racial status of Jews extends back into the colonial period. In colonial censuses, "sometimes Jews were 'white' (albeit of a different religion), sometimes they stood alone in a quasi-racial category between 'blacks' and 'whites,' sometimes they were a religious group." See Laura A. Leibman, "The Crossroads of American History: Jews in the Colonial Americas," in *By the Dawn's Early Light: Jewish Contributions to American Culture from the Nation's Founding to the Civil War*, ed. Adam Mendelsohn (Princeton, NJ: Princeton University Library, 2016), 20.

14 William Dunlap, *New York Weekly Magazine*, March 4, 1795, 129, quoted in Edward D. Coleman, "Plays of Jewish Interest on the American Stage, 1751–1821," *Publications of the American Jewish Historical Society*, no. 33 (1934): 18 n20.

15 Despite the paltry number of American plays featuring Jewish characters in the post-independence period that Harap studies, Edward D. Coleman identifies twenty-eight productions on the American stage that included Jewish characters in the more expansive period of 1752 to 1821. The vast majority of these productions were British, with Shylock being by far the most well-known "stage Jew." Heather Nathans points to the fact that "Shylock" was a common epithet in early national political discourse as evidence of how that character and the stereotypical traits he represents was adopted and "Americanized." Coleman, "Plays of Jewish Interest," 172; Nathans, "A Much Maligned People: Jews on and off the Stage in the Early American Republic," *Early American Studies: An Interdisciplinary Journal* 2, no. 2 (Fall 2004): 310–342.

16 Julie Kalman, *Orientalizing the Jew: Religion, Culture, and Imperialism in Nineteenth-Century France* (Bloomington: Indiana University Press, 2017), 119, 121. Kalman notes that the concept of orientalism has long had a fraught relationship with Jewishness. Within Edward Said's paradigm and in the scholarship that built on it, Jews fall into the categories of "eastern victim" or "western, European oppressor," with little space in between to acknowledge the interconnected nature of communities across the diaspora. Kalman, *Orientalizing the Jew*, 4. It is not surprising that much of the scholarship surrounding the American Barbary crises, built on Said's foundational concept and often focused specifically on Muslims and Islam, would overlook the complexity of Jewish figures; Jews play, for example, only a bit part in Timothy Marr's concept of Islamicism, even while they are present in many of the texts he discusses.

17 Aamir R. Mufti, *Enlightenment in the Colony: The Jewish Question and the Crisis of Postcolonial Culture* (Princeton, NJ: Princeton University Press, 2007), 39, 38, 40.

230 **NOTES TO PAGES 92–98**

18 Jonathan Senchyne, "Bottles of Ink and Reams of Paper: *Clotel*, Racialization, and the Material Culture of Print," in *Early African American Print Culture*, ed. Lara Langer Cohen and Jordan Alexander Stein (Philadelphia: University of Pennsylvania Press, 2012), 142, 145.

19 Kalman, *Orientalizing the Jew*, 118. By the early nineteenth century, France had accrued a massive debt to the Bacri and Busnach families, and historians have suggested that the 1830 invasion of Algiers was at least in part motivated by the need to wipe out that debt.

20 Harap, *Image of the Jew*, 35.

21 Peskin, "From Shylocks to Unbelievers," 270.

22 "London, Sept. 10.," *Columbian Herald* (Charleston, SC), November 21, 1785.

23 "Barbary," *Daily Advertiser* (New York), May 25, 1786.

24 Peter Markoe, *The Algerine Spy in Pennsylvania*, ed. Timothy Marr (Yardley, PA: Westholme Publishing, 2008), 37. The brief reference to Mendez's previous travels in America raises the intriguing possibility that the character may have been, in part, inspired by the reports of the three Algerines with which I began this chapter.

25 Markoe, *Algerine Spy*, 18–19.

26 Markoe, *Algerine Spy*, 51, 39.

27 In the previous chapter I mentioned that *The Algerine Spy in Pennsylvania* was inspired by a late seventeenth-century epistolary novel, *Letters Writ by a Turkish Spy*. A trans-European Jewish spy network features prominently in that novel as well, with the titular spy, Mahmut, introducing a Jewish character, Eliachim, in the very first letter. In fact, *The Turkish Spy* became particularly well known as a referent in the legend of the Wandering Jew that circulated throughout the seventeenth and eighteenth centuries. Mahmut supposedly meets this legendary figure, in the novel named Michob Ader, in Paris. See Jacob Crane, "The Long Transatlantic Career of *The Turkish Spy*," *Atlantic Studies* 10, no. 2 (2013): 228–246.

28 Pencak, "Jews and Anti-Semitism," 369.

29 Markoe, *Algerine Spy*, 39.

30 *Independent Gazetteer* (Philadelphia), March 20, 1784, quoted in Pencak, "Jews and Anti-Semitism," 395.

31 Markoe, *Algerine Spy*, 17, 39.

32 Markoe, *Algerine Spy*, 113.

33 Royall Tyler, *The Algerine Captive; or, The Life and Adventures of Doctor Updike Underhill: Six Years a Prisoner among the Algerines* (1797; reprint New York: Modern Library, 2002), 194, 195. Tyler's novel includes these quotation marks, but there is little indication of what Underhill or Tyler would be quoting from.

34 Tyler, *Algerine Captive*, 201, 203.

35 Tyler, *Algerine Captive*, 201, 203.

36 Jared Gardner, *Master Plots: Race and the Founding of American Literature, 1787–1845* (Baltimore: Johns Hopkins University Press, 1998), 48.

37 Tyler, *Algerine Captive*, 204.

38 Richard Cumberland, "The Jew; A Comedy," in *The Plays of Richard Cumberland*, ed. Roberta F. S. Borkat (New York: Garland, 1983), 5:12.

39 Royall Tyler offers an interesting case study in the difference between representations of biblical and modern Jews in early American literature and drama. Today

NOTES TO PAGES 98–103   231

Tyler's reputation as a playwright rests almost completely on *The Contrast* (1787), but he also completed three biblical plays that are extant: *The Origin of the Feast of Purim, Joseph and His Brethren*, and *The Judgement of Solomon*.

40 As Ed White puts it, "The novel's final conflict revolves not around slavery . . . but around the question of whether or not to trust a Jew." White, "Divided We Stand: Emergent Conservatism in Royall Tyler's *The Algerine Captive*," *Studies in American Fiction* 37, no. 1 (Spring 2010): 24–25.

41 Tyler, *Algerine Captive*, 223.

42 Sarah Sillin, "'Made to Feel Wretched': Royall Tyler and the Trouble with Global Sympathy," *Early American Literature* 51, no. 1 (2016): 117.

43 Tyler, *Algerine Captive*, 226.

44 Sillin, "Made to Feel Wretched," 113.

45 James Butler, *Fortune's Foot-Ball; or, The Adventures of Mercutio: Founded on Matters of Fact: A Novel of Two Volumes* (Harrisburg, PA: John Wyeth.1797), 1:27, 145.

46 Mufti, *Enlightenment in the Colony*, 37.

47 Harap, *Image of the Jew*, 205.

48 Heather Nathans, *Hideous Characters and Beautiful Pagans: Performing Jewish Identity on the Antebellum American Stage* (Ann Arbor: University of Michigan Press, 2012), 25, 27.

49 Elizabeth Maddock Dillon, "Slaves in Algiers: Race, Republican Genealogies, and the Global Stage," *American Literary History* 16, no. 3 (2004): 418. The play's message of Anglo-American reconciliation must have resonated with some audiences. While Rowson's play was not often staged after 1800, there is at least one instance of the drama being performed as part of a program celebrating the end of the War of 1812. *Albany [NY] Register*, March 31, 1815.

50 *Massachusetts Gazette* (Boston), September 7, 1787.

51 Elizabeth Maddock Dillon, *New World Drama: The Performative Commons in the Atlantic World, 1649–1849* (Durham, NC: Duke University Press, 2014), 56.

52 It is unknown how much money Hallam's efforts raised, although a report later that year noted that he hosted several such benefits. *Columbian Herald*, August 16, 1787.

53 *Philadelphia Gazette*, March 19, 1794.

54 For more on benefit performances to raise ransom funds for Barbary captives, see David J. Dzurec III, *Our Suffering Brethren: Foreign Captivity and Nationalism in the Early United States* (Amherst: University of Massachusetts Press, 2019), 71–72.

55 Susanna Rowson, "New Song" (Philadelphia: Mathew Carey, 1794).

56 In the preface to the printed version of the play, Rowson confesses that the work was "not more than two months from the first starting of the idea, to the time of its being performed," pointing to the influence of the theatre's fundraising effort. Rowson, *Slaves in Algiers; or, A Struggle for Freedom* (Philadelphia: Wrigley and Berriman, 1794), i. Benilde Montgomery points to another potential inspiration for the work in the passage of the Navy Act on March 27, 1794, which authorized the construction of five frigates to protect American merchants from Barbary corsairs. Montgomery notes that, within debates over this new American navy, Rowson clearly positions herself on the side of ransom payments over the possibility of full-scale war. Montgomery, "White Captives, African Slaves: A Drama of Abolition," *Eighteenth Century Studies* 27, no. 4 (Summer 1994): 618–619.

232 NOTES TO PAGES 103–110

57 Rowson, *Slaves in Algiers*, ii, 4.

58 Dillon, "Slaves in Algiers," 416.

59 Rowson, *Slaves in Algiers*, 16.

60 Nathans, *Hideous Characters and Beautiful Pagans*, 21–22.

61 Rowson, *Slaves in Algiers*, 17.

62 Nathans, *Hideous Characters and Beautiful Pagans*, 319–320. Even as Jewish figures became increasingly racialized in the nineteenth century, the ambiguities of Jewish identity and the prominence of religious difference remained. As Nathans comments, "I have found little consensus among my sources whether 'Jewish' connoted a race, a religion, an ethnic identity, or even a collection of character traits. Eighteenth- and nineteenth-century Americans used the terms to mean multiple things, sometimes all at the same time." Nathans, *Hideous Characters and Beautiful Pagans*, 9.

63 Rowson, *Slaves in Algiers*, 15. Nathans observes that "little" was a popular adjective attached to Jewish men on both the British and American stages. Nathans, *Hideous Characters and Beautiful Pagans*, 23.

64 Rowson, *Slaves in Algiers*, 6, 8.

65 Rowson, *Slaves in Algiers*, 31–33.

66 Dillon, "Slaves in Algiers," 419.

67 Rowson, *Slaves in Algiers*, 39.

68 Rowson, *Slaves in Algiers*, 68.

69 Dillon, "Slaves in Algiers," 421.

70 Spires, *Practice of Citizenship*, 35.

71 Rowson, *Slaves in Algiers*, 8, 32.

72 Charles Brockden Brown, "What Is a Jew?" in Charles Brockden Brown, *Arthur Mervyn; or, Memoirs of the Year 1793*, ed. Philip Barnard and Stephen Shapiro (Indianapolis: Hackett, 2008), 358.

73 Charles White contested the claims that racial characteristics are shaped by climate, attempting instead to establish human "gradations" as discrete, immutable categories within a clear hierarchy topped by European man. In his discussion of skin color, he acknowledges that "those naturalists who contend that the colour of the human species is caused by climate, advance, that there cannot be a more striking instance of this than in the Jew." White dismisses the claim of phenotypical diversity among global Jewish communities entirely, stating simply, "The truth is, that Jews are generally swarthy in every climate." White, *An Account of the Regular Gradation in Man and in Different Animals and Vegetables* (London: C. Dilly, 1799), 104.

74 Stephen Shapiro, *The Culture of Commerce of the Early American Novel: Reading the Atlantic World-System* (State College: Pennsylvania State University Press, 2008), 263.

75 Sean X. Goudie, "On the Origin of American Specie(s): The West Indies, Classification, and the Emergence of Supremacist Consciousness in *Arthur Mervyn*," in *Revising Charles Brockden Brown*, ed. Philip Barnard (Knoxville: University of Tennessee Press, 2004), 82.

76 Michael J. Drexler, "*Arthur Mervyn; or, Memoirs of the Year 1793*," in *The Oxford Handbook of Charles Brockden Brown*, ed. Philip Barnard, Hilary Emmett, and Stephen Shapiro (New York: Oxford University Press, 2019), 80.

77 Shapiro, *Culture of Commerce*, 264.

NOTES TO PAGES 111–115   233

78 William Dunlap, *The Life of Charles Brockden Brown* (Philadelphia: James P. Parke, 1815), 2:40.
79 Goudie, "On the Origin of American Specie(s)," 81.
80 Louis Harap, "Fracture of a Stereotype: Charles Brockden Brown's Achsa Fielding," *American Jewish Archives* 24, no. 2 (November 1972): 188, 195.
81 Shapiro, *Culture of Commerce*, 287, 290.
82 Brown, *Arthur Mervyn*, 306; Samuel Otter, *Philadelphia Stories: America's Literature of Race and Freedom* (New York: Oxford University Press, 2010), 69.
83 Brown, *Arthur Mervyn*, 320.
84 Shapiro, *Culture of Commerce*, 267–268; Carroll Smith-Rosenberg, *This Violent Empire: The Birth of an American National Identity* (Chapel Hill: University of North Carolina Press, 2010), 440.
85 Brown, *Arthur Mervyn*, 113.
86 Charles Brockden Brown, *Edgar Huntley; or, Memoirs of a Sleep-Walker* (New York: Barnes and Noble, 2007), 172.
87 Benjamin Franklin, *Observations Concerning the Increase of Mankind, People of Countries, &c* (Tarrytown, NY: William Abbott, 1918), 10.
88 Mathew Carey, *A Short Account of Algiers and of Its Several Wars against Spain, France, England, Holland, Venice, and Other Powers of Europe, from the Usurpation of Barbarossa and the Invasion of the Emperor Charles V. to the Present Time* (Philadelphia: Mathew Carey, 1794), 11–12.
89 Mungo Park, "Selections: An Account of Mr. Park's Journey into the Interior Parts of Africa," *Monthly Magazine, and American Review* (New York), July 1799, 306.
90 John Foss, *A Journal, of the Captivity and Sufferings of John Foss; Several Years a Prisoner in Algiers*, 2nd edition (Newburyport, MA: Angier March, 1798), 74.
91 Drexler, "*Arthur Mervyn*," 76.
92 Brown would have had several opportunities to see *Slaves in Algiers* in Philadelphia or in 1796 when it was staged multiple times in New York's John Street Theatre, managed by his close friend William Dunlap.
93 Smith-Rosenberg, *This Violent Empire*, 440.
94 Brown, *Arthur Mervyn*, 239.
95 "Selections: Condition of the Female Sex at Constantinople," *Monthly Magazine, and American Review*, August 1799, 381.
96 Brown, *Arthur Mervyn*, 320.
97 Timothy Marr, *The Cultural Roots of American Islamicism* (New York: Cambridge University Press, 2006), 48, 52.
98 Brown, *Arthur Mervyn*, 271, 306.
99 That Fielding's Jewishness remains unrecognizable for much of the novel signals Brown's departure from his British source material: William Godwin's novel *Caleb Williams* (1794). A gothic tale about innocence and political corruption, the novel follows the titular protagonist as he is pursued by the vengeful aristocrat Ferdinando Falkland. At one point in the novel, Williams attempts to evade Falkland by hiding in the Jewish neighborhood of London, announcing to the reader, "The exterior which I was now induced to assume was that of a Jew. One of the gang of thieves upon——forest, had been of that race; and by the talent of mimicry . . . I could copy their pronunciation of the English language." As with Rowson's Ben Hassan,

234 NOTES TO PAGES 115–122

Jews are distinctly marked by their strange accent. Williams proceeds to apply a subtle Blackface: "One of my cares was to discolour my complexion, and give it the dun and sallow hue which is in most instances characteristic of the tribe to which I assumed to belong." Williams hides in the Jewish ghetto of London, secure in his anonymity, until he becomes so overwhelmed with the urge to tell his story that he prints his own account of his flight from Falkland, which eventually gives away his disguise. Godwin, *Caleb Williams* (1794; reprint New York: Oxford University Press, 2009), 246–247. In *Caleb Williams*, the protagonist assumes a Jewish identity to hide because Jews are depicted as socially invisible and racially known—the boundary between Jewish and Gentile identities is fixed. Brown reverses the figuring of Jewish identity in his text. In *Arthur Mervyn*, Fielding is socially visible (indeed, wealthy and prominent) while remaining racially unidentifiable.

100 Michael Warner, *Letters of the Republic: Publication and the Public Sphere in Eighteenth-Century America* (Cambridge, MA: Harvard University Press, 1990), 169.

101 Brown, *Arthur Mervyn*, 307, 308.

102 Goudie, "On the Origin of American Specie(s)," 81.

103 Brown, *Arthur Mervyn*, 317.

104 Peskin, "From Shylocks to Unbelievers," 281.

105 James Ellison, *American Captive; or, Siege of Tripoli* (Boston: Joshua Belcher, 1812), A2, 38.

106 Ellison's play alters the history of the Tripolitan War and of Eaton's expedition in a number of ways that place American operations in a more positive light. Immorina's father, identified in the play as Ali-Ben-Mahadi, was inspired by Hamet Karamanli, the deposed bashaw of Tripoli who allied with the United States against his usurper brother Yusuf Karamanli. Eaton's expedition intended to take Tripoli and restore Hamet to the throne; however, after Eaton and Hamet captured Derne, about four hundred miles east of the city of Tripoli, Yusuf sued for peace. The United States accepted the peace agreement over the protests of some who felt the country was forsaking its ally. Frank Lambert, *The Barbary Wars: American Independence in the Atlantic World* (New York: Hill and Wang, 2007), 152–155. By having the heroes in his play succeed in capturing Tripoli and reinstalling its former bashaw, Ellison revises what for some had been a source of national shame even as the country had been able to negotiate favorable terms from Yusuf.

107 Jonathan B. Smith, *The Siege of Algiers; or, The Downfall of Hadgi-Ali-Bashaw* (Philadelphia: J. Maxwell, 1823), 5.

108 Harap, *Image of the Jew*, 209. Harap also points out that Smith's play was never performed, and he speculates that it likely was not meant to be performed, given the massive amount of dialogue and the comparatively few stage directions. The printed version of the play reads more like a novella.

109 Smith, *Siege of Algiers*, 23.

CHAPTER FOUR: PERFORMING DIASPORA IN NOAH'S *TRAVELS*

1 "Subjects for Engravings," *New-York Mirror*, September 27, 1836.

2 Regarding the lack of scholarship on the *Travels*, even Noah's biographers, Isaac Goldberg and Jonathan D. Sarna, have little to say about the work. Sarna's

NOTES TO PAGES 122–124   235

biography, still the most comprehensive account of Noah's life, treats the text and the public response to it in just two pages, noting it as "a curious, fairly well written, and quite entertaining mixture of travel stories, history, and apologetics." Sarna, *Jacksonian Jew: The Two World of Mordecai Noah* (New York: Holmes and Meier, 1981), 31. See also Goldberg, *Major Noah: American-Jewish Pioneer* (Philadelphia: Jewish Publication Society of America, 1936), 146–147.

3 Sarna, *Jacksonian Jew*, 27.

4 Mordecai Manuel Noah, *Travels in England, France, Spain, and the Barbary States, in the Year 1813–14 and 15* (New York: Kirk and Mercein, 1819), 376–377.

5 Joel Barlow to David Humphreys, April 5, 1796, in Charles Burr Todd, *The Life and Letters of Joel Barlow, LL.D.* (New York: G. P. Putnam's Sons, 1886), 129. Lawrence A. Peskin argues that, while much of the correspondence from diplomats in North Africa was not available to the public, the opinions (and prejudices) expressed were central to the shaping of official perceptions in the period. Peskin, "From Shylocks to Unbelievers: Early National Views of 'Oriental' Jews," *Journal of the Early Republic* 39, no. 2 (Summer 2019): 277.

6 Lotfi Ben Rejeb, "A Jewish-American Consul in Tunis in 1815: Mordecai Noah, Jews, Islam, and the United States," *CELAAN: Review of the Center for the Study of Literatures and Arts of North Africa* 7, nos.1–2 (Spring 2009): 9–10.

7 James Clifford, "Introduction: Partial Truths," in *Writing Culture: The Poetics and Politics of Ethnography*, ed. James Clifford and George E. Marcus (Berkeley: University of California Press, 2010), 14, 24.

8 "Editor's Cabinet," *National Register, a Weekly Paper* (Washington, DC), March 20, 1819.

9 Julian Levinson, "Encountering the Idea of America," in *The Cambridge History of American Jewish Literature*, ed. Hana Wirth-Nesher (New York: Cambridge University Press, 2016), 37. In identifying this moment of textual and performative intersection, I intend to build on Joseph Roach's influential concept of oceanic interculture, a transnational formation consisting of multiple and overlapping circum-Atlantic genealogies of performance and memory. In his seminal work *Cities of the Dead* (1996), Roach argues that the genealogies of circum-Atlantic performance carry with them the often-forgotten moments of contact among races in the Atlantic World: "Representations of these encounters show how Europeans, Native Americans, and Africans, real or imagined, acting in one another's presence . . . performed not only their identity but also their threatened continuity." Roach, *Cities of the Dead: Circum-Atlantic Performance* (New York: Columbia University Press, 1996), 122. Missing from Roach's triangulation is, of course, the "Jew."

10 Here again I am drawing on recent work on African American citizenship in the late eighteenth and early nineteenth centuries. See my discussion of Spires and Bonner in the previous chapter.

11 For *The Cambridge History of Jewish American Literature*, Edna Nashon writes that "Jewish American drama is a rubric with elastic parameters," encompassing a wide variety of styles and subgenres. Nevertheless, Nashon, like many other critics, locates the genesis of Jewish American drama decisively in the "early years of the twentieth century." Nashon, "Jewish American Drama," in Wirth-Nesher,

236 **NOTES TO PAGES 124–127**

ed., *Cambridge History of Jewish American Literature*, 242. Such histories imagine Jewish American drama as almost exclusively in conversation with Ashkenazi, Yiddish-language theatre. By extending that timeline to include early nineteenth-century figures like Noah, I argue, we can recover the more complex origins of Jewish American performance in the dynamic relationship between Ashkenazi *and* Sephardic communities at both a national and circum-Atlantic level.

12 Lori Harrison-Kahan, *The White Negress: Literature Minstrelsy, and the Black-Jewish Imaginary* (New Brunswick, NJ: Rutgers University Press, 2011), 2. See also Michael Rogin, *Blackface, White Noise: Jewish Immigrants in the Hollywood Melting Pot* (Berkeley: University of California Press, 1996).

13 Like *Salmagundi, The Trangram* was the product of a collaboration of three authors: Noah, lawyer Alexander Coxe, and an unknown third contributor. Also like *Salmagundi, The Trangram* hosted a cast of characters including the main protagonist, Christopher Crag, and a theatre critic named Solomon Solemn (likely to have been Noah's pseudonym in the magazine). Only three issues of *The Trangram* were ever published, but the periodical was seen by prominent printer Philadelphia William Duane to be worth republishing in a single bound copy of the three issues that included Duane's own handwritten explanatory notes identifying the many local and timely references in the work. That copy is currently in the Historical Society of Pennsylvania's rare books collection. On a side note, to illustrate what a small world Philadelphia was at the time, Alexander Coxe's father, rich merchant Tench Coxe, once received a polite letter from a struggling author in jail for his debts requesting a loan to bail him out. That author was Peter Markoe, four months after the publication of *The Algerine Spy*.

14 Sarna, *Jacksonian Jew*, 10–11.

15 Jeffrey H. Richards, *Drama, Theatre, and Identity in the American New Republic* (New York: Cambridge University Press, 2005), 155.

16 In his 1832 *History of American Theatre*, William Dunlap includes a short letter from Noah in which he describes his early engagement with Philadelphia theatre culture. Noah relates that he was "a regular attendant of the Chestnut-street theatre," during the management of Wignell and Reinagle. Although Noah was only nine years old when he moved to Philadelphia around 1794–1795, his frequenting of the theatre in which Rowson's *Slaves in Algiers* was first performed and his later interest in American productions suggest that it was very likely he would have encountered that play, in print if not on stage. Additionally, Noah's writings frequently referenced him studying at "Franklin's library," suggesting that he may have also encountered Markoe's novel at some point. Dunlap, *The History of the American Theatre* (New York: J. and J. Harper, 1832), 381.

17 See my discussion of Ben Hassan in the previous chapter.

18 Stuart Hall, "Cultural Identity and Diaspora," in *Colonial Discourse and Post-Colonial Theory*, ed. Patrick Williams and Laura Chrisman (Durham, NC: Duke University Press, 2016), 392.

19 Henry Bial, *Acting Jewish: Negotiating Ethnicity on the American Stage and Screen* (Ann Arbor: University of Michigan Press, 2005), 3, 17.

20 Mordecai Manuel Noah, "Oriental Correspondence," *The Times* (Charleston, SC), April 15, 1812.

NOTES TO PAGES 128–134   237

21 Mordecai Manuel Noah, "Oriental Correspondence," *The Times*, June 6, 1812.

22 Mordecai Manuel Noah, "Oriental Correspondence," *The Times*, June 20, 1812.

23 In his 1936 biography, Isaac Goldberg includes a chapter on Noah's activities in Charleston, but only briefly quotes from the Muly Malak letters. Goldberg, *Major Noah*, 50–56. Jonathan Sarna's 1981 biography, still the most complete source on Noah's life, merely reproduces Goldberg's citations without going back to the articles. It would seem that Noah's sojourn in Charleston and his Muly Malak letters constituted a minor episode in the writer's career, yet in truth, the Muly Malak letters from this period were so popular that locals began to refer to Noah himself as Muly Malak. Noah was so strongly associated with his Turkish pseudonym that Howard Haycraft and Stanley Kunitz's biographical dictionary of American authors, originally published in 1938, includes an entry under "Malak, Muley," that reads simply, "See Noah, Mordecai Manuel," in *American Authors, 1600–1900: A Biographical Dictionary of American Literature*, ed. Howard Haycraft and Stanley Kunitz (New York: H. W. Wilson, 1938), 504.

24 Samuel A. Hay, *African American Theatre: An Historical and Critical Analysis* (Evanston, IL: Northwestern University Press, 1998), 8.

25 Noah, *Travels*, v–vi.

26 Ralph Waldo Emerson, "The American Scholar," in *The Portable Emerson*, ed. Carl Bode (New York: Penguin Books, 1981), 51.

27 "American Literature," *Mercantile Advertiser* (New York), February 1, 1819.

28 Noah, *Travels*, 1.

29 "Editor's Cabinet."

30 Janine Barchas, "Prefiguring Genre: Frontispiece Portraits from Gulliver's Travels to Millennium Hall," *Studies in the Novel* 30 (Summer 1998): 260, 265.

31 For a discussion of stereotypical images of Jewish features, see Heather Nathans, "A Much Maligned People: Jews on and off the Stage in the Early American Republic," *Early American Studies: An Interdisciplinary Journal* 2, no. 2 (Fall 2004): 310–342. For an extensive study of the popularity of physiognomy in the period, see Christopher Lukasik, *Discerning Characters: The Culture of Appearance in Early America* (Philadelphia: University of Pennsylvania Press, 2011).

32 Heather Nathans, *Hideous Characters and Beautiful Pagans: Performing Jewish Identity on the Antebellum American Stage* (Ann Arbor: University of Michigan Press, 2017), 2.

33 Barchas, "Prefiguring Genre," 123.

34 See Joseph Rezek, "The Racialization of Print," *American Literary History* 32, no. 3 (Fall 2020): esp. 418–419.

35 Pere Gifra-Adroher, *Between History and Romance: Travel Writing on Spain in the Early Nineteenth-Century United States* (Madison, NJ: Fairleigh Dickinson University Press, 2000), 69–70; Mary Louise Pratt, *Imperial Eyes: Travel Writing and Transculturation* (New York: Routledge, 1993), 77–78.

36 Noah, *Travels*, 9.

37 Aamir R. Mufti, *Enlightenment in the Colony: The Jewish Question and the Crisis of Postcolonial Culture* (Princeton, NJ: Princeton University Press, 2007), 38. One does wonder why a British captain, during wartime, would accommodate the celebration of an earlier American victory over the British.

238　**NOTES TO PAGES 134–139**

38　Noah, *Travels*, 51, 53.

39　Noah, *Travels*, 125.

40　Gifra-Adroher, *Between History and Romance*, 75.

41　Noah must have assumed that the Spanish setting would provide him with some cover, as in this section he comes closest to criticizing Christianity. At least one reader, writing in the *Christian Spectator*, took offense at Noah's lightly mocking observation that a particular wine vault resembled the arrangement of a church. The commentator asserted that "this passage does Mr. Noah no honour. A reader may indeed learn from it, that he is not a believer in the New Testament, but no one will consider him as a man of liberal principles." "Remarks on a Passage on Noah's *Travels*," *Christian Spectator, Conducted by an Association of Gentlemen. For the Year 1820* (New Haven, CT: Howe and Spalding, 1820), 2:20.

42　Noah, *Travels*, 345.

43　Mary Louise Pratt, "Fieldwork in Common Places," in Clifford and Marcus, eds., *Writing Culture*, 32.

44　Take, as just one example, John Foss's account of entering Algiers in 1784: "We were conducted to the Dey's palace, by a guard, and as we passed through the streets, our ears were stunned with the shouts, clapping of hands, and other acclamations of joy from the inhabitants." Foss, *A Journal, of the Captivity and Sufferings of John Foss; Several Years a Prisoner in Algiers* (Newburyport, MA: Angier March, 1798), 13.

45　Pratt, *Imperial Eyes*, 81–83. Notably, Pratt describes reciprocal vision in Mungo Park's narrative with a reference to Montesquieu's *Persian Letters* (1721), a forerunner to Peter Markoe's *The Algerine Spy*, Irving's Mustapha Letters, and Noah's "Oriental Correspondence."

46　Ben Rejeb, "Jewish-American Consul," 12.

47　Noah, *Travels*, 307–308, 300, 313.

48　Donald J. Ratcliffe, "Selling Captain Riley, 1816–1859: How Did 'Narrative' Become So Well Known?" *Proceedings of the American Antiquarian Society* 117 (2007): 178–179. While critics agree that Riley's *Narrative* was very well-known throughout the nineteenth century, Ratcliffe notably contests the oft-repeated claims, originating from the publishers of the sequel to the *Narrative*, that more than 1 million copies of the original text had been sold and circulated. In fact, Ratcliffe credits excerpts and references to the text for spreading Riley's fame, despite the comparatively limited print run of his work. Ratcliffe, "Selling Captain Riley," 208–209.

49　James Riley, *An Authentic Narrative of the Loss of the American Brig Commerce* (New York: T. and W. Mercein, 1817), 414, 468, 469. Earlier versions of Riley's manuscripts contained more direct representations of Barbary Jews as Shylock-like according to many of the prevailing literary stereotypes of the day, but his editors censored those comments. Peskin suggests that the anxiety of Riley's editors might have reflected a fear that negative depictions of North African Jews might affect public views of America's domestic Jewish population, a theme I explore more extensively in the previous chapter. See Peskin, "From Shylocks to Unbelievers," 291–292.

50　Noah, *Travels*, 314n.

51　Noah, *Travels*, 376–377.

52　Noah, *Travels*, 379.

NOTES TO PAGES 139–143   239

53 The eleventh article of the 1794 Treaty of Tripoli was already a controversial text when Noah cited it in 1819, having been deployed in various debates over issues of church and state. The *Travels* is the first of many instances over the treaty's history in which its language was used to argue for Jewish American inclusion. See Jacob Crane, "Reading American Secularism in the 1797 Treaty of Tripoli," *American Quarterly* 72, no. 2 (June 2020): 403–422.

54 Christopher James Bonner, *Remaking the Republic: Black Politics and the Creation of American Citizenship* (Philadelphia: University of Pennsylvania Press, 2020), 18–21.

55 I base this conclusion on the fact that the London *Times* from 1819 to 1822 makes no mention of Noah's *Travels* either in an article or an advertisement.

56 *Narrative of the Proceedings of the Jews, in Their Attempt to Establish Their Right to the Elective Franchise in Jamaica* (Belfast: A Mackay Jr., 1823), 29–30.

57 The melodrama seems to have provided a particular form of access to the national imaginary for early American Jewish writers; perhaps it is no coincidence that the three most prominent Jewish writers in the early nineteenth century—Noah, Isaac Harby, and Noah rival Samuel Benjamin Helbert Judah—all wrote melodramas. Critic Douglas A. Jones Jr. notes that in the United States, melodramas often contested "the historical actualities of antebellum society" by offering social outcasts such as African Americans, Native American, women, and the poor as heroes and heroines. However, as appealing as these characters might be, Jones argues that the melodramatic form is deeply conservative, allowing an audience to, through the "immolation of the victim," legitimate "their humanity and the ideology of white supremacy." Jones, "Aesthetics, Ideology, and the Use of the Victim in Early American Melodrama," *Journal of American Drama and Theatre* 22, no. 1 (Winter 2010): 53; 70. Along these same lines, theatre historian Bruce McConachie locates Noah's works along with many of his contemporaries at the end of a period in which melodramas, including Rowson's *Slaves in Algiers*, were invested in preserving an elite paternalism against encroaching ideologies of egalitarianism. McConachie, *Melodramatic Formations: American Theatre and Society, 1820–1870* (Iowa City: University of Iowa Press, 1992), 2. It is perhaps the ability of early national melodrama to mitigate a white audience's responsibility for the welfare of the suffering Other and its nostalgia for patriarchal values that made the form so popular with audiences.

58 "Yusef Caramalli," *New-York Literary Journal, and Belles-Lettres Repository*, June 5, 1820, 140.

59 *Saturday Evening Post* (Philadelphia), January 26, 1822, quoted in Nathans, *Hideous Characters and Beautiful Pagans*, 45.

60 Nathans, *Hideous Characters and Beautiful Pagans*, 44.

61 See note 106 on the context of Ellison's *American Captive* in the previous chapter.

62 Elizabeth Maddock Dillon, "Slaves in Algiers: Race, Republican Genealogies, and the Global Stage," *American Literary History* 16, no. 3 (2004): 421.

63 Mordecai Manuel Noah, "The Ararat Proclamation and Speech," in *The Selected Writings of Mordecai Noah*, ed. Michael Schuldiner and Daniel J. Kleinfeld (Westport, CT: Greenwood Press, 1999), 109. I have written elsewhere at length about

240 **NOTES TO PAGES 143–151**

the circulation and impact of the texts and images of the Ararat project. See Jacob Crane, "Ararat Revisited," *Multi-Ethnic Literature of the United States* 44, no. 1 (Spring 2019): 43–64.

64 Levinson, "Encountering the Idea of America," 27, 37.

65 Michael Hoberman notes that critics in Jewish American Studies have become so taken with the symbolic importance of Noah's failed colony that in the most recent edition of *The Cambridge History of Jewish American Literature* (2016), Ararat takes up more column inches in the index than Philip Roth, Emma Lazarus, or Orthodox Judaism. Hoberman, "Parking the Ark in Niagara Falls: Mordecai Manuel Noah and the Imposition of Meaning in Jewish American Literary History," *Studies in American Jewish Literature* 37, no. 1 (2018): 69–70.

CHAPTER FIVE: "THE ADVANTAGE OF A WHIP-LECTURE"

1 Erik J. Chaput and Russell J. DeSimone, "Strange Bedfellows: The Politics of Race in Antebellum Rhode Island," *Common-Place: The Journal of Early American Life* 10, no. 2 (January 2010), http://commonplace.online.

2 Erik J. Chaput, "Proslavery and Antislavery Politics in Rhode Island's 1842 Dorr Rebellion," *New England Quarterly* 85, no. 4 (December 2012): 670. Dorr himself remained staunchly in favor of African American rights and was able to later introduce a provision that guaranteed fugitive slaves the right to a jury trial.

3 Chaput and DeSimone, "Strange Bedfellows."

4 William Brown, *The Life of William J. Brown of Providence, R.I.* (Freeport, NY: Books for Libraries Press, 1971), 173, 162–163.

5 Chaput and DeSimone, "Strange Bedfellows."

6 Within existing scholarship, Timothy Marr does the most to explore antebellum-era references to the Barbary, mentioning many of the works I read below, but he is primarily interested in American views on Islam more broadly. Nevertheless, my survey is deeply indebted to his work. See Marr, *The Cultural Roots of American Islamicism* (New York: Cambridge University Press, 2006), 147–159.

7 Martha Schoolman, *Abolitionist Geographies* (Minneapolis: University of Minnesota Press, 2014), 1, 20.

8 It is worth noting that Garrison was a native of Newburyport, Massachusetts, born less than a decade after the return of Barbary captive John Foss. While Foss died in 1800, we might speculate that Garrison grew up hearing about the experiences of that famous former resident.

9 Garrison's *Liberator* did report on events in French Algeria, often from the French perspective, noting the heavy cost in lives and treasure to secure the colony. A short piece in 1845 remarks, "Never did [a] colony cost so dear and make so poor a return." *The Liberator* (Boston), December 5. Less often the paper reported on the cost to colonial Algerians, as when it decried the massacre of a thousand Arabs who had been hiding from the French military in a cave. *The Liberator*, August 8, 1845. Much more work needs to be done to explore the position the antislavery press took on the occupation of Algiers.

10 James Riley, *An Authentic Narrative of the Loss of the American Brig Commerce* (New York: T and W Mercein, 1817), 532. I quote the longer passage in chapter 6.

NOTES TO PAGES 151–158   241

11 Archibald Robbins, *A Journal, Comprising an Account of the Loss of the Brig Commerce, of Hartford, (Con.) James Riley, Master, upon the Western Coast of Africa, August 28th, 1815*, 20th edition (Hartford, CT: Silus Andrus, 1831), 91, quoted in Paul Baepler, Introduction, in *White Slaves, African Masters: An Anthology of American Barbary Captivity Narratives*, ed. Paul Baepler (Chicago: University of Chicago Press, 1999), 29.

12 Charles S. Watson, *The History of Southern Drama* (Lexington: University of Kentucky Press, 1997), 46.

13 Sarah Pogson, *The Young Carolinians; or, Americans in Algiers*, in *Essays Religious, Moral, Dramatic and Poetical* (Charleston, SC: Archibald E. Miller, 1818), 66.

14 Pogson, *Young Carolinians*, 66, 96.

15 Douglas A. Jones Jr., "Slavery's Performance-Texts," in *The Cambridge Companion to Slavery and American Literature*, ed. Ezra Tawil (New York: Cambridge University Press, 2016), 158.

16 Pogson, *Young Carolinians*, 91.

17 Harriet Jacobs, *Incidents in the Life of a Slave Girl*, ed. R. J. Ellis (1861; reprint New York: Oxford University Press, 2015), 30.

18 Susanna Rowson, *Slaves in Algiers; or, A Struggle for Freedom* (Philadelphia: Wrigley and Berriman, 1794), 1:69.

19 Rather than a daughter of Columbia, Pogson's Ellinor is literally a daughter of (the) States.

20 Although for centuries it was common practice for Europeans enslaved on the Barbary Coast to be ransomed by either aristocratic families or religious orders, I have found no evidence that this occurred during the United States's conflicts with North Africa. All American captives were freed either through treaty or by ransom paid by a government official.

21 Several variations of this phrase appear in the newspaper, including "slavery worse than Algerine," "worse than Algerine bondage," and "worse than Algerine servitude." The constant in all these instances is the use of the antiquated term "Algerine," which was used more frequently to refer to an inhabitant of the semi-autonomous city of Algiers than the later French colony of Algeria. *The Liberator* did use the term "Algerians," but with few exceptions, it did so in reference to the resistance against French colonialism. Otherwise, Algerines and Algerians shared space on the pages of Garrison's paper as well as other newspapers of the period, such as the *Anti-Slavery Standard*, as distinct spatio-temporal references.

22 Marr, *Cultural Roots of American Islamicism*, 147–148.

23 Robert Fanuzzi, *Abolition's Public Sphere* (Minneapolis: University of Minnesota Press, 2003), xv, xxxv.

24 "Non-Resistance," *The Liberator*, November 20, 1840.

25 "For the Voice of Freedom," *Voice of Freedom* (Montpelier, VT), June 22, 1839.

26 "The Amistad," *Colored American* (New York), October 5, 1839. In the article the writer describes Noah's allegations.

27 "Exciting Slaves to Rebellion," *Colored American*, November 10, 1838.

28 "The Africans of the Amistad," *Daily National Intelligencer* (Washington, DC), December 9, 1839; "The Captured Africans," *Hampshire Gazette* (Northampton, MA), September 11, 1839.

242 NOTES TO PAGES 158–166

29 "The Black 'Pirates,'" *Hampshire Gazette*, September 4, 1839.

30 Richard Peters, *Reports of Cases Argued and Adjudged in the Supreme Court of the United States, January Term 1841* (New York: Banks Law, 1903), 15:556.

31 Marcus Rediker, *The Amistad Rebellion: An Atlantic Odyssey of Slavery and Freedom* (New York: Penguin Books, 2012), 143.

32 *A True History of the African Chief Jingua and His Comrades* (New York: The Booksellers, 1839), 32.

33 "The N.Y. American," *The Liberator*, 8 April 1842.

34 William Boelhower, "The Rise of the New Atlantic Studies Matrix," *American Literary History* 20, nos. 1–2 (Spring–Summer 2008): 96.

35 Frederick Douglass, *The Heroic Slave: A Cultural and Critical Edition*, ed. John R. Kaufman-McKivigan, Robert S. Levine, and John Stauffer (1852; reprint New Haven, CT: Yale University Press, 2015), 162–163, 158.

36 Ivy Wilson, "On Native Ground: Transnationalism, Frederick Douglass, and *The Heroic Slave*," *PMLA* 121, no. 2 (2006): 466.

37 Carrie Hyde, "From 'Climates of Liberty,'" in Douglass, *Heroic Slave*, 246.

38 "The Ransom," *The Liberator*, January 29, 1847.

39 William Garrison, Preface, in *Narrative of the Life of Frederick Douglass, an American Slave*, ed. Ira Dworkin (New York: Penguin Books, 2014), 7.

40 "From a Speech," *The Liberator*, March 25, 1842.

41 O'Connell's description of Adams's having lost his native language seems to reference British official Joseph Dupuis's description of meeting Adams in Mogadore, Morocco, which was appended to publication of Adams's narrative: "The appearance, features and dress of this man . . . so perfectly resembled those of an Arab . . . when I spoke to him in English, he answered me in a mixture of Arabic and broken English, sometimes in Arabic only. . . . Like most other Christians after a long captivity and severe treatment among the Arabs, he appeared upon his first arrival exceedingly stupid and insensible." Dupuis, "Introductory Details Respecting Robert Adams," in *The Narrative of Robert Adams, a Barbary Captive: A Critical Edition*, ed. Charles Hansford Adams (New York: Cambridge University Press, 2005), 15.

42 In Douglass's second autobiography, he describes an instance in which a white abolitionist remarks to him, "Give us the facts, . . . we will take care of the philosophy." Douglass, *My Bondage and My Freedom, ed. John David Smith* (New York: Penguin Classics, 2003), 266. I return briefly to this moment again at the end of chapter 6.

43 Teresa A. Goddu, *Selling Antislavery: Abolition and Mass Media in Antebellum America* (Philadelphia: University of Pennsylvania Press, 2020), 81.

44 James McCune Smith, Introduction, in Douglass, *My Bondage and My Freedom*, 18.

45 James McCune Smith, "The Destiny of the People of Color," in *The Works of James McCune Smith*, ed. John Stauffer (New York: Oxford University Press, 2006), 50.

46 John Aikin, "A Dialogue between a Master and a Slave," in *The Columbian Orator*, ed. Caleb Bingham (New York: J. C. Totten, 1816), 240–242.

47 Douglass, *My Bondage and My Freedom*, 117.

48 Richard Walser identifies ten plays before 1800 that included characters speaking in African American dialect, although in several cases, such as in Thomas Forrest's

NOTES TO PAGES 167–170 243

The Disappointment (1767), the character is a European colonial from the Caribbean rather than an African American. Everett's play is one of the few works that came after independence. Walser, "Negro Dialect in Eighteenth-Century American Drama," *American Speech* 30, no. 4 (December 1955): 270–271. While the play would have a long life as part of Bingham's anthology, there is no evidence that it was ever actually performed on stage.

49 David Everett, *Slaves in Barbary; A Drama in Two Acts*, in Bingham, ed., *The Columbian Orator*, 103, 108.

50 As in the case of Ben Hassan from Rowson's *Slaves in Algiers*, Sharp is the only character in Everett's play to speak in dialect.

51 Everett, *Slaves in Barbary*, 113–115.

52 Several previous critics have noted that Douglass must have encountered the play and even read it aloud, probably multiple times. After briefly summarizing the play's antislavery message with an emphasis on the work's oriental pageantry, biographer William S. McFeely simply comments, "What the Baltimore boy made of this costume-party piece is anybody's guess." McFeely, *Frederick Douglass* (New York: Norton, 1991), 36. Robert J. Allison cites McFeely's text but takes his speculations much further, asserting that Douglass "relished" the work. Allison, *The Crescent Obscured: The United States and the Muslim World, 1776–1815* (New York: Oxford University Press, 1995), 101.

53 Paul Gilroy, *The Black Atlantic: Modernity and Double Consciousness* (Cambridge, MA: Harvard University Press, 1993), 60.

54 Douglass, *My Bondage and My Freedom*, 180.

55 Gilroy notes the importance of Egypt to many African Americans, including Douglass, as "evidence of the greatness of pre-slave African cultures." In particular, he argues that "Egypt . . . provided the symbolic means to locate the diaspora's critique of Enlightenment universals outside of the philosophical repertoire of the West," most notably Hegel's dismissal of Africa and Africans in his view of universal history. Gilroy, *Black Atlantic*, 60.

56 Margaret Kohn, "Frederick Douglass's Master-Slave Dialectic," *Journal of Politics* 67, no. 2 (May 2005): 501.

57 Gilroy, *Black Atlantic*, 63.

58 There are also several known instances when Douglass invoked Algerine pirates in his speeches. The year before publishing his first autobiography, he declared in a speech that one would sooner "[seek] a union with Algerine pirates" than remain in the union with John C. Calhoun and Henry Clay. "Communications. Report of the New England Convention," *National Anti-Slavery Standard* (New York), July 25, 1844.

59 Douglass, *Heroic Slave*, 4.

60 While his narrative may not be among the most prominent slave narratives of the period, Lewis Clarke is today best known for being the inspiration for the character of George Harris in *Uncle Tom's Cabin* (1852). See Harriet Beecher Stowe, *A Key to Uncle Tom's Cabin* (Boston: John P. Jewitt, 1858), 13.

61 While critics have questioned just how extensively Tyler's novel circulated after its initial publication in 1794, *The Algerine Captive* did in fact continue to appear in the mid-nineteenth century, with several newspapers reprinting sections. One writer

244 **NOTES TO PAGES 170–177**

described reading over the novel in 1849, although he admitted that, "till last week, [he] had not seen a copy of it for fifty years." "A New Englander of the Last Century," *National Anti-Slavery Standard*, June 7, 1849.

62 Lewis Clarke, *Narrative of the Sufferings of Lewis Clarke, during a Captivity of More Than Twenty-Five Years. Among the Algerines of Kentucky* (Seattle: University of Washington Press, 2012), 11.

63 "From the British and Foreign A.S. Reporter," *The Liberator*, June 10, 1842.

64 "Barbary not Barbarian," *Emancipator and Free American* (Boston), July 28, 1842.

65 "The Bey of Tunis," *Emancipator and Free American*, May 19, 1842.

66 Dana Luciano, *Arranging Grief: Sacred Time and the Body in Nineteenth-Century America* (New York: New York University Press, 2007), 170–171, 185.

67 Schoolman, *Abolitionist Geographies*, 22.

68 Charles Sumner, *White Slavery in the Barbary States: A Lecture before the Boston Mercantile Library Association, Feb. 17, 1847* (Boston: John P. Jewett, 1853), 4, 12.

69 Sumner, *White Slavery*, 6.

70 "Abolition in Tunis—Slavery in the United States," *National Era* (Washington, DC), October 14, 1847.

71 John Greenleaf Whittier, "The Crisis," in *Poems by John G. Whittier* (Boston: Benjamin B. Mussey, 1850), 378.

72 John Greenleaf Whittier, "The Christian Slave," in *Poems*, 148.

73 Marr, *Cultural Roots of American Islamicism*, 154.

74 John Greenleaf Whittier, "Derne," *National Era*, September 26, 1850.

75 William Eaton was a divisive figure in the wake of the Tripolitan War, as he bitterly opposed the treaty that ended the war and prevented his ally from overthrowing his brother. Robert J. Allison writes that Eaton "remained at best an ambiguous hero and would not be transformed into a fabled character until after his death" in 1811. Allison, *Crescent Obscured*, 204.

76 Whittier, "Derne."

77 Frederick Douglass, "A Letter to the American Slaves from Those who Have Fled from American Slavery," in *The Life and Writings of Frederick Douglass: Supplementary Volume*, ed. Philip S. Foner (New York: International Publishers, 1975), 5:166.

78 "The Domestic Slave Trade," *Frederick Douglass' Paper* (Rochester, NY), October 27, 1854.

79 "John Brown Meeting at Florence Mass," *The Liberator*, December 31, 1859.

80 Wendell Phillips, "John Brown and the Spirit of Fifty-Nine" in *The World's Best Orations: From the Earlier Period to the Present Time*, ed. David J. Brewer (Chicago: Ferd. P. Kaiser, 1899), 3183–3184.

81 "Observance of the Day in Albany," *The Liberator*, January 13, 1860.

82 Frederick Douglass, "John Brown and the Slaveholders' Insurrection: An Address Delivered in Edinburgh, Scotland, on 30 January 1860," in *The Frederick Douglass Papers, Series One: Speeches, Debates, and Interviews*, ed. John W. Blassingame (New Haven, CT: Yale University Press, 1985), 3:317.

NOTES TO PAGES 179–182   245

CHAPTER SIX: PETER PARLEY IN TRIPOLI

1 An earlier version of this chapter appeared in the journal *ESQ* as "Peter Parley in Tripoli: Barbary Slavery and Imaginary Citizenship," *ESQ: A Journal of Nineteenth-Century Literature and Culture* 65, no. 3 (2019): 512–551, Copyright 2022 by the Board of Regents of Washington State University.

2 Samuel Griswold Goodrich, "The Story of Robert Seaboy," in *Peter Parley's Short Stories for Long Nights. Revised by Peter Parley, Jun. with Engravings* (London: Mirror Press, 1837), 54, 60–61.

3 Barbary pirates make frequent appearances in Anglo-American works written and adapted for children throughout the nineteenth century, including geography and ethnography textbooks, histories of the Tripolitan War and the career of Stephen Decatur, dime novels, and retellings of *Robinson Crusoe*. Thomas Mayne Reid's *The Boy Slaves* (1865) borrowed heavily from James Riley, and even Doctor Doolittle in *The Story of Doctor Doolittle* (1920) is briefly captured by Algerian corsairs.

4 Traditionally, the relationship between Frederick Douglass and William Lloyd Garrison has been seen as exemplifying the "benevolent paternalism" of white abolition as it sought to control and deploy Black bodies for its own purposes. Douglass himself once described his relationship to Garrison as "that of a child to a parent." Douglass to Charles Sumner, September 2, 1852, in *The Life and Writings of Frederick Douglass*, ed. Philip S. Foner (New York: International Publishers, 1950), 2:210, quoted in Russ Castronovo, *Fathering the Nation: American Genealogies of Slavery and Freedom* (Berkeley: University of California Press, 1996), 211. Descriptions of Garrison's relationship to Douglass as "paternalistic" and "filial" in the critical literature are far too common to list comprehensively. See also Waldo E. Martin Jr., *The Mind of Frederick Douglass* (Chapel Hill: University of North Carolina Press, 2000), 47, and Robert S. Levine, *The Lives of Frederick Douglass* (Cambridge, MA: Harvard University Press, 2016), 51.

5 For more on the relationship between liberalism and sentimentalism in abolition, see Christine Levecq, *Slavery and Sentiment: The Politics of Feeling in Black Atlantic Antislavery Writing, 1770–1850* (Hanover, NH: University Press of New England, 2008), 190–208. See also Christopher Castiglia, *Interior States: Institutional Consciousness and the Inner Life of Democracy in the Antebellum United States* (Durham, NC: Duke University Press, 2008), 101–135. For a discussion of liberalism and race in children's literature, see Caroline Levander, *Cradle of Liberty: Race, the Child, and National Belonging from Thomas Jefferson to W. E. B. Du Bois* (Durham, NC: Duke University Press, 2006), 12–15.

6 This siloing of children's literary criticism is particularly evident in studies of nineteenth-century abolitionism. Although the last decade has seen a significant rise in critical interest in children's literature generally and abolitionist narratives for children specifically, the field remains partitioned off from mainstream nineteenth-century studies. It is still rare to see studies of antebellum abolitionism reference the ways in which antislavery texts and arguments were also presented to younger readers, while even the growing body of scholarship on children's literature often concedes that the discourse of children's abolitionism merely reflected the adult version. Rarely are these discourses put into direct conversation. Children's

literary studies has recently gained ground within mainstream criticism, however, as evidenced by the awarding of the 2017 Early American Literature Book Prize to Patricia Crain for *Reading Children: Literacy, Property, and the Dilemmas of Childhood in Nineteenth-Century America* (Philadelphia: University of Pennsylvania Press, 2017).

7 Daniel Roselle, *Samuel Griswold Goodrich, Creator of Peter Parley: A Study of His Life and Work* (Albany: State University of New York Press, 1968), 53–54.

8 Gillian Avery, *Behold the Child: American Children and Their Books, 1621–1922* (New York: Random House, 1994), 72.

9 Katherine Pandora, "The Children's Republic of Science in the Antebellum Literature of Samuel Griswold Goodrich and Jacob Abbott," *Osiris* 24, no. 1 (2009): 78.

10 Deborah C. De Rosa, *Domestic Abolition and Juvenile Literature, 1830–1865* (Albany: State University of New York Press, 2003), 2.

11 Paula T. Connolly, *Slavery in American Children's Literature, 1790–2010* (Iowa City: University of Iowa Press, 2013), 24–25.

12 Levander, *Cradle of Liberty*, 48–49.

13 Lydia Maria Child in particular might serve as a useful foil for understanding Goodrich's approach to antislavery rhetoric. In 1826, Child founded the *Juvenile Miscellany*, one of the country's first monthly children's magazine. For the eight years to follow, Child edited and contributed to the magazine, writing under her familial alter-ego, "Aunt Maria." By the early 1830s, she was well established as a major figure in the growing market of children's literature; however, her career as an editor ended abruptly as a result of her increasingly active involvement in Garrisonian abolitionism, and she was forced out of her position not long after the publication of *An Appeal in Favor of That Class of Americans Called Africans* in 1833. As a result, Child is far better known today for her abolitionist activities and her editing of Harriet Jacobs's narrative than for her role in the development of American children's literature. Nevertheless, given the recent emphasis in childhood studies on the comparison between rhetorical constructions of the child and the slave, a more comprehensive view of Child's career raises questions concerning how her editorial and authorial positioning as a children's writer might have influenced how her later works approach questions of racial paternalism, sympathy, and empowerment. For comparisons of the child and the slave as rhetorical figures, see Courtney Weikle-Mills, *Imaginary Citizens: Child Readers and the Limits of American Independence, 1640–1868* (Baltimore: Johns Hopkins University Press, 2013), 172–176, and Crain, *Reading Children*, 89–108. While a further study of Child's work lies beyond the scope of this chapter, I want to suggest that such questions might help us develop a more complex and comprehensive understanding of the development of nineteenth-century antislavery rhetoric across multiple audiences and modes of address. Child's early career provides a cautionary tale that might help explain Goodrich's approach to race and slavery in his Peter Parley books.

14 Connolly, *Slavery in American Children's Literature*, 35.

15 Edwin Heriott, quoted in Connolly, *Slavery in American Children's Literature*, 35.

16 Lawrence A. Peskin parallels the popularity of several of the most popular Barbary narratives with the circulation of Olaudah Equiano's autobiography in the 1790s

NOTES TO PAGES 185–189 247

and notes the consistency with which those held in North Africa referred to themselves as "slaves" rather than "captives." See Peskin, *Captives and Countrymen: Barbary Slavery and the American Public, 1785–1816* (Baltimore: Johns Hopkins University Press, 2009), 71–89; Robert J. Allison, *The Crescent Obscured: The United States and the Muslim World, 1776–1815* (Chicago: University of Chicago Press, 1995), 87–106; and Paul Baepler, Introduction, in *White Slaves, African Masters: An Anthology of American Barbary Captivity Narratives*, ed. Paul Baepler (Chicago: University of Chicago Press, 1999), 29–31.

17 Crain, *Reading Children*, 201.

18 Lesley Ginsberg, "Of Babies, Beasts, and Bondage: Slavery and the Question of Citizenship in Antebellum American Children's Literature," in *The American Child: A Cultural Studies Reader*, ed. Caroline F. Levander and Carol J. Singley (New Brunswick: Rutgers University Press, 2003), 89.

19 Samuel Griswold Goodrich, *The Young American; or, Book of Government and Law* (New York: William Robinson, 1842), 40.

20 Weikle-Mills characterizes nineteenth-century debates over citizenship as contested between those, following Rousseau, who characterized citizenship as manifest in natural law and those who saw it as a result of education and allegiance to patriarchal authority. Weikle-Mills places Goodrich squarely in the latter group, noting that many of the writer's texts, particularly those focused on natural history, depicted the dangers of "using nature as a model for citizenship." Weikle-Mills, *Imaginary Citizens*, 197. For more on the rethinking of the terms of citizenship in the antebellum era, see Derrick R. Spires and Christopher James Bonner, cited in chapters 3 and 4.

21 Weikle-Mills, *Imaginary Citizens*, 66.

22 Michael Warner, *The Letters of the Republic: Publication and the Public Sphere in Eighteenth-Century America* (Cambridge, MA: Harvard University Press, 1990), 174.

23 Lauren Berlant, *The Queen of America Goes to Washington City: Essays on Sex and Citizenship* (Durham, NC: Duke University Press, 2002), 5.

24 Weikle-Mills, *Imaginary Citizens*, 66, 6.

25 Connolly, *Slavery in American Children's Literature*, 34.

26 Samuel Griswold Goodrich, *The Tales of Peter Parley about Africa: With Engravings* (Philadelphia: Desilver, Thomas, 1836), 18.

27 Although certainly an embarrassing incident, the grounding of the *Philadelphia* resulted in the most enduring image to emerge from the Tripolitan War, the burning of the captured ship by Stephen Decatur, who led a nighttime raid to prevent Tripoli from using the ship against the American blockade. Seen somewhat ironically as a major victory in the war, many depictions of the event exist, including most famously Edward Moran's *Burning of the Frigate Philadelphia in the Harbor of Tripoli, February 16, 1804*, painted almost a century after the incident in 1897.

28 Hester Blum, *The View from the Masthead: Maritime Imagination and Antebellum Sea Narratives* (Chapel Hill: University of North Carolina Press, 2008), 51.

29 Jonathan Cowdery, *American Captives in Tripoli*, in Baepler, ed., *White Slaves, African Masters*, 172.

30 Goodrich, *Tales about Africa*, 29.

248 **NOTES TO PAGES 190–202**

31 John Foss, *A Journal, of the Captivity and Sufferings of John Foss; Several Years a Prisoner in Algiers*, 2nd edition (Newburyport, MA: Angier March, 1798), 74.

32 Jacob Rama Berman, *American Arabesque: Arabs, Islam, and the 19th-Century Imaginary* (New York: New York University Press, 2012), 21.

33 Goodrich, *Tales about Africa*, 29.

34 Goodrich, *Tales about Africa*, 36, 97–98, 109, 111–112.

35 Connolly, *Slavery in American Children's Literature*, 36.

36 Goodrich, *Tales about Africa*, 113.

37 See Baepler, Introduction, 27–28.

38 Goodrich, *Tales about Africa*, 81–82.

39 Goodrich, *Tales about Africa*, 86, 90, 93–94.

40 Goodrich, *Tales about Africa*, 95.

41 While previous critics have investigated the role of Riley's narrative in the *Tales about Africa*, they have also misinterpreted Goodrich's source material to fit a more stable Black-white binary. In one notable example, Caroline Levander focuses on the role of Riley's *Narrative* as a "slave-ship story" through which contact between white America and Black Africa results in the loss of racial identity for both through the enslavement of James Riley. She argues that "with the knowledge that slavery does not contain but, rather, produces and perpetuates the threat that racial others pose, Peter Parley is able not only to free the wrongfully enslaved Captain Riley and his crew but to consider the impact of the slave trade on U.S. national identity." Levander, *Cradle of Liberty*, 48–49. Interestingly, Levander identifies Riley as a slave trader, which he was not, in order to present the captain's capture as a cautionary tale that emphasizes his role as an intermediary between whiteness and Blackness.

42 Castronovo, *Fathering the Nation*, 294–295.

43 Brigitte Fielder, "Black Girls, White Girls, American Girls: Slavery and Racialized Perspectives in Abolitionist and Neoabolitionist Children's Literature," *Tulsa Studies in Women's Literature* 36, no. 2 (October 2017): 325.

44 Goodrich, *Tales about Africa*, 93.

45 Samuel Griswold Goodrich, *The Story of Captain Riley, and His Adventures in Africa* (Boston: Carter, Hendee, 1834), 5, 7.

46 See my discussion of antifiction critique in Royall Tyler's *The Algerine Captive* (1797) in the introduction.

47 Goodrich, *Story of Captain Riley*, 22–23.

48 James Riley, *An Authentic Narrative of the Loss of the American Brig Commerce* (New York: T. & W. Mercein, 1817), 20.

49 Goodrich, *Story of Captain Riley*, 62.

50 Riley, *Authentic Narrative*, 85.

51 Goodrich, *Story of Captain Riley*, 150, 219.

52 Goodrich, *Story of Captain Riley*, 42, 235, 159.

53 Riley, *Authentic Narrative*, 532.

54 Goodrich, *Story of Captain Riley*, 239–240.

55 Crain, *Reading Children*, 101.

56 Frederick Douglass, *My Bondage and My Freedom*, ed. John David Smith (New York: Penguin Classics, 2003), 266.

CODA: SELIM'S ARCHIVE FEVER

1 See Sylvaine A. Diouf, *Servants of Allah: African Muslims Enslaved in the Americas* (New York: New York University Press, 1998), and Michael A. Gomez, *Black Crescent: The Experience and Legacy of African Muslims in the Americas* (New York: Cambridge University Press, 2005). Gomez does touch on several instances in which enslaved Africans were identified as "moors," although, as in the case of Omar ibn Said, it is difficult to tell whether there was any actual connection to North Africa. Gomez also briefly mentions the case of Selim, discussed below.

2 See Herbert Asbury, *The Barbary Coast: An Informal History of the San Francisco Underworld* (New York: Thunder's Mouth Press, 2002).

3 For a discussion of post–Civil War Barbary works, see Paul Baepler, "The Barbary Captivity Narrative in American Culture," *Early American Literature* 39, no. 2 (2004): 217–246.

4 "Selim, or the Algerine in Virginia," *Graham's Illustrated Magazine*, November 1857, 434.

5 "Selim," 434–435.

6 "Selim," 437.

7 "Selim," 435.

8 Laura Doyle, *Freedom's Empire: Race and the Rise of the Novel in Atlantic Modernity, 1640–1940* (Durham, NC: Duke University Press, 2008), 6–8.

9 "Selim," 436.

10 Jacques Derrida, *Archive Fever: A Freudian Impression*, transl. Eric Prenowitz (Chicago: University of Chicago Press, 1998), 11, 19.

INDEX

Adams, John, 14, 139

Adams, Robert, 54, 164–165

The Algerine Captive (Tyler), 5–12, 15, 17, 34, 89–91, 95–100, 117

The Algerine Spy in Pennsylvania (Markoe), 25, 59, 65–75, 80, 88–95, 100, 128, 135, 224n31, 226n48

Allen, Richard, 89, 108

The Allied Despots; or, The Friendship of Britain for America (Verax), 17–18, 20–21

Allison, Robert J., 88, 210n12, 227n3, 244n75

The American in Algiers; or, The Patriot of Seventy-Six in Captivity, 5, 24, 39–49, 53, 56, 102

La Amistad (ship), 6, 149, 156–158, 160

Apap, Christopher, 24

Apter, Emily, 60

Arthur Mervyn (C. B. Brown), 108–117, 233n99

Ashton, Susanna, 48

Baepler, Paul, 4, 7, 32, 60, 149, 192, 210n12

Barlow, Joel, 39, 70, 123, 223n15

Ben Ali, Mahomed, 58, 221n7

Ben Benjamin, Adonah, 96–98, 100

Ben Hassan. *See* Rowson, Susanna

Ben Rejeb, Lotfi, 123, 136

Berlant, Lauren, 71, 186

Berman, Jacob Rama, 58, 190

blood (descriptions in narrative texts), 41–42, 48, 102–103

Boelhower, William Q., 16–17, 162

Brown, Charles Brockden, 4, 21–22, 233n92; *Arthur Mervyn*, 108–117, 233n99

Brown, John, 16, 177

Brown, William Hill, 21

Butler, James, 99–100

Carey, Mathew, 1–6, 21, 49, 59, 63, 209n1, 209n8, 218n15, 220n53; *A Short Account of Algiers*, 35–36, 41, 112–113, 217n5

Carthage, 69–71, 215n59, 225n41

Child, Lydia Maria, 53, 184, 246n13

children's literature, 27–28, 166, 179–202

Chiles, Katy, 6

Clarke, Lewis, 170, 243n60

Clay, Henry, 2, 155–156

Connolly, Paula T., 183–184, 187, 192

Constitutional Convention, 25, 59, 65, 72, 75

Creole (ship), 16–17, 149, 160–162, 170

Crèvecoeur, J. Hector St. John de, 74

critical aporia, 21

Cumberland, Richard, 90, 96–97

Davis, Lennard J., 12

Decatur, Stephen, 3, 24, 76, 122, 138, 142, 177

Defoe, Daniel, 218n12

dialect (in characters' speech to denote difference), 105, 118, 129, 152, 168, 242n48, 243n50

DiCuirci, Lindsay, 9, 12, 60

Dillon, Elizabeth Maddock, 101–103, 106–108, 118, 143

251

INDEX

Dorr, Thomas William, 147–148, 240n2
Douglass, Frederick, 27, 37, 163–169, 172,
177, 195, 202, 243n52, 243n58, 245n4;
The Heroic Slave, 4, 16–17, 162, 169
Doyle, Laura, 17, 206, 218n12
Dunlap, William, 90, 111, 233n92,
236n16

Eaton, William, 24, 76, 89, 118–119,
175–177, 188–189, 234n106, 244n75
Ellison, James: *The American Captive;
or, Siege of Tripoli*, 118–120, 234n106
Equiano, Olaudah, 47, 246n16
Everett, David, 166–169, 243n50

Faherty, Duncan, 51, 65, 220n53
fake news, 13–14, 212n40
Fetnah. *See* Rowson, Susanna
fictionality, 8–9, 12–15, 34, 53, 60–61, 157,
203, 211n21
Fielding, Achsa, 26, 108–117, 233n99
Foss, John, 5, 37, 39, 58, 217n5, 217n9;
*A Journal, of the Captivity and
Sufferings of John Foss*, 31–34, 112,
190, 238n44
Foushee, William, 87–88
Franklin, Benjamin, 97–98, 112, 213n46;
alleged capture and enslavement
of, 12–14; "On the Slave Trade," 25,
61–64, 72, 156, 161

Gallagher, Catherine, 8
Gardner, Jared, 6, 10, 97, 217n9
Garrison, William Lloyd, 53, 149,
154–155, 163–166, 184, 240n8, 245n4
Gifra-Adroher, Pere, 133–135
Gilroy, Paul, 16, 168–169, 243n55
Goodrich, Samuel Griswold, 28, 179–202,
212n26, 247n20; *The Story of Captain
Riley, and His Adventures in Africa*,
193–202; *Tales of Peter Parley about
Africa*, 187–193
Goudie, Sean X., 110–111, 116
Grimes, William, 48
Gustafson, Sandra M., 21–23, 66,
222n8

Haitian Revolution, 65, 110, 150
handwriting, 48, 56. *See also* print
Hanson, Joseph, 76
Harap, Louis, 89, 101, 111, 119, 234n108
Hegel, Georg Wilhelm Friedrich, 19,
168–169, 172, 215n59, 243n55
Henry, Patrick, 65, 87–88
The Heroic Slave (Douglass), 4, 16–17,
162, 169
*Humanity in Algiers; or, The Story of
Azem*, 34, 49–53, 220n53
hypocrisy in American attitudes to
slavery, 34–37, 42, 47–50, 154, 168, 172

ibn Said, Omar, 25, 53–55, 203
Ibrahim, Sieur, 58, 221n7
Irving, Washington, 20, 25, 75–83, 125, 128
Irving, William, Jr., 25, 75–83, 125, 128

Jackson, James, 62–63, 80
Jackson, Scipio, 32–34, 52
Jacobs, Harriet, 53, 152–153, 182
Jefferson, Thomas, 3, 21, 42, 80, 139,
214n48; *Notes on the State of Virginia*,
46, 109, 211n16
Jewish diaspora, 90–100, 118–119,
129–130, 140. *See also* racial identity:
Jewish
Jewish futurity, 90, 94, 98–99, 109, 113,
117. *See also* racial identity: Jewish
Jones, Absalom, 89, 108
*A Journal, of the Captivity and Sufferings
of John Foss* (Foss), 31–34, 112, 190,
238n44

Kalman, Julie, 90–92, 229n16
Khan, Mustapha Rub-a-Dub Kelli. *See*
Mustapha letters
Koenigs, Thomas, 8–9, 12–13

logocracy, 25, 79–83, 128
Lopez, Aaron, 96–97
Loughran, Trish, 22, 61, 222n8, 223n16

Macklin, Charles, 101
Marana, Giovanni Paolo, 66

Markoe, Peter, 65; *The Algerine Spy in Pennsylvania*, 25, 59, 65–75, 80, 88–95, 100, 128, 135, 224n31, 226n48
Marr, Timothy, 32, 114, 154, 174, 211n14, 240n6; on *The Algerine Spy in Pennsylvania*, 70, 73; on *The Allied Despots; or, The Friendship of Britain for America*, 17; on the Mustapha letters, 80
Mather, Cotton, 36–37, 215n60
Mendez, Solomon. *See* Markoe, Peter
Mervyn, Arthur. *See* Brown, Charles Brockden
Mikveh Israel synagogue, 88, 94
Monroe, James, 122, 139–140
Montaigne, Michel de, 82
Moro, Prince. *See* "Story of Prince Moro"
Mufti, Aamir R., 91, 100
Muslim invasion, fear of, 59, 64–65
Muslim-Jewish conspiracy, fear of, 88, 93, 118, 125, 139
Mustapha letters (W. Irving), 25, 59, 75–83, 125, 128

Nathans, Heather, 101, 142–143, 229n15, 232n62
Naturalization Act (1790), 89
Noah, Mordecai Manuel, 26, 121–144, 203; author portrait, 130–133; diplomatic career, 122–123; "Oriental Correspondence," 125–129, 237n23; plays authored by, 122–124, 140–143; *Travels in England, France, Spain, and the Barbary States*, 26, 129–140
novel-news matrix, 12, 15, 67

O'Brien, Richard, 10–12, 15–17, 52
O'Connell, Daniel, 164–165, 242n41
"On the Slave Trade" (Franklin), 25, 61–64, 72, 156, 161
orientalism, 58, 75, 154, 175, 229n16

Park, Mungo, 112, 133
Parley, Peter. *See* Goodrich, Samuel Griswold

passing (racial), 37, 69, 74, 93, 111
Paulding, James Kirke, 25, 75, 78
periodization, 21–24, 206
Peskin, Lawrence A., 10–12, 217n5, 228n8, 235n5, 238n49, 246n16
Pethers, Matthew, 8
Pieh, Sengbe, 6, 156, 159–160
Pogson, Sarah, 151–154
print: access to, 8, 12, 14–15, 49; authority of, 51–52, 61, 66, 100, 105, 196; production of, 43–44, 47, 67–68, 74, 131; racialization of, 40, 93
pseudonyms, 59–63, 125, 222n8, 237n23
publication. *See* print

racial identity, 5, 7, 88; American, 76; Jewish, 89–91, 108, 115, 124
Rhode Island and the Constitutional Convention, 73, 147–148, 154
Riley, James, 4, 137–138, 150–151; narrative adaptation by Goodrich, 181–182, 193–202
Rowson, Susanna, 6, 90, 153, 231n56; *Slaves in Algiers; or, A Struggle for Freedom*, 5, 90–91, 100–108, 114, 117–118, 125, 142

Salmagundi. See Mustapha letters
Salomon, Haym, 94
Sancho, Ignatius, 46, 211n16
satire, 13–14, 36–38, 62–66, 71, 79–81, 155–156, 212n40, 218n16
Schoolman, Martha, 7, 149, 172
Schueller, Malini Johar, 62, 71, 81, 214n48
Selim the Algerine, 204–206
Shalev, Eran, 60, 70, 225n41
Shays, Daniel, 73, 148
Shylock stereotype, 90–104, 117–119, 144, 229n15, 238n49
Sillin, Sarah, 98–99, 217n10
slave advertisements (escaped or runaway), 35–39, 219n19
Slaves in Algiers; or, A Struggle for Freedom (Rowson), 5, 90–91, 100–108, 114, 117–118, 125, 142

Smith, James McCune, 165–166
Smith, Jonathan S., 89, 119
Spires, Derrick R., 89, 108
spy/observer narratives, 66, 125–126, 129, 224n29. *See also* Markoe, Peter
"Story of Prince Moro," 25, 53–56
Sumner, Charles, 63, 172–173

textual authority. *See* print
Travels in England, France, Spain, and the Barbary States (Noah), 26, 129–140
Truxton, Thomas, 13–16, 213n41, 213n47
Tyler, Royall: *The Algerine Captive*, 5–12, 15, 17, 34, 89–91, 95–100, 117

Underhill, Updike, 5–12, 21, 34, 95–99, 197, 217n10, 224n24

Verax, Valentine: *The Allied Despots; or, The Friendship of Britain for America*, 17–18, 20–21

Warner, Michael, 22, 59–61, 115, 186–187, 222n8, 223n16
Washington, George, 42, 46, 161
Washington, Madison, 160–162, 169
Webster, Daniel, 160–161
Weikle-Mills, Courtney, 181, 186, 201, 247n20
Wheatley, Phillis, 43–48, 211n16
White, Charles, 109, 232n73
White, Ed, 51, 220n53, 231n40
Whittier, John Greenleaf, 173–176

yellow fever epidemic (1793), 36, 89, 108, 110